THE GAMBLING TIMES GUIDE TO

GREYHOUND RACING

By
William E. McBride

A Gambling Times Book
Distributed by Carol Publishing Group

THE GAMBLING TIMES GUIDE
TO GREYHOUND RACING

Copyright © 1984 by Gambling Times Incorporated

MCBRIDE, WILLIAM E.
THE GAMBLING TIMES GUIDE TO GREYHOUND RACING

ISBN: 0-89746-007-3

Manufactured in the United States of America

First Carol Publishing Group Edition 1990

Distributed by Carol Publishing Group
120 Enterprise Avenue
Secaucus, NJ 07094

Carol Publishing Group books are available at special discounts for bulk purchases, for sales promotions, fund raising, or educational purposes. Special editions can also be created to specifications. For details contact: Special Sales Department, Carol Publishing Group, 120 Enterprise Ave., Secaucus, NJ 07094

All material presented in this book is offered as information to the reader. No inducement to gamble is intended or implied.

OTHER *GAMBLING TIMES* BOOKS
AVAILABLE—CURRENT RELEASES

BLACKJACK BOOKS

The Beginner's Guide to Winning Blackjack by Stanley Roberts
Gambling Times Guide to Blackjack by Stanley Roberts
Winning Blackjack by Stanley Roberts
Million Dollar Blackjack by Ken Uston

POKER BOOKS

According to Doyle by Doyle Brunson
Caro on Gambling by Mike Caro
Caro's Book of Tells by Mike Caro
Free Money: How to Win in the Cardrooms of California by Michael Wiesenberg
New Poker Games by Mike Caro
Poker for Women by Mike Caro
The Railbird by Rex Jones
Tales Out of Tulsa by Bobby Baldwin
Wins, Places and Pros by Tex Sheahan

CASINO GAMING BOOKS

The GT Guide to Casino Games by Len Miller
The GT Guide to Craps by N.B. Winkless, Jr.
How to Win at Casino Gaming Tournaments by Haven Earle Haley

GENERAL INTEREST BOOKS

Gambling and the Law by I. Nelson Rose
The GT Guide to Bingo by Roger Snowden
The GT Guide to European and Asian Games by Syd Helprin
The GT Guide to Systems that Win, Vols. I and II
The GT Guide to Winnings Systems, Vol. II
GT Presents Winning Systems and Methods, Vols. I and II
The GT Quiz Book by Mike Caro
Golf, Gambling and Gamesmanship by Gary Moore
The Mathematics of Gambling by Dr. Edward O. Thorp
P$yching Out Vegas by Marvin Karlins, Ph.D.

Winning by Computer
by Dr. Donald Sullivan

SPORTS BETTING BOOKS
Fast Track to Thoroughbred Profits
by Mark Cramer
The GT Guide to Basketball Handicapping
by Barbara Nathan
The GT Guide to Football Handicapping
by Bob McCune
The GT Guide to Greyhound Racing
by William McBride
The GT Guide to Harness Racing
by Igor Kusyshyn, Ph.D., Al Stanley
and Sam Dragich
The GT Guide to Jai Alai
by William R. Keevers
The GT Guide to Thoroughbred Racing
by R.G. Denis

Acknowledgements

My most sincere appreciation to the many people who helped in the preparation of this book. I enjoyed excellent cooperation and hospitality from the management of every racetrack that I approached. Special thanks, too, to the specific individuals who helped me with background material and gave me encouragement: Ted Colton, at the Palm Beach Kennel Club; Mildred Hopkins, Business Manager of the *Greyhound Racing Record;* George Johnson, Executive Director of the AGTOA; Peggy MacKinnon, with the Hill & Knowlton Co.; and Edmond Markel, of the Hollywood Greyhound Track in Florida. Many, many others contributed by sending me material and granting permission for its use in this book.

Thanks, too, to my lovely wife Alice, for her help, encouragement and patience. And a special kind of thanks to the folks who invented the lovely word processor that I originally typed this on—it's like a magic typewriter!

Table of Contents

"Intruder Entry" (from another track). Running characteristics (inside, outside, etc.). Tip sheets and morning odds.

About the Author

Author Bill McBride was a handicapper of harness horse races for years before becoming "converted" to the greyhounds. The research for this book on dog racing took three years, and has been gathered from tracks throughout the country.

Bill has proven that good logic can "beat" the greyhound races and produce a good profit for the thinking fan. In this book, he examines the sport from A to Z for the beginner, and then reveals and details a handicapping and wagering system that will provide the astute reader with a sound and dynamic plan for profit.

Bill has authored numerous books and articles associated with his trade, the sporting goods business. He built a small basement operation into a successful three-store chain, and conducts wholesale business in 14 states. His business involves travel all over the United States, and it was during these travels that he gathered information on most of the 44 dog tracks in operation. Most handicappers become expert only at a small number of tracks. In this book, Bill shows the reader how to tailor a profitable system to *any* track.

Bill also travels around the world—for business, for pleasure, and in his occasional role as a guide and host for travel groups. Most of these groups are scuba-diving oriented, as Bill has been a scuba instructor for 18 years. During these visits to foreign lands, Bill also enjoyed visiting the race tracks. The outline for this book was compiled while Bill was in Manila in the fall of 1982.

Bill and his wife Alice live in Ohio. They enjoy gardening, being grandparents, and learning about the care and feeding of wild horses. Mrs. McBride and her daughter recently "adopted" two wild mustangs from the range, through a government program, to prevent them from being used as dog food.

Chapter 1
The Sport of Queens

Eight powerful dogs hit the sharp first curve in a pack at a velocity of over 45 miles per hour. Dogs collide, dirt flies. One dog—the favorite!—spins out and almost hits the fence! The crowd rises and roars! A brindle bitch streaks through the chaos in the curve and emerges in the lead. She hits the next curve with the highest-odds greyhound in the race on her flank, and gaining! It's a close race in the stretch. Every dog is watching the speeding lure, and everybody in the screaming crowd is watching the dogs! The favorite has regained his stride and is now closing for third. They hit the spotlighted finish line in a group of three—it's a photo finish for all three spots! In a few seconds, the results flash on the board. The crowd roars again! The long-shot dog has won, and pays $48.40! The trifecta payoff is $2260.30! The crowd soon quiets, and almost immediately the betting lines start forming for the next race, which will start in exactly 14 minutes. There will be 13 races tonight, and the one that just finished was only the first! Excitement is high, and the fans are talking, laughing, bright-eyed and totally involved...

This scene is repeated year-round at greyhound racing tracks throughout the United States and several other countries. Called the "Sport of Queens," dog racing has become the sixth-largest spectator sport in the United States, and it's still growing. It is fast-paced, exciting to watch, colorful, *and is the only sport on which pari-mutuel betting is conducted in which no human being participates in the actual competition!* (Many fans have come to dog racing because they like this aspect of it.)

Even in the economic hard times of 1981 to 1983, many tracks expanded, remodeled, or otherwise prospered and grew. The modern greyhound racetrack provides facilities equal to many of the best horse tracks: Clubhouses with gourmet dining, enclosed air-conditioned grandstands, beautifully landscaped grounds, and a large courteous staff. Adequate, convenient, low-cost parking is provided, and admission rates are quite low at most tracks. All in all, a most comfortable atmosphere is provided, and the fans seem to feel welcome and appreciated, unlike some of the older horse tracks where fans seem to need brute strength just to fight their way to a seat or into a betting line.

Dog racing provides jobs for over $100,000 people annually, and in 1981 the sport provided over $156 million to the general funds of the 14 states in which it is conducted. This was from the mutuel handle alone, and was above and beyond the sales taxes, payroll taxes, etc., which were also generated. Over 2½ million people attended the dog races in 1981 alone, at the 45 tracks in the 14 states in which it was conducted.

The industry itself takes great pains to see that every race is conducted in an absolutely fair manner, recognizing that instances of race-fixing have damaged the image of other types of racing. Further, state officials are present at every race to likewise assure that no manipulation takes place. It is somewhat more difficult to handicap dogs than it is horses, but one can feel sure that the outcome of each race has not been "adjusted" to anyone's benefit. And, because of the competitive nature of the dogs, which have been bred to *run,* and the lack of any "rules of conduct" once the race is underway, the payoffs tend to be somewhat larger than for horses.

Is the racing of greyhounds cruel or harmful to the dogs in any way? Sometimes people who have never seen a dog race ask about this. The answer is that you will seldom see an animal *enjoy* a race more! From the time the dogs are brought onto the track for the post parade, you'll see that they are absolutely *eager* to run! Admittedly, most would probably rather get started by some other means than being placed in the starting boxes, but even that is not in any way hurtful—they just don't like the delay! It is obvious from the outset that these creatures have not been whipped, abused, or spirit-broken in any way. You will see from the way the dogs behave with their *lead-outs* (the young people who bring each dog onto the track), that you are looking at joyful, competitive, eager creatures who love what they are doing. Back in the early days of racing, live rabbits were used as lures. This was a bit cruel to the rabbit, even though he never really got caught, so an artificial lure was devised. It vaguely resembles a rabbit, but the dogs know that it's not real. But that doesn't matter—they just want to chase *some*thing, because that's what they were *raised* to do!

Another question sometimes asked is, "What happens to the dogs that get too old to race, or are injured, or prove to be not fast enough?" The dogs with good bloodlines, or course, are often kept by the kennel for breeding purposes. In the past, the "excess" dogs were, indeed, sometimes euthanized if homes were not readily available for them. Presently, the various organizations of track owners, kennels, and dog owners are actively seeking more ways to find recipients for these dogs. They make fine pets, and are in no way vicious or high-strung.

That you're reading this book indicates you have some interest in the sport. If you haven't yet been "to the dogs," go! You'll probably be most pleasantly surprised. And while you're there, look at the faces of the other fans. You'll be sure to see a lot of smiles and enthusiasm.

Chapter 2

How It All Started

The sport of dog racing probably wouldn't work if there hadn't been a breed of dog developed especially for running. Just like the beagle is bred for his "nose" and persistance in hunting, and the labrador is bred for his instinctive retrieval of waterfowl, the greyhound was developed for its speed. It is a breed that is literally "born to run."

The greyhound's origins date back to over 4000 years ago. Ancient Egyptian pharohs rated them first among all animals as pets, and as hunters. Likewise, in Arabian, Persian, Roman and Greek countries, the greyhound was held in high esteem, and a new litter of pups was cause for great celebration. In fact, the greyhound is the only breed mentioned in the Bible!

In the 1700s, the first formal rules for greyhound *coursing* (the pursuit of hares) were initiated by Queen Elizabeth I; thus, dog racing became known as the "Sport of Queens."

In the late 1800s, greyhounds were introduced to the United States to help control the jack rabbit, a troublesome pest that was destroying crops. Before long, competitive events were being conducted ("My dog's better than your dog . . . ").

In about 1912, circular racing of dogs around a track was made possible by the invention of a mechanical lure by Owen Patrick Smith. In 1919, the first public track opened in Emeryville, California. Though this track didn't survive, it paved the way for the present sport.

Though the sporting public quickly took to the dog races, the industry suffered through many growing pains. Part of the problem was that many people felt it must somehow be cruel to the animals involved, and pressured the state legislatures to disallow it. From the start, the industry suffered not from lack of attendance, but rather from legal roadblocks to the opening of tracks. Often, the opposition either had a misconception of the way dog races were conducted—feeling that the animals were somehow being mistreated or abused—or there was concern about legalizing pari-mutuel wagering.

As of this writing, dog racing is legal in 14 states, and several others have the matter under consideration. In general, the sport has gained a far better image than it had while suffering through its early years. And rightfully so, for it has policed itself well and made every possible effort to protect the betting public and to avoid unkind treatment of the animals.

Race meetings today are regulated by state statute, and these laws are enforced by members and officials of the various state racing commissions. The public is assured of fair practices and honest conduct of the pari-mutuel process at every track.

Furthermore, each state receives a substantial return from the greyhound tracks, just as they do from the horse tracks or from other forms of legal wagering. Of the total amount wagered at a track, the *handle,* about 6% to 8% of the total goes to the state. Each state usually has representatives present at the tracks to assure that this is accounted for properly.

Chapter 3

How the Greyhounds Are Raced

How does it all work? There are almost always eight dogs in each race. Each one is assigned a number and a color, and wears a saddle-type "blanket" for identification. Each dog also wears an identical muzzle. Other than for the obvious purpose of preventing any possible nipping, the muzzles are designed to provide a sharp and high-contrast image for the photo finish camera.

About eight to 10 minutes prior to each race, the dogs are brought onto the track. Each is held by a short leash by a *lead-out,* usually a young person, who is in charge of controlling the dog during the post parade, placing the dog into the starting box, and collecting the dog again when the race is over. The lead-outs are under strict instructions to avoid talking with any fans, or each other, during this process.

At most tracks, the dogs are paraded on the track, in view of the crowd, for about six to eight minutes. This gives the public an opportunity to look over the contestants. It also gives the dogs a chance to work off some of the nervous energy they may have built up while waiting. Every dog has been individually penned in a supervised lock-up area for at least two hours before the program starts. During this period, the dogs have been carefully observed, their identification checked (56 points, including ear tattoos, etc.), and urine samples collected. No greyhound may be raced while under any type of medication. The dogs' weights are carefully checked, and any dog with too much variance from its normal weight is scratched from the competition.

The post parade also gives the dogs one last opportunity to relieve themselves, should they feel the need. All that one has to do is signal "I gotta go!" to his lead-out, and he will be taken to an appropriate area; within sight of the crowd, though, so that no one has a reason to wonder if "his dog" was taken behind the fence and kicked in the leg. Likewise, there are some handicappers who might take this potty break into consideration as a factor in a dog's performance.

As the time approaches, the dogs are taken to the starting area, and lined up for another minute or so behind the row of starting boxes. The row of boxes, all connected, have been placed in the appropriate position for the length of the course to be run. The most common courses are set up for approximately 5/16-mile, 3/8-mile, or 7/16-mile, though some tracks may vary these distances slightly. Generally, a program will involve a few races run on each of the two or three courses. The number-one box is on the inside of the track, number eight is on the outside.

Each dog in every race has been placed in the proper grade or "class" of competition by a very fair method. The placement rules were established by the universally accepted Hartwell Grading System, initiated in 1950. Basically, when a dog wins a race, it is moved *up* a grade. If it doesn't place in the money for three races in a given class, it is then moved *down* a grade, and so forth. (Table 3-1 illustrates the details.) This system ensures that all of the dogs in a race are of nearly the same class. The actual placing of the dogs in a given race of the appropriate grade is determined by a random lot drawing, as is each dog's post position. In short, everything possible is done to assure a fairly run and closely contested race.

The dogs have a mandatory "retirement age" of five years at most tracks, and most dogs aren't entered until the age of 17 months.

Table 3-1

THE GREYHOUND GRADING SYSTEM

Confused by the grading system used at greyhound tracks across the country? Well you shouldn't be. . . as a matter of fact it's really simple.

—There are six grades of greyhounds, indicated by A,B,C,D,E and M (Maiden)

—The winner of any race is advanced one grade until reaching Grade A.

—If a greyhound fails to finish 1st, 2nd or 3rd in three consecutive starts (except in Grade D) or fails to earn more than one 3rd in four consecutive starts in the same grade, that greyhound shall be lowered one grade. In Grade D, a greyhound may fail to finish 1st, 2nd, 3rd or 4th in four consecutive starts before being lowered.

—Any greyhound, racing in Grade E, for four (4) consecutive starts that fails to finish 1st, 2nd, 3rd or 4th in those four starts, shall be dropped from further racing at the meeting.

—Any greyhound finishing 2nd, 3rd or 4th in Maiden (M) events may at the request of the owner or trainer to the Racing Secretary be moved into Grade D races and then must abide by all the provisions of the grading system. Maidens shall be designated by the letter "M" on the program after the name of the greyhound.

—All races "made up" by the Racing Secretary shall be designated by the letter "T" in the program. All stake races shall be designated by the letter "S" in the program.

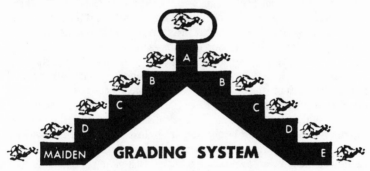

THE GREYHOUND GRADING SYSTEM

Table 3-1 (courtesy of the Hollywood Greyhound Track) describes the concept of the Hartwell Grading System. This is the concept used by all modern tracks, though a few tracks use different terminology for the various grades. Listed below is the comparison:

Most Tracks	Taunton and Lincoln	Colorado Springs	Multnomah	Wheeling Downs
A	AA	A	A	AA
B	A	BB	B	A
C	BB	B	C	B
D	B	C	DD	C
E	C	D	D	D
M	J	M	M	M
	M			

Back to the starting boxes... About 30 seconds before the race is to start, the sliding backs of the (odd-numbered) 1, 3, 5, and 7 boxes are raised, and those dogs are placed inside—*bodily,* in many cases, since most of them aren't too crazy about *this* part. These boxes are then closed, and the remaining four (even-numbered) dogs are then placed in their boxes. Usually, there is a small window in the front door of each box. This allows the dogs to see out, and also keeps them from wanting to turn around, though they couldn't, anyhow, without great difficulty. Soon, they'll see the rabbit *(lure)* coming around the track. They know that the front door is going to flip wide open at any second, and the race will be on. Every dog *knows,* deep in its heart, that *this* will be the time they will *catch* that dumb rabbit and find out what's inside! Some are starting to bay and howl, though they'll stop barking the instant the race starts.

The lure approaches the starting box... In an upstairs control room, a human hand is on the lever that controls the speed of the lure. The operator must watch the progress of the race closely, to keep the lure at just the right distance in front of the lead dog. The rabbit dare not be caught, but the dogs must be allowed to get close enough to be convinced that they *are* going to catch it—this time. The lure itself is usually a cotton facsimile, and is mounted on a horizontal rod extending into the center of the track from a miniature electric go-cart that rides on electric trolley rails. These rails can be either on the inside rail of the track (inside lure), or on the outer edge (outside lure). The majority of tracks use an inside lure. In some cases, there may be two lures attached to the rod. (One rabbit for every four dogs?)

Usually, the lure has a nickname, and as it approaches the starting boxes, the announcer intones, "H-e-r-e c-o-m-e-s S-P-U-N-K-Y! (Or Rusty, or Sparky, or whatever...)

As the lure swings in front of the boxes, the entire front of the starting box assembly swings up swiftly, opening all eight boxes at precisely the same instant. Attendants beside the boxes are poised and alert to assist any dog that might slip or fall at the start—or decide to head for the barn, instead of for the rabbit! In perhaps one race in 300 (more often than not in a maiden race with new, inexperienced dogs) a dog might simply choose to stay in the box, or stroll out and casually watch the other seven dogs peel out. Hope that *your* money's not on *that* one, 'cause there are no refunds.

Prior to the opening of the boxes, the lead-outs leave the starting area and position themselves near the finish point, out of sight, so that the dogs won't be distracted during the race by seeing them.

As the doors flip up, the dogs leap out in a powerful surge. In the first few strides it is often apparent which dog will reach the first turn in the lead—a definite advantage, especially in the shorter races. The greyhounds' large feet and claws get a good grip on the track for this fast start, and the dirt literally flies.

More often than not, the majority of the dogs hit the first turn in a pack. Usually, some contact is made: No courtesy or right-of-way applies here—it's every dog for himself! Sometimes hard collisions occur. Now and then one or more dogs can fall, stumble, tumble, crash, or otherwise clobber or get clobbered. Seldom do serious injuries occur, however, even if the speeding dog wipes out and actually rolls over several times. Any dog that falls is certainly done with for *that* race, even though after a bad tumble most dogs will get back up and take off again after the pack. Attendants are positioned at various points around the track to gather up any dog that might seriously need help.

Through the back straightaway and into the next curve, every dog is trying its best to get to the front of the pack. He wants *his* teeth to be the first to sink into that crazy lure! This is bred into them, and it's what they *live* for. They are at their best right here, and they're doing exactly what they would rather do more than absolutely anything else! Go inside! Go outside! Cut 'em off! Squeeze through! Bump 'em out! Anything is fair! There is no "Excuse me" or "Oops—I'm sorry!" It's hell-bent for election, and no dog can pull dirt better than the greyhound.

They're in the stretch now, and the dogs that favor the outside of the track are swinging out there and turning on even more dog-power. *Anything* can happen in the stretch. More often than not, the dog that comes out of the final turn in the lead will finish in the money—but not always, by any means! And a truly strong dog that may have experienced some minor trouble at the start can speed into the stretch from dead last and win—if he's got the heart and the stamina.

On a 5/16-mile course, the dogs will hit the finish line about 30 seconds after the boxes flipped open. A 3/8-mile race takes about 40 seconds, and a 7/16-mile course usually clocks in at about 46 seconds. (Most tracks vary slightly from one another in exact distance, track surface condition, and other factors.)

The lure continues moving, past the finish line, and about one-third of the way into the next curve it will fold up and "disappear" into a trap box. The dogs decelerate and follow it right to the trap. By now, most

The greyhound is a perfect four-legged running machine. With his eye firmly on the lure, he is at full speed plus. Note how the muzzle coloration provides a sharp "nose" for the photo finish. Courtesy: Hollywood Greyhound Track, Florida.

tails are wagging. They realize that once again they've failed to catch that dumb bunny, but at least they made it hole up! Well, maybe next time . . .

In a typical race, the winning dog will be awarded 55% of the race's purse for its owner. The second-place dog will share 25%, third place 15%, and fourth place will earn 5%. At the major tracks, purses range from about $1750 for Grade A races to around $600 for maiden races. Championship races, of course, can range far above this, to as much as $100,000 or more. Most high-stakes races also divide the purse beyond fourth place.

Once the race is over, the track surface will usually receive a light grading and smoothing out before the next post parade starts—that is, unless it is raining (or snowing!). The next race will go off *exactly* as scheduled, usually in 15 minutes. There will be no delays for balky dogs, tardy jockeys, broken equipment, or anything else. Most fans appreciate this reliability, and realize that they must get into the betting lines in plenty of time to avoid being shut out.

The races will go on regardless of *any* weather conditions, short of a violent electrical storm that could endanger the staff or the dogs. (Or cause a power outage that would darken the lights and stall the electric rabbit. This has happened a few times, and it was hell on that cotton rabbit, muzzles or not! Makes for eight *really* happy dogs, though.) In the north, some of the tracks that operate in the winter months have steam-heat pipes buried under the surface of the track to prevent freezing. Otherwise, snow, sleet, downpours, fog, nor much else will cause a race cancellation, unless the roads are so bad that the dogs and the crowd simply can't get to the track. The dogs apparently don't mind in the least if it is raining (cats and dogs?), or snowing, or whatever. In fact, they often seem to thoroughly enjoy slogging through a muddy track, and rarely slip or fall because of it; some tracks even record *faster* times on a muddy track than on a track in good condition.

All in all, the dog races are a most enjoyable experience for nearly everyone. Often, after a horse race or a jai alai game, the losers are quite vocal, often in abusive language, about the darn jockey or driver or player who they think caused their loss through poor effort or for some foul reason. Somehow, losers at the dog track just can't get as angry or nasty about the affair. They picked the right dog, and the dog did his level best, but it was just that poor luck of being involved in that collision in the final turn! Oh well, who to pick for the next race. . . It seems to make for a far more pleasant atmosphere, and many folks who take their first look at the dog races go back again and again.

Positive Identification
—How it Works

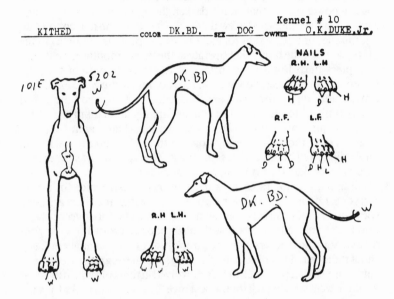

Greyhound racing has every safeguard possible to assure the sport's complete honesty and the security and protection of the patrons. One of the most valuable safety measures is the Bertillion Card, pictured here.

Greyhounds look pretty much the same to most people. But each animal is different, with distinguishable markings. It is the responsibility of the Paddock Judge to make sure that the proper greyhound will run in the proper race and in the proper position.

Every greyhound on the racing list at Hollywood has his own Bertillion Card. The card shown here is a copy of the one for the legendary *Kithed*. It provides complete information.

Table 3-2: *The Positive Identification System used by all U.S. tracks. Courtesy: Hollywood Greyhound Track.*

The top line of the card includes the name of the greyhound *(Kithed),* the color of the greyhound (DK, BD-dark brindle), the greyhound's sex (Dog, denoting a male), the greyhound's owner and the kennel number to which he belongs.

The tattoo numbers are the most important of all and each greyhound must have them in accordance with Florida law.

The numbers on the right ear (101E) stand for the month (October) and the year (1971) *Kithed* was whelped. The initial "E" alongside signifies that *Kithed* was No. 5 tattooed in the litter. The figures (5202) on the left ear stand for the litter registration number, filed with the National Greyhound Association.

Coloration and all markings of the greyhound are then drawn in detail, even including the color of the toenails. The "W" underneath signifies the coloring under the chest.

R.H. and L.H. (at right) stand for *Kithed*'s right hind and left hind feet. The initials D, L and H show where the toenails are dark (D), light (L), and horn (H). Directly below are R.F. and L.F. for right front and left front.

At left are R.H. and L.H. again with the "W" standing for partial white feet.

It's all part of the complete safety measures that keep greyhound racing the cleanest and most honest of sports.

Chapter 4
Pari-Mutuels and Betting Information

"Pari-mutuel" is a French-derived term for "Betting among each other, or ourselves." This is exactly what one does at the race track, be it a greyhound track or horse track. A common misconception is that when one places a bet one is betting against "the track." Those who believe this feel that "the track" then sets the odds, and can arbitrarily pay off whatever it chooses. This philosophy generates some rather ill feelings toward the track when the payoffs are smaller than the ill-informed bettor felt they should be. In fact, you will sometimes overhear these people discussing various tracks in terms of which ones are "stingy" or "generous." If this were actually the case, human nature being what it is, we probably wouldn't have any racetrack betting today. Your author, for one, certainly wouldn't participate in any betting in which the odds were computed to serve the track's profit or expense needs.

The fact is that when we make a bet on a race, we are betting against our fellow fans. To see how this works, let's bring it down to the smallest scale. Suppose eight of us are about to watch a dog race. I say to the other fans, "I'll bet $100 that number 4 will win this race." The other fans each pick a different dog, and put $100 on their selection. A representative from the track is standing by, and says, "I'll hold the money. From it, I will remove 18% to pay the dog owners for racing their dogs, the expenses involved with maintaining the grandstand and track, the wages of those who work here, the taxes to the state for our license to conduct races, and some profit for the track owners." This gentleman takes our $800, and we all watch the race together. Another gentleman, a state official, is standing in the background watching all of these proceedings, and his fellow employee is down at the paddock area to make sure the race is run fairly. Number 4 wins! I get my $100 back, plus the $100 from each of the fans that bet on other dogs, right? A total of $800, right? Wrong! The gentleman from the track will pay me $656. He had collected and held our total bets of $800. From this, he withheld 18%, or $144, as per the agreement made earlier. He, or the track, could not care less about which dog wins. He will not make a nickel more or less, regardless of the outcome.

This example, of course, is over-simplified. In a real-life situation, the odds on each dog will be different. These odds are arrived at purely by the amount wagered on each dog, compared to what amounts have been wagered on the other dogs. As a simple example, suppose that six fans bet on number 4, one fan bets on number 3, and one fan bets on number 8. Number 4 wins. This time, six bettors need to be paid off. The track was holding the same $800 total, and will be deducting the same $144 "take." Each of the six winning bettors will get their original $100 back, and will share the remaining $56 evenly, (except that the track will keep the odd pennies, or *break*). This means that the winners will collect $109.30 each. Not much profit, eh? The problem was that too many folks bet on that number 4 dog, and made him the *favorite*.

If that number 3 dog had won, the holder of that one winning ticket would have collected all $656, because he was betting on a *long shot*. Nothing about the dog automatically made him a long shot. The "morning odds" in the program had nothing to do with it—that was just one man's guess as to how *he* thought the crowd would *probably* bet. Nothing that the track decided had anything to do with the odds—*they get the same $144 no matter which dog wins.* (If you owned a racetrack, you would likely be pleased to see nice big payoffs occur now and then, to whet the appetite of the bettors to wager more so that your cut of the total [the handle] would be more.)

Again, this is greatly simplified to illustrate the principle of pari-mutuel wagering. In reality, the process becomes somewhat more involved because of the need to share winnings for the *place* and *show* positions, along with the *win* position.

The "pool" however, for the *quiniela* betting, as well as the dollars bet on the *perfecta* and *trifecta,* is held separate from the monies bet on win, place or show. Therefore, the payoffs on these bets are not determined by the odds reflected in the win, place or show betting. The payoffs are, however, determined in exactly the same manner—the amount of money the winners share is in direct proportion to the amount of money made available by those who bought losing tickets. It is not a matter of the track simply figuring that it is time for a fat or a slim payoff.

Coming out of the final curve, the two lead dogs are focused entirely on the lure. Notice how close the inside dog is to the rail. Courtesy: Palm Beach Kennel Club.

The Tote Board

Every track has a lighted display board in the infield in view of the wagering public. The information appearing here is also shown on similar lighted boards and/or television screens at various locations around the grandstand, clubhouse, and betting areas.

This information is constantly being updated, usually about every 20 to 30 seconds. The most prominent display is of the odds currently in effect for the win bet. The tote board is connected to the computer center, which monitors every ticket machine in the facility. At all times, this "brain" knows exactly how much is being bet on each dog. It quickly deducts the track's take from this figure, and computes what the payoff would be if that dog won. It then displays this figure in the form of odds on the tote board. These odds are constantly changing, as bettors place more or less on one dog or another. They will become *final* only when the starting box flips open. At this instant, the betting machines are automatically locked, and no further betting can take place.

If, for example, the final odds on the winning dog are 5-2 when the race starts, holders of $2 tickets on that dog will be paid 2½ times what they bet, plus the amount of their bet, or $7, in this example. If a favorite dog had very short odds, say of 1-5, the $2 ticket would pay only $2.40. (Winnings of 40 cents, plus the amount bet.) This is simply because so many people bet on that dog, and had to share the bets of the few that didn't, that there just wasn't much to be shared. By the way, in most states, if *everyone* bet on the winner, and there were no "losings" for the winners to share, the track *still* has to make a minimum payoff of $2.10 or $2.20 on a $2 bet. This is the only time that a track can actually lose money because of the outcome. It happens only very rarely, usually on show tickets on a very strong favorite.

A $2 ticket will pay off the following amounts, at the odds shown:

Odds	Pays	Odds	Pays
1-5	$ 2.40	7-2	$9.00
2-5	2.80	4-1	10.00
1-2	3.00	9-2	11.00
3-5	3.20	5-1	12.00
4-5	3.60	6-1	14.00
1	4.00	7-1	16.00
6-5	4.40	8-1	18.00
7-5	4.80	9-1	20.00
3-2	5.00	10-1	22.00
8-5	5.20	12-1	26.00
9-5	5.60	15-1	32.00
2-1	6.00	18-1	38.00
5-2	7.00	20-1	42.00
3-1	8.00	22-1	46.00

Most toteboards don't show the odds, payoffs, or amounts wagered on place and show. In this case, the bettor can only observe the win odds, and project this to probable odds on the other two positions. The payoffs on place and show depend not only on the amount wagered, but also on which other dogs finish in which positions. In other words, the payoff on a show bet will depend not only on which dog showed, but also on which dogs finished first and second. Since a ticket will pay off if the dog bet on comes in first, second, *or* third, a favorite coming in in any of these positions, with a lot of show bets made on him, will dilute the show payoff for everyone, whether they bet on him to show, or on the dogs that finished second or third. If all three positions are won by long shots, the payoff for show will be far larger, unless a lot of people bet a lot of money to show on one of the dogs, even though he was a long shot to win.

Let's review the basics for a moment. A *win* ticket bought on a dog will pay off only if that dog does win. If he comes in second or third, that ticket loses. A *place* ticket bought on a given dog will pay off if that dog comes in second *or* first. If the dog comes in third, that ticket loses. A *show* ticket bought on a given dog will pay off if that dog comes in third *or* second *or* first.

At first thought, logic seems to dictate that one should buy nothing but show tickets, since the ticket will pay off if the selected dog gets third or better. After all, there are only eight dogs in the race, and pure chance gives any dog a 37% chance of at least showing. In fact, if one bought show tickets on all eight dogs in the race, three of the eight tickets would win money and only five would lose! If that sounds like a winning program to you, you'll need to look a little further into the facts of racing. The "catch" is that the payoffs on show average out so small that one would still lose his bankroll, even if cashing in three tickets out of every eight. In fact, even if you get so good at handicapping that you can cash *six* show tickets out of eight, you would still likely lose money.

Looking at the program, one can tell which dogs *he* thinks are the best of the lot. Looking at the tote board, one can instantly see which dogs the *crowd* thinks are the best of the lot, in order of preference. This is a true consensus of the betting selections made by everyone present. Sometimes you will note that a certain dog appears to be a strong favorite early on in the betting, and then seems to "cool off," with the odds increasing more with each flash of the board. This can happen if an early bettor places a large amount on that certain dog, say $100, $500, or more. That bet alone will affect the odds enough to send them way down. If not many other bettors agree with that one, the odds on that dog will start back up, as more people bet more on other dogs.

However, a certain number of fans will notice that bet, and be influenced by those odds, and put some of their money on that dog simply because they think that somebody must "know something" that they don't, even though the dog doesn't seem that strong to them. This may hold the odds down, or even drive them further down, as the crowd is affected more by what they think they see in the board than what their own handicapping knowledge tells them. For this very reason, large bettors often wait until the last minute to place their big bet, so that other fans will not have time to notice and put a lot more money on that dog and drive the odds down even more. Frankly, that is usually of no special disadvantage to others, for this "smart" bet is not that "smart" that often. In fact, it is sometimes a foolish dog owner who is putting a chunk of his money where his heart is. Or it may be someone who "heard something" from someone who "heard something" from his friend's cousin, whose brother works in the restaurant at the track, and heard that one of the dogs really looked good in a schooling race the other afternoon. . .

One feature presented by the tote boards at many tracks, or shown on TV monitors, is the probable odds of the various quiniela and/or perfecta payoffs. Odds will be indicated on all of the various combinations. This is not only of interest, but can be of real advantage to the studious bettor. By looking at these odds, one can also see that there indeed is not always a firm and logical connection between these odds and those that are reflected on the win odds; it is purely a matter of how many fans are betting on which combinations of numbers. The *trifecta* odds cannot be shown, simply because there are too many possible number combinations—336 combinations in an eight-dog race, to be exact. (However, some tracks do show how much is being bet in the trifecta pool on each dog, which does give a fairly accurate preview of the probable size of the payoff.)

Types of Bets

We have already discussed the win, place, and show bets. One can bet as many dogs as he wishes to do any of the above. In fact, one can bet a dog to do all three, which would be a *combination bet* or betting *across the board*. In this case, the bettor would cash all three tickets if the dog won; cash the place and show tickets if the dog placed; and cash the show ticket if the dog showed. Or one can bet one dog or several to win, another one or more to place, and the same ones or another, or others, to show. In short, one can bet any way one likes. (But if one bets too many ways in one race, one is bound to lose.)

One can bet nearly any amount desired on any type of bet desired, as long as the increments are in the amount required by the track. Most tracks have a $2 minimum bet to win, place or show. From this point on, bets can be made in dollar increments, that is, $3, $4, $5 or whatever. A few tracks, without electronic ticket machines, still sell tickets in $2, $5 or $10 increments.

Quinielas

Nearly every track offers quiniela betting on most, if not all, races. In this bet, the bettor attempts to select the two dogs that will come in first and second. *He will win if they come in in either order,* and the payoff will be the same, no matter which order they come in. The size of the payoff will be determined purely by how many other people bet the same combination, and how much "loser's money" there is to share from those people who put money into the pool for losing combinations. The average quiniela payoff at most tracks is around $28 for a $2 ticket, though it can range from as little as $4 to as much as $200, or even far more.

Of course, one may bet as many combinations as desired on quiniela bets in any race. In fact, if you wanted to cover *all* of the combinations, you could say, "Box 'em all." Your ticket would cost $56, and you'd have a sure winner. You're gambling that the payoff would be larger than your outlay. Over a span of time, it won't average out, obviously. You can instead box three dogs ($6 or multiples thereof) or box four dogs ($20 or more), or 5, or 6, or 7.

You may also *wheel* a quiniela. You can select one dog and wheel him with all of the rest. (Seven bets, costs $14.) Or, you can *partial wheel* one dog with only *some* of the others. If one of your first two choices, or the crowd's, is in first or second place more than about 60% of the time, try wheeling the first choice with the second, third and fourth choices, and the second choice with the third, fourth and fifth. This will cost $12 (or multiples thereof) and may well return a profit over a span of time (especially if the selections are yours, by means of a good handicapping system, and score better than those of the crowd).

Perfectas

Perfectas are also known as *exactas* at some tracks. This works just like the quiniela, except that to win you must pick the winner and the second-place dog *in order*. This, of course, is more difficult, and therefore fewer bettors will be successful at it, but the average payoffs will be larger. In fact, they will usually be two to three times larger than the quiniela payoff, though this is only an average and not a firm rule. (Under certain circumstances, it is possible for the quiniela payoff to be larger than the perfecta payoff for a given race. This is quite rare, however, and is purely a factor of how the other bettors bet.)

You may also box or wheel perfecta bets, just as you do in the quiniela; however, box bets cost more since you are buying two tickets on each combination—one with one of the dogs on top, and one for the other order. Likewise, in the wheel, the dog you wheel with the others must win, not place, or you lose. Again, you may wheel or box as many combinations as you choose, in whatever increments the track requires. (Note: at a few tracks, the basic perfecta bet is for $3, instead of $2.) One cannot afford to habitually cover all of the combinations and hope for big payoffs. A $2 perfecta box of all eight dogs, for example, would cost $112, and over a span of time would very likely lose money.

Trifectas

Also known as the *Pick 3* or *Big 3*, the trifecta involves selecting the top *three* dogs in the finish. You may bet them straight (in order), or box them (which means that you win if they come in in any order). At tracks where the basic straight trifecta bet is $2, a three-dog box ticket is $6, but pays only half of the payoff amount of the straight ticket. One may box four dogs ($24), five dogs ($60), or six or seven or even all eight.

The average trifecta payoff at the average dog track is around $400; the average box payoff is therefore around $200. It is a very popular form of betting, and recommended by many professional handicappers.

Occasionally, the size of the trifecta payoff seems to bear no relationship to the odds shown in the win column on the tote board. A long shot may win, and the payoff be far smaller than would seem logical, or the reverse may happen. It must be remembered that the trifecta pool is kept separate from the other pools, and the payoff is in direct proportion to how people bet *on the trifecta,* not how they bet to win.

The Big Q

The Big Q is also known as the double quiniela. Here, the bettor buys a quiniela ticket on a given race (often the next-to-last race of the program). If that ticket is a winner, instead of cashing it in, he exchanges it for another selection on the following race. If he hits that, it's usually a large payoff, since this pool is held separate and no one else can buy into it once the first half is underway. Of 1000 tickets purchased, for example, perhaps only 50 are winners on the first half, and are allowed to exchange for a ticket on the next race. The other 950 buyers have lost and are out. Their money will be shared only by those in the remaining 50 who select the right combination. Of the 50 lucky bettors who were still "alive" going into the second race, if only five pick the right combination in the last race, those five are going to share the whole pool.

Those who regularly play the Big Q usually buy multiple tickets on the first race. If they are boxing selections for the first race, they may buy the same box two, three, or more times. Then, if they win on that first race, they have several winning tickets to exchange on multiple selections in the second race. For example, if it is their habit to box four dogs in a quiniela, they would likely box their four selections *six times* on the first race, costing them $72. If they won, they would then have six winning tickets to exchange for the second race, so that they could likewise box four dogs in that race at no additional cost. That's a bunch of money, for most folks, but the Big Q payoffs are usually quite large, very seldom under $200 and often far more.

The Pick Six

This is an exotic bet in which the bettor attempts to select the *winners* of six sequential races. It is, of course, nearly impossible to do with one bet. One bet may cost as little as $1 or $2. The near impossibility of it is evidenced by the huge payoffs often achieved ($250,000 or more has been paid off in some cases). If there is not a winner on a given program, as is often the case, consolation prizes are paid to those who come the closest by selecting five or four of the six. This bet was introduced within the last few years and is becoming increasingly popular due to the publicity given to the tremendous payoffs. It is not, in this author's opinion, much different from a random lottery. Many folks who "go for it" do so as they do for the lotteries, by boxing and betting many combinations. This practice, of course, runs up the cost.

Superfectas

This is a step beyond the trifecta, in that the bettor attempts to select the first *four* dogs across the finish line. Since this is far more difficult to do, the payoffs are accordingly much larger. Boxing and wheeling may be done, just as for the trifecta or other combination bets.

Other Types of Bets

The track's printed program outlines the various types of betting available along with the amounts accepted in each kind of bet, the rules pertaining to refunds, false starts, etc. Read these directions carefully, for once you leave the betting window you will never get a refund for any error made by you or the clerk. Make sure you know how things work *before* you make your bet. If you are not clear on something, go to the information window, where a clerk is present to help you understand. Don't hesitate to ask, and remember that some tracks may vary from the methods described here.

The Bettor and the IRS

In the track's program is a section about the process of handling your winnings if they are of an amount to come to the interest of the Internal Revenue Service.

Basically, if you cash a ticket for more than 300 times what that ticket cost you ($600 on a $2 bet, $900 on a $3 bet, etc.) you must give the track your name and Social Security number and sign a receipt for the winnings. The track will send a copy of the form to the IRS, and you must report that as gambling winnings on your next return. (You may be able to offset those winnings with losses, but you can never deduct more losses than winnings.)

In most states, if your total winnings on one ticket are $1000 or more, regardless of what it cost you, you will not only need to fill out the form, etc., but the track will deduct 20% of your winnings right then and there, and send this amount to the IRS "for" you. (Under certain circumstances, you may be able to sign certain other forms, and get your hands back on that 20% on the spot.) Certain exceptions might apply if more than one bettor owns a winning ticket, but your odds of legally bypassing this proposition are slim. At some tracks are certain fans who, because of their tax bracket of whatever, are willing to take the "big" winning tickets to the window for the real winners, and sign the form in *their* name, instead of the winner's. They do this for a percentage. It is an illegal practice for both parties.

Betting Methods

Many tracks are installing computer-controlled mutuel machines which allow any type of bet to be made at any window, and winning tickets can be cashed at the same window. Often, a sign is displayed asking the bettor to call out first the amount of his bet, then the type of bet and the number or numbers of the dog(s) he wishes to bet on. (Not the *name* of the dog.) This might be "Five dollars to place on number 7," or "A one-dollar trifecta box on 4, 7 and 8." Always call out the smallest number first, except with perfectas, in which case the first number you say is the one which you intend to bet to win.

Again, the track's program will contain complete betting instructions. You will find that everything is done to make wagering simple, easy and quick. The track also intends that each clerk is friendly and helpful to you. If one of them is not, be sure to let management know.

Do be sure to look at your ticket before you leave the betting window. If an error has been made, and mistakes can happen, you must catch it *then*. If you go long enough to the races, you will slip up some day and when the dogs cross the finish line *think* that you have a winning ticket in your pocket, but then find out that the clerk didn't give you what you ordered (or you called it out wrong, or whatever). Even if the ticket *would have been* worth $1000, don't bother trying to collect or get a refund. The clerk certainly didn't do it on purpose, since he or she could not possibly have anything to gain by punching the wrong numbers. One thing is sure—you'll be checking your tickets at the window for a long time afterward. Likewise, if you buy a winning ticket, then lose it, that's tough luck. You might get someone to listen to your sob story, but you ain't gonna talk anybody into paying you for it.

Many tracks have advance wagering, whereby you can place your bets for following races prior to the time the previous race is done. That is, you could go to the track, place all your bets for the whole evening, and just stay in your seat and (hopefully) cash all of your winners at the end of the evening. . . Or even leave the track and cash your tickets the next night, or later. In some cases, you can even go to the track on the afternoon of the races and place your bets. These features are not available at all tracks, but will be explained completely in the program.

Examples of some types of bets involving multiple selections. Courtesy of Wheeling Downs.

BOX AND KEY ENTRY BETTING

QUINIELA BOX . . . Pick at least three or more dogs and if 2 of the dogs finish 1st and 2nd - YOU ARE A WINNER.

Number of dogs	Quiniela Box	Number of bets	$2.00 Base Bet Total Cost
3	DOG BOX	3	$ 6.00
4	DOG BOX	6	12.00
5	DOG BOX	10	20.00
6	DOG BOX	15	30.00
7	DOG BOX	21	42.00
8	DOG BOX	28	56.00

PERFECTA BOX . . . Pick at least three or more dogs and if 2 of the dogs finish 1st and 2nd - YOU ARE A WINNER.

Number of dogs	Perfecta Box	Number of bets	$2.00 Base Bet Total Cost
3	DOG BOX	6	$ 12.00
4	DOG BOX	12	24.00
5	DOG BOX	20	40.00
6	DOG BOX	30	60.00
7	DOG BOX	42	84.00
8	DOG BOX	56	112.00

TRIFECTA BOX . . . Pick at least three or more dogs and if 3 of the dogs finish 1st, 2nd and 3rd in any order - YOU ARE A WINNER.

Number of dogs	Trifecta Box	Number of bets	$1.00 Base Bet Total Cost	$2.00 Base Bet Total Cost
3	DOG BOX	6	$ 6.00	$ 12.00
4	DOG BOX	24	24.00	48.00
5	DOG BOX	60	60.00	120.00
6	DOG BOX	120	120.00	240.00
7	DOG BOX	210	210.00	420.00
8	DOG BOX	336	336.00	672.00

TRIFECTA KEY . . . Pick at least three or more dogs. Your KEY dog must finish in the position selected and 2 of the other dogs can finish in any order - YOU ARE A WINNER.

Number of dogs	Trifecta Key	Number of bets	$1.00 Base Bet Total Cost	$2.00 Base Bet Total Cost
3	Dog Key	2	$ 2.00	$ 4.00
4	Dog Key	6	6.00	12.00
5	Dog Key	12	12.00	24.00
6	Dog Key	20	20.00	40.00
7	Dog Key	30	30.00	60.00
8	Dog Key	42	42.00	84.00

IMPORTANT . . . When placing your bet always state the Base Amount of your Bet.

For Example: $2 Quiniela Box on #1, 2, and 3
$2 Perfecta Box on #1, 2, and 3
$1 Trifecta Box on #4, 5, and 6
$1 Trifecta Key - #1 to win and
#5, 6, and 8

Chapter 5

The Printed Race Program

The thoroughbred fan has his *Racing Form,* the baseball fan has his sports pages and statistics, the stock market player has his financial reports . . . and the greyhound fan has his *program.*

The track prints a program for each racing day, usually about 24 hours in advance. Generally, these are available at various sales points around the track area (drug stores, newsstands, etc.), and sold to the public for about $1 to $2. At most tracks, one can purchase a program for the following day before leaving the track but usually not until after the eighth race, to make it less likely that someone will use the wrong program for the wrong date.

The program usually includes a chart of the race results from a day or two before. This is helpful information for the handicapper; even if he was there himself, he may wish to read the chartwriter's comments on certain races. (Note: the track's chartwriter is paid to write that brief synopsis of what happened to each dog during each race, i.e., "Collided first turn," "Box to wire," "Flew wide," etc. While the fan has only seconds to see all of this develop, the chartwriter has the benefit of re-playing tapes of each race, until he can note each dog's circumstances and comment on them.)

The results charts printed in the program also note the exact odds that each dog went off at, the condition of the track, the times of each race, and other information. This is generally more information than is provided in newspaper reports, and may well be of specific interest to certain types of handicapping which involve record-keeping. The program also contains much more useful data concerning the track facilities, types of betting, and post position records.

The *most important* information included in the program, however, is the listing of the entries for the races on the present date, and the *past performance charts* for each of the dogs entered. This is far more than just a listing of the names and weights of the contestants—though that alone seems to be adequate information for some of the casual bettors that one often overhears!

31

Most programs list the details of the last six or eight races that each dog ran. A virtual mountain of information is contained here, some of which is pertinent, some not. Which *is* and which *isn't* is a point of great debate among various handicappers. In later chapters we will help the reader sort this out for himself. In this chapter, we will simply address how to interpret the material itself.

Basically, what one will find, race by race, dog by dog, includes:

(1) The date of each race, and whether it was a matinee or evening race. An "x" after the date signifies a matinee.

(2) The condition of the track and, in some cases, the weather and /or temperature.

(3) The odds that each dog went off at in each past race.

(4) The post position that each dog started from in each of the past races.

(5) How each dog got out of the box, in relationship to the other dogs in each of the races. (The *break*.)

(6) How each dog was in position at the "1/8 call" and the "stretch call" in each race.

(7) How each dog finished in each race.

(8) What course each race was run on.

(9) What the winning time was for each race.

(10) What each dog's *computed* time was for each race.

(11) How many dogs were in each race.

(12) What each dog weighed in each race.

(13) Who the owner of each dog is.

(14) Who the trainer of each dog is.

(15) Which kennel entered each dog.

(16) Who each dog's parents were.

(17) How old each dog is. (When they were born.)

(18) Each dog's color.

(19) Each dog's gender. (Male = D, Female = B.)

(20) What track each race was run at.

(21) What grade each race was run at.

(22) If the race shown was not a race at all, but was really a "schooling race."

(23) The record of each dog for the year to date, and also for the last year. Number of total races entered, and the number of wins, places, and shows. Some programs also list the number of fourth-place finishes.

(24) The names of the dogs the winning dog beat in each race, or the names of the dogs that came in ahead of that dog in those races. (Note: unlike horse race programs, the name of this dog is not listed at this point.)

(25) The chartwriter's comments on each of the races shown.

(26) The post positions and blanket colors for the present day's race.

(27) The "morning odds" for each dog. (This is not the track's odds-maker's idea of who *he* thinks is the best; it is his notion of how he thinks the *crowd* will bet. Some programs also show the theory of a local handicapper, usually not employed by the track, to show how *he* thinks the dogs will finish.)

(28) Some programs provide the number of the race that each dog ran in on each date, i.e., the first race of the night, the eighth race, etc.

That's a *lot* of information—far more, really, than most people can absorb—and a lot of it isn't very useful. Those studious bettors who manage a profit at the track, though, have learned which information to use and which to discard. Even so, it takes them a certain amount of time to put it all into meaningful order. If you buy a program on the way into the track and simply glance at it just before each race, you won't have much chance to gather enough information for intelligent wagering. It does take some study.

Save your programs when you're done with them. If you've marked them in any way, there is something to learn by studying them again later, whether you won or lost. The track's floor and parking lot are littered with discarded programs when the races are finished; many were thrown down in disgust by "fans" who lost. If they come back again, they'll very likely lose again, for they haven't learned from their mistakes. Your old programs can be your best source of information for developing a winning system at any track.

Following are two samples of the instructions printed in programs for the interpretation of the past performance charts:

How To Read Past Performance Chart

An explanation of the past performance chart is shown below. It gives information for use in studying the past performance.

MKC LORINE (59) HOL 20 7 4 3 2 / BIS 14 3 3 4 0 — Owner—Ralph Long; Kennel—Ralph Long 18; Trainer—Kathy Krips

Brindle B., January, 1979. Sandy Printer—Dixie's Donna.

Date and Race Previous Event	Distance	Track Condition	Time of Winner	Weight at Post Time	Post Position	Start	One-Eighth Lengths Back	Stretch Call	Finish—Lengths From Winner	Actual Running Time	Odds	Grade	Comment	Order of Finish
3-21^{13}	5-16	F	31.34	59	7	5	1^{2}	1^{3}	1½	31.34	7.40	SA	World champ	DJRagener,FlyingRoger,DDsJackie
3-14^{10}	5-16	F	31.26	58½	5	2	3	3	1^{hd}	31.26	2.60	SA	Up last step	Clerked,FlyingRoger,GHsChuck
3-11^{10}	5-16	F	31.30	59	2	4	3	3	3^{3½}	31.55	5.40	A	Gd.effrt.wd	SkihiElse,DJQuesto,Reunited
3- 7^{10}	5-16	F	31.18	59½	6	5	3	3	2^{2}	31.31	8.00	A	Tried hard wd.	DDsJackie,DJQuesto,Reunited
3- 4^{7}	5-16	F	31.57	59½	6	6	4	2	2^{nk}	31.60	4.20	A	Bold bid wd	DJQuesto,RickBick,DocsMoonshadw
2-28^{12}	5-16	F	31.43	59½	4	4	2	1^{1}	1^{ns}	31.43	8.50	B	Up on outside	TopQuality,Kingsford,BonkysFirst

The above grouping embraces all the essential points on each greyhound in the program. The number to the right of the greyhound's name is its set weight. Next is the record at Hollywood, (Number of starts first, second, third, fourth) while the greyhound's record at the track he performed at before Hollywood is immediately below (BIS-Biscayne). Next is the owner and kennel. Below is the trainer. Beneath the greyhound's name is its color, sex, whelping date and breeding. Reading across the first past performance line, MKC Lorine last ran on March 21 in the thirteenth race over the 5-16 Mile Course. "F" indicates the track surface was Fast. "S" means Slow; "M" indicates Muddy. The time of the winner was 31.34, MKC Lorine's post weight was 59 pounds, she broke from the seven box, she broke fifth, was first by two lengths at the 1/8 mile call, was first by 3 lengths at the head of the stretch and crossed under the wire first by 1/2 length. Her time was 31.34 and her equivalent odds to the dollar were 7.40. The chartwriter's comment on the race the greyhound ran follows immediately while the SA denotes MKC Lorine ran in grade A company while the "S" signifies it was a stakes race. The three names on the end were the top three finishers after MKC Lorine in the race. The line under March 21 shows MKC Lorine last ran on March 14 in the tenth race and won the race by a head (HD) over Clerked who ran second in the race. If the grade of the race is preceded by a capital "S" it was a stakes race; if preceded by a "T" that race was put together by the Racing Secretary matching eight of the finest greyhounds at the track.

An "s" following the date indicates a schooling race and if there is a number after the three finishers the figure is the number of greyhounds in the schooling race. An asterik after a greyhound's name means imported; "M" means graded maiden; "OOP" in running times means 'out of picture'; "X" after the date indicates matinee. (WL) after the greyhound means weight loser.

Courtesy of the Hollywood Greyhound Track.

HOW TO READ THE PROGRAM

***MISS BISCAYNE** (59) Kennel—Bluebell Kennel; Owner—John Smith; Trainer—Richard Roe — BIS 8 6 1 0 / TAU 2 0 1 1

Fawn B., Jan. 1973. Stout Fellow—Good Producer

Post Position Blanket Number	Date and Race Previous Event	Distance	Time of Winner	Weight at Post Time	Post Position	Start	One-Eighth Lengths Ahead	Stretch Call	Finish—Lengths From Winner	Actual Running Time	Odds	Comment Pertaining to Effort Made	Grade of Race	ORDER OF FINISH SHOWING FIRST THREE DOGS If dog finishes first, second or third its name is omitted and the fourth dog to finish is shown.
1	10-27^{11}	Mar	48.51	59½	6	5	4	3	2^{1}	48.58	3.10	Driving outside	SA	Riata, Strictly, Upperhand
	10-20^{10}	Mar	48.53	59	3	7	5	2	1^{2}	48.53	2.20	Handily	TA	Upperhand, Rope, Review
	10-15^{2}s	Mar	48.55	59	2	6	1^{1}	1^{1}	1^{3}	48.55	— —	Easily		Tootie, MarMar, Ida^{7}
	10- 5^{10}	BC	33.33	59½	8	5	4	3	1^{5}	33.33	4.20	Pulled out	A	Sweetie, NonSense, Rajah
	x9- 8^{10}	BC	33.32	59	7	7	7	6	4^{8}	33.88	*.80	Bumped early	A	NonSense, Pluto, Ibid

Top line shows Dog's name and racing weight; color and sex; date whelped; sire and dam; owner, kennel and trainer. At right is the Dog's record at Biscayne (top line), and at the last meeting at which it raced. Record shows number of starts and number of firsts, seconds and thirds.

The letters A, B, C, D, E, M, T and S appearing at the end of the race comment line indicate the Grade of the race: (M-Maiden; S-Special, or Stakes Race; T-Mixed Grades. In an S or T race the actual grade of the dog is listed following S or T—S(A)—T(B).

Small "x" preceding date and race in past performance lines denotes Matinee, small "s" after date indicates schooling race; small figure in the one-eighths column denotes lengths ahead if in the lead; small figure in the finish column shows number of lengths by which the dog won, or the number of lengths behind the winner at the finish. *In front of odds denotes favorite in race. *In front of dog's name indicates foreign-born.

Times given in past performances are those of the winner and actual running time of the dog shown. (OOP means Out of Picture).

Small figure in the "order of finish" column shows the number of dogs in the race when less than eight.

Weights shown in past performances and charts are the actual weights of greyhounds as they went to the post for each race. The weight shown in the parenthesis beside the dog's name is the established racing weight of that dog.

Chart Calls: In all races the 1/8th call is made as the dogs enter the backstretch, on a line with the Marathon Course box. In all races the stretch call is made as the dogs enter the stretch, approximately at the Biscayne Course box.

Courtesy of Biscayne Dog Track.

Some tracks vary slightly in the exact spot on the track where each "call" is reported. This is a rather important factor in accurate interpretation of the information, so be sure to learn the particulars about the specific track which you attend. Following are two illustrations of this:

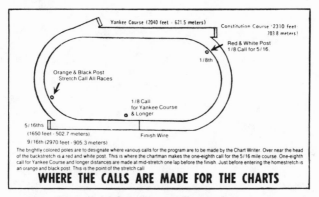

WHERE THE CALLS ARE MADE FOR THE CHARTS

Plainfield Greyhound Track, Conn.:

Where Calls Are Made:

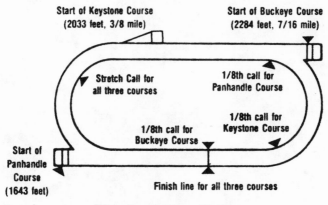

Wheeling Downs, W. Va.:

Chapter 6

Simple Methods of Basic Handicapping

Most fans go to the dog races to wager. If you are a real sports fan, or just enjoy the excitement of racing, or owned some dogs or had an interest in them, it is possible that you would enjoy the races without betting. The vast majority of the people that you'll see at the track, though, are there to *bet*. You'll probably want to bet, too . . . Better yet, you'll probably want to bet and *win!*

It is always possible that by betting on your house number, a dog with a cute name, or some other "dumb" selection, you could hit a jackpot with your very first bet on the dogs. That's called "dumb luck," and there are, indeed, a *few* people who manage to come out ahead on that alone. But of those who look no further than making "fun" bets, 999 out of 1000 will lose, lose, lose. That phrase, "fun bet," is misleading, because it usually means just picking out a dog by chance, and playing by luck. In reality, though, a fun bet is far more fun if it wins! Do a little homework on the program, while those around you are having too much fun to take it "that serious," and you will go home with some of their money in your pockets. (Take a poll the next day, and see who had the most "fun"!)

In short, if you're going to bet, and you'd rather win than lose, you'll have to pay attention to the factors that can give you an edge over your fellow fans. You don't have to become the smartest handicapper at the track—you just have to become "smarter" than about half of the other fans in attendance. That isn't too difficult.

You'll need to allow some time to weigh the factors printed in the program. It's best if you get a program *prior* to the start of the races, or at least arrive early enough to have some time to get started on "figuring" it.

The edge that basic handicapping can give you is minimal. You can lose this edge with hurried handicapping that is not thorough enough, or that produces errors. Take enough time to do it adequately, even if you must skip a few races to do so.

Mark your program to highlight the factors which you are going to use to make your selections. Few people can keep all of this information in their head. Don't worry about whether people think you're taking it all too seriously if you're seen scratching figures in a program. It probably took some serious work to get that money that you're going to bet with, and it is worth some study to keep it, or multiply it.

It is possible to become so involved in handicapping that you begin to think handicapping is the key to winning. If you should start to feel that way, back up! Handicapping is important, and one must develop this ability in order to come out ahead, but good handicapping alone does not assure success. One must also develop a *betting* plan and method if the handicapping system is to make profit. Remember this:

> *YOU CAN LOSE WITH GOOD HANDICAPPING AND POOR BETTING, BUT YOU CANNOT WIN WITH POOR HANDI- CAPPING AND GOOD BETTING!*

In other words, you must have and use *both,* together, or no system will work.

No matter how casually you wish to get involved with successful betting, you must keep some form of written record of your results, experiments, successes and errors. Without a record, no matter how scant, it is nearly impossible to learn from your experiences. Invest early in the basic tools of the trade: some notebooks for record-keeping, and a container, if no more than a cardboard box, in which to keep old programs.

The only other investment to consider would be an assortment of books on handicapping methods. Few, including this one, have *all* the answers, but most good books will have *some* good angles to investigate. You *can* reach a point where you actually "know too much" and out-handicap yourself, but you must at least get a good grip on the basics.

Beginning with the next chapter, we will deal with some major and rather studious methods for refining customized systems to win at specific tracks. Because tracks and factors vary considerably, it's difficult to generalize about reliable handicapping factors. The more a system/ method can be tailored to a particular track, the better the outcome. If you want to learn to do this well, read the rest of the book; if you are only interested in modest success, the rest of this chapter will get you started.

In handicapping any race, you must determine how *the eight dogs stack up against each other.* Even if you've been following a certain dog, or made some money on him in the past, don't bet him for those reasons alone. He has never been up against *these* seven other dogs together before, starting from *this* post position. Also, if you've bet on a certain dog before and *lost,* don't lay off of him out of hard feelings. Against another field, he may do much better.

In other words, look at one race alone, and the history that the eight dogs are bringing into it. Compare all the factors that you feel matter, each dog with the other seven. When you've done this, rate the field from one to eight. Select a dog which your intelligence says has the *best* chance to win. Place other dogs second, third, and so on. The easiest way to do this is numerically, giving certain numbers of "points" for the fastest dog, the strongest-finishing dog, etc., thereby ending up with a numerical sequence of point values for each dog.

Once you've done this, you're about half-way to a profitable series of bets. Next, you have to determine *how* to bet on your selections. It is not enough to simply bet your first choice to win, race after race; even the world's handicapping experts couldn't make a profit doing this. The fact is, you simply won't be that correct that often. Perhaps one of your first two or three choices does win nearly all the time. Even so, how would you bet? All three dogs to win, each time? That would be a losing system. All three dogs to show? There's no profit in trying to cover three dogs, or even two.

Does your system score better on the 5/16-mile course than on the 3/8-mile course? Does it score better or worse in certain grade races than others? The answer is almost certain to be yes to both of these questions, so your records had better tell you which courses and grades you do the best and worst on. And you will very likely find that there are certain grades on certain courses in which your facts say to not bet. In fact, that may be the case a full one-third or even one-half of the time. When your system says don't, *don't!* This may well be the best service that a good system provides for you: proving when it is dumb to bet.

Here are some basic keys to handicapping:

Speed. Average out the speed of each dog in recent races, as shown in the past performance chart. If there is much of a spread in these averages, it can mean important pluses and minuses. If there is not much of a spread, don't try to make much of a factor of it. Remember, it doesn't matter how fast the dogs are averaging compared to other races the same night, or to the track record, or another time of year, or another track. It matters *only* how their average speed compares to the other dogs in the *same* race.

Post position. In certain grades, and/or on certain courses, certain starting boxes tend to be "hot" or "cold." The printed program often includes a chart showing general post position results tables. This is a little too vague to be of specific use, and an individual will do better to make up his own such table. It can be done by checking past records, programs and charts. This advantage or disadvantage changes from time to time, so make sure that your table is fresh and current.

Late speed. This is also known as *stretch speed,* or *finish.* In other words, how does each dog usually do in the stretch, *compared to the other dogs in this race?* Look at the past performance charts and note the final two columns showing a dog's position in recent races. You will see if he gains in the stretch, loses, or holds his own. This is more of a factor on longer courses than on shorter courses.

Recent performance. This is also known as *form.* How has each dog done *lately?* Look closely at the most recent two, three or four races, than at the year-to-date record. Ignore last year's record altogether. Has the dog been in the money much lately? More or less than the other dogs *in this race?* Is he hot, or not?

Grade. Each dog in each race will be in the *same* grade as in his last or last several races; or in a grade *higher,* because he won his last race out; or in a grade *lower,* because he hasn't been in the money for the last several races. All of this matters, but not to the extent that the average fan usually considers. A dog winning a B race, for example, moves up to the A grade. Compare that dog with another one in the same race that finished fifth, fourth and eighth in his last Grade A races. Who's hot and who's not? The answer is not always this simple, and there are few rules of thumb. It can be a large factor in some grades on some courses, and a little factor in others. A little study of this factor at your track will clue you in. Don't go with the general rule of thumb that up is bad and down is good—the reverse can sometimes be true.

Early speed. This, of course, means how well a dog has been doing *early* in the race. Some handicappers look at how the dog *breaks;* that is, how fast he is at getting out of the starting box. The first column in the past performance chart indicates this. Other handicappers, including this author, feel that it is more pertinent to study how the dog does in getting into and through the first curve. This position is found in the second column.

As you study this, you will spot some dogs that have terrible early speed, but great late speed, or the reverse. This may or may not be a factor, depending on the pattern of the other dogs in the same race. On the other hand, some other dogs may have both adequate early *and* late speed, and these dogs often are in the money, even if they don't always win.

Inside or outside runner. Some dogs just naturally run better on the inside, outside, or middle of the track. You can sometimes get a clue to this from the chart-writer's comments, i.e., "Wide for show," "Inside late rush," etc. Many feel the outcome of a race can be forecasted by judging this factor alone. If an outside dog is starting from an inside box, won't he be more likely to collide, or at least be at a disadvantage? The answer, according to this author's studies, is that you cannot use this as a consistent factor.

Indeed, there are a few dogs who simply do not like certain boxes —outside, inside, or middle—and will do poorly from that position almost every time. Of course, one wants to be aware of this, and judge accordingly; but just because the program indicates that a dog who ran a "mid-track route" in most of his recent races is tonight starting from the –2 box is not a reason to downgrade the dog on that alone.

There are books written entirely about this, and they all seem to take it for granted that immediately upon the break all of the inside dogs are going to head for the rail, even if they are in the #7 or #8 boxes, and all of the wide, or outside, dogs are going to head immediately *there,* no matter what box they start from. This would definitely create a mass collision, and would give a tremendous advantage to an inside dog starting from the #1 box, and to a wide-running dog starting from the #8 box, and so on. However, most inside dogs who start from the outside boxes are smart enough not to go for the rail until the traffic thins out a little. Likewise for most outside dogs starting from inside boxes—few make an immediate break for the outside, but instead like to run there once the race is under way. In that chart-writer's three or four words, though, there simply isn't room to say "Started strong inside, moved to the middle of the track on the backstretch, and finished wide in the stretch." Instead, the comment might be something like "Strong finish outside." This, to many handicappers, would indicate an outside dog, and they would deduct points if that dog started from an inside box.

In short, watch for those few cases when a dog really does suffer from an unfavorable post position, but do not be too heavily swayed by those who would have you drawing collision courses on your program.

Ignore. Ignore schooling races and races in which the dog was bumped, or collided, or was otherwise impeded. Simply cross those races off of the program lines, and pay no attention to the times, speed, finish, or anything else about those races. Do your computing from the other races shown. If this leaves too little meaningful information about the dog to make an adequate judgment on him, and you cannot afford to include him in your bet "just in case," then pass on that race. You will notice that this will cause you to pass nearly all maiden races. Good! It is nearly impossible to apply intelligent handicapping to any race of eight dogs (or horses, for that matter) who have never won a race in their lives.

How to Bet, Once
You've Done Your Handicapping

If you are good enough at handicapping at a certain track, it is possible to turn a modest profit by betting your first two choices to *win,* especially if you have enough willpower to pass on those types of races which your system indicates you'll do poorly on. You won't get *that* much profit, though, because you'll have to beat the 16% to 18% house "take" just to break even. If you can manage a 5% to 10% profit above this, you'll have done extremely well, for win-betting. Chances are that you'll find it quite difficult to profit from a win-bet program.

For moderate but fairly reliable profit, the *quiniela* bet offers the best chance. Begin by *boxing* your three ($6) or four ($12) top selections in a quiniela bet. In a way, you'll be eliminating the four or five dogs least likely to win or place, and betting that any two of the remaining dogs come in first and second. Your average win will be around $27 at most tracks. If you're boxing four dogs, you'll have to win more than 50% of the races you bet on, to make a profit. That means you must pass those no-bet races, when your system says so, or you will riddle your averages. When you can handicap well enough to need to box only three dogs, you will need to win only 30% of your races, to make even more profit.

A refinement of this method, once your system gets enough history to rely on, is to instead make a *partial wheel* quiniela bet. You can, for example, bet your #1 selection with your #2, your #3, and your #4 selections; and your #2 selection with your #3 and #4 selections. This covers four dogs for only $10, if your first or second choice finishes first or second.

If your system indicates that your top selection is strong enough to almost certainly either win or place, you may wheel that selection with all seven of the other dogs, for a total cost of $14 (or for $12 or $10, if one or two of the dogs are absolute wash-outs and can be eliminated from your bet). This won't usually produce as many wins as does boxing, but you will get a $75 to $120 quiniela payoff now and then.

Once again, be advised that *no one's* system works equally well on all tracks, on all grades, and on all courses. Any "system" that claims to bypass this truth is not a complete system and will likely not be profitable. Likewise, if your study gives you this information, but you then ignore it and bet the poor-bet races anyhow, you can easily turn a good profit potential into a loss. Remember to have the willpower to resist betting when you can't bet intelligently.

Once your system starts showing some consistency, the *trifecta* wager can provide an even larger return. However, to make it work, more capital is required, along with a larger amount of patience and persistence since fewer tickets will be cashed.

Forget the *straight* trifecta bet, under most situations. The world's best handicapper might cash one out of 300 straight trifecta tickets he buys, but most of us would simply lose the thrill if we cashed only one ticket every five to ten nights, profit or not.

Instead, think in terms of the trifecta *box* wager. Here, you box three, four or five dogs (for $6, $24 or $60), and you win if three of those dogs come in first, second, and third, *in any order*. The amount you win will be half the amount that the straight tickets collect, but the median box trifecta payoff, at the typical dog track, is around $200! This means that if you're boxing four dogs in your "good" races, you'll need to win only about one out of eight to make a profit! Some payoffs, of course, will be tiny—maybe $50 or less—but some will be $400 to $500 or more. Over a span of time, with decent handicapping, good record-keeping, and willpower, a good profit can be made from the trifecta.

Progressive Betting

Books have been written solely on the subject of the *increasing wager* method of profiting at the races. Investigate this if you wish, but this author feels that it is a mechanical and dangerous way to attempt to make up for lazy handicapping.

The theory simply states that if one loses a bet, the next bet should be made in a larger amount, perhaps even doubled. If *that* bet doesn't win, then the next bet is even larger, or double again. Another loss, another increase, and so forth. The theory is that when one finally does score a win, the amount of that win will counterbalance the previous losses.

There are many hazards inherent in this philosophy—some obvious, some invisible. If it worked unfailingly, one wouldn't have to use any time for handicapping, but could simply bet "at will," using house numbers or whatever, over and over. Try it, if you wish, but not until you study the method very closely, and have a hefty bankroll to experiment with.

Crashes, Collisions, and Pile-ups

A horse racing fan who goes "to the dogs" for the first time is often aghast at the number of races that involve bumps or problems for several of the dogs. In horse racing, contact rarely occurs. If a driver's or jockey's horse interferes with another, an "objection" or "inquiry" usually occurs, and the results of the race are often adjusted to reflect this infringement of etiquette. The astute and skillful horse handicapper will cash more of his tickets than the expert dog handicapper will, because of collisions inherent in the dog races, but the dog fan's tickets will tend to have substantially larger payoffs, for that very same reason.

Add the fact that no human error or manipulation is going to occur during a dog race, and it's apparent why more and more fans are going to the greyhounds.

If you really want to outsmart the "average" dog race fan, and put some money in your pocket, or even make a living at the dog races, read on. . .

Chapter 7

Making a Good Profit at the Greyhound Track

"Hey, that was a lot of fun even if we did lose a little money!"

How many times have you heard someone say something like that on the way out of the grandstand at the end of a night's racing? The excitement of racing is exhilarating—few "spectator sports" get the fan so involved. Many fans go to the track fully expecting to lose some money, but anticipating that they'll still have more fun, per dollar, than many other forms of entertainment could provide. If they managed to cash a few tickets during the course of the program, so much the better, although they may still have a net loss for the evening.

Well, that's great! More power to 'em, bless their hearts! These folks, and the serious but ill-advised "handicappers" whose "systems" consistently lose, are the ones who make it possible for others to take home a profit from the track. Casual players just don't want to take time out from their evening's fun to do much thoughtful selection, and the vast majority of those who do consider themselves handicappers are not willing to spend the time and effort it takes to handicap adequately. Both types just keep bringing more money for the track owners and the studious players to share. Do *you* want some of it to take home? To bank? To vacation with? Buy a new car with? Then read on. . .

A typical medium-sized greyhound track, on an average week-night, might have a *handle* of around $300,000. This is the total amount wagered through the windows for the evening's races. Of this, the track and the state share a *take* of around 17% to 19%, or about $54,000. Approximately 2000 people will have attended, about eight out of 10 of whom will go home losers at an average of about $60 each. On the average, this means that the 400 or so fans who go home with profits will be sharing winnings of about another $50,000, which is around the same amount as the track's take, and averages about $135 per winner. Obviously, this won't be divided evenly—some will win far more, others scarcely enough to pay their transportation.

In any case, a number of folks *are* going to make some money, but about four times as many will lose. The vast majority of folks go back and forth from one group to the other. It is estimated that far less than 5% can consistently stay on the winning side and show an actual profit after a certain number of weeks or months. The rest of this book will show you how you can join that minority.

On any given night, a substantial number of the 20% who go home winners will have managed to do so by simply playing their house numbers, lucky numbers, lottery numbers, age, license numbers, cute names, hunches, etc. We know that they will most likely lose these winnings, and probably much more, by continuing to bet so haphazardly. But they'll still have fun, if they don't lose the farm, and you can bet their friends will hear a lot of bragging about "the time they won the $600 trifecta at Superdog Downs."

However, a small percentage of those who went home winners came to the track fully expecting to make a profit, and had done some preliminary work to help ensure that. They had done their homework and they came to the track with a *plan,* and enough capital to follow that plan. The fact that you're reading this book indicates you'd like to join that group. You *can,* and you're on your way!

Does this mean that those who go to the track to win don't have time to have any fun? They have even *more* fun than the losers, believe me! You can bet they get just as excited as any fan, for every race. In fact, the studious player usually gets even more exhilaration from seeing more finishes develop as he predicted. The person who goes to *win* usually isn't with a party of people, probably isn't drinking much, and most likely won't indulge in much social interaction with his neighboring fans, as do those who go mainly just for a good time. And, it's likely that the studious player either arrived early at the track or had already invested part of his day in preparation, to increase his odds of winning. But he certainly doesn't need to be a grouch or a long-face to be a winner. Those who say that they'd like to win, "but it just isn't worth taking the fun out of it to do so" don't realize that it's more fun to *win* than to *lose!*

In short, there *is* money to be made at the dog track. The track doesn't "get it all," as many fans think; the smart bettor gets his share, too. Anyone of average intelligence can quite consistently take some home, and have fun doing it. But it does take some thought, some work, and a certain amount of capital, as does virtually any enterprise that is to succeed.

Handicapping does not work as well for dog races as it does for horse races! And that is precisely why you *can* make a profit at the dog track.

Horses, horse racing, and horse race handicappers have been around for many, many years. The race horse—with its driver or jockey to guide it, think for it, whip it, and coax the very best from it—is a far more definable factor to handicap. Good handicappers, including your author, can often pick five to seven winners on an evening's card! Furthermore, there are often one or sometimes several horses in many races which have virtually no chance of winning, unless there is an accident or a crash, which there seldom is. Any undue interference is usually caught, and results in disqualifications. The result is that the finish (at least 75% of the time, at most tracks) is purely a result of the comparative quality, grade, speed, form, and condition of the horse, relative to the other horses in that race.

Therefore, it is quite possible to develop good skills in horse handicapping. You can brag about the percentage of winners you've predicted, and the number of tickets cashed, *but you will still have to have another source of income to finance your losses at the race track,* because you will almost certainly lose. The catch is that because there are often so many other good handicappers present, the odds on the logical selections will be too low to allow you to turn a profit. You will have to score 75% to 85% in your selections to just barely break even, and that is a nearly impossible percentage.

Greyhound races, on the other hand, are much less predictable—not *impossible* to handicap, but more difficult. The world's best dog handicapper cannot pick more than 30% to 35% winners, over a span of time, and even that would be fantastic success. Why? Because once the dogs are placed into the starting boxes, the human element is out of the picture. The only human hand involved, once the boxes open, is the one on the speed control of the lure, and this is a very small factor.

The dog has been (hopefully) bred to the best advantage; it has been (hopefully) conditioned to the trainer's best ability; it has been nurtured (hopefully) on the best diet; it has been (hopefully) transported and handled in the best manner; it has been (hopefully) treated with the appropriate medications to avoid illness or disease; and it has been entered in a race grade consistent with its recent performance.

But, when the box opens, the dog is purely on its own. It has no ability to judge how to best run its race based on the comparative early or late speed of the other contestants. It doesn't know just how important it is to have at least its nose in front of another dog's nose by the finish line—in fact, it doesn't really know *what* a finish line is, let alone *where* it is. It doesn't know that its owner will receive more money if there are only one or two dogs ahead of it at the end of the race, instead of three or four. If by nature it tries to be the first to catch the lure, then it doesn't care about being polite or courteous to any other dogs that happen to get in the way along the route. Nor is it concerned about getting disqualified if it bumps another dog. Nobody is there to crack it on the rump along the way to urge it to a faster performance. Nor does it have any way to tell its owner or trainer that tonight it has a deep ache in its groin from a mis-step, collision, or over-effort in the last race.

And, in truth, there isn't even a great deal of difference in how *fast* the dogs can run. The difference in average speed between a Grade A dog and a Grade C dog, at most tracks, is usually less than 8/10 of one second. And many dogs that usually run in Grade D or C can occasionally log a faster time than the track's average Grade A race! Likewise, you will even see times when, on the same night, a Grade A race is won, with a clean race, in a slower time than was a Grade D race with some collisions.

Add to all of this the fact that *very few* dog races do not include at least some instances of bumping, colliding, interfering, crashes, wrecks, tumbles, falls, etc. (Can you imagine this happening at the horse track?)

To put it simply, in nearly any greyhound race, from championship to Grade D (let alone maiden races), nearly *any* dog in the race is capable of winning, and absolutely any dog in any race can easily finish in the quiniela, perfecta or trifecta.

All of these inconsistencies in dog racing result in much larger payoffs, and not just for the "fluke" races, but for nearly every race on the card. Your author has won, by boxing four horses in most races, as many as five or six trifectas in one program of horse racing, several times, and still lost money! Using the trifecta as an example (and you will see that the trifecta can be a profitable betting plan), the median box trifecta payoff at most horse tracks ranges around $75, whereas at most dog tracks, the median is around $225! To box four selections usually costs $24. This means that at the horse track, you would have to win about one out of three trifectas just to break even. But in dog racing, you would only need to win about one in nine, and it is entirely possible to average three or even four out of nine. The trifecta offers the best opportunity for profit, in most cases, at most tracks. To box only three selections, however, is futile. Boxing four selections, though costing four times as much, is many times more profitable, as you will discover later in this book.

Don't be misled by the occasional "giant trifectas" at either the dog or the horse tracks—you can be sure that no serious handicapper is cashing that whopper ticket. It was won by the guy who played his house number, and you can be sure he'll eventually lose it all back wagering this way. There are no handicappers who apply some formula to pull down one of these biggies. They are just flukes, and you must not feel that your system has failed you when you miss these.

Likewise, logic dictates that the payoffs the good handicapper does grab are generally going to be smaller than average, since his reasoning is also being used, to some degree, by many of the other handicappers who are present. However, the same inconsistency that makes it difficult to handicap the dogs also ensures that occasionally one's fourth choice is going to win, and that is when you grab a few of those $400 or $600 payoffs, and collect some of the money that the straight-trifecta buyers have deposited for you.

Because of the factors that make the payoffs larger, one must be content to score a smaller percentage of wins at the dog track. If cashing tickets is your thrill, you'll certainly cash a larger number at the horse track, but they'll be too small to profit from. At the dog track you'll win much larger amounts but less often. In fact, one must be mentally (and financially) prepared to suffer the *big skunk* now and then at the dog track and not be destroyed by it, for it is this very factor that makes it possible, in the end, to come out on top.

Chapter 8

Developing Your Own System

The next few chapters will teach you how to develop your own system for profiting from the dog races. You will learn how to make it work for *you,* so that you can point to that new car, that garden tractor, or those vacation tickets, and say, "The doggies bought it for me!"

You must first realize that it takes determination. Just like the smoker who tries to stop smoking, but can only do so when he finally *really* wants to stop, you can win at the dog races only when you *really* decide that you want to. Any fan would say he wants to win, but very few want to win bad enough to go about it in a logical manner.

There is no easy way. There are spot plays, number systems, and parlay methods that can create some action, if used intelligently, but because most of these are played by lazy handicappers, they will result in no profit in the long run. Beware of any plan that doesn't involve computation of the program. I have read about schemes which declare that you don't even need a program—you simply make your selections from the odds board. That would certainly be quick and easy, so try these plans, if you like. You can surely get them into gear quicker than you will the methods to be discussed here. But eventually you will discover that you'll have to put much more than this into it if you're going to be a consistent winner.

The fact is that there is simply no formula, scheme, diagram, plan or method that will work at all tracks, in all grades, at all times. That statement alone, if you accept it, is worth the price of this book. Nothing that applies "in general" will work well enough to make you money. For a plan to work, it must be specifically designed for a *certain* track, a *certain* grade, a *certain* course, and be absolutely up to date. Few factors remain unchanged from season to season and meet to meet; a profitable method must be constantly updated. Therefore, any system put forward in a book, sold to you, divulged to you, developed by you, or devised in any manner, is not going to work forever. If you follow the directions in this book, you will spend many hours tailoring a system that will work. But, once having done so, you must *not* carve it in stone and consider it to be a permanent system. If you do so, it is almost certain that it will gradually deteriorate into a losing system. You must constantly freshen it up and modernize it to keep it alive and profitable. This is the reason why no one can give you a printed, prepared formula, in this book or any other, and guarantee that it will work for you.

There will be three steps covered. Skip any one of them, and it will not work.

In Step 1, you will learn how to develop your own system, tailor-made for a specific track. This takes time, but will cost little—you don't have to bet money while you are in the process of developing it.

In Step 2, you will learn how to use your system to score your program and develop your plan.

In Step 3, you will learn how to wager by using your system and your scored program.

(The final step—how to spend what you take home—you can devise for yourself.)

Of the three steps, Step 1 is by far the most time-consuming and exacting. Here is where you set your course. The expertise and patience that you apply here will be repaid in direct proportion in your later winnings. Steps 2 and 3 (and certainly Step 4) cannot work without an adequate job done on the first step. Here is where you will determine whether or not you *really* want to win. Frankly, few will spend the time and effort to do this, and it is on this presumption that I decided to write this book. If you really want to win, you will see the logic of this reasoning, and follow through with it. (In doing so, you may very well become my competitor, because some day you and I will surely be at the same track, using the same logic, and thereby splitting some of the pots!)

Step One:
System Development

One more time, that all-important statement: *No system will work at every track every time, in any grade.* If you have tried any systems that purport to do so, you have already discovered this truth, probably at great expense.

Tracks vary in a number of ways. The Racing Secretary, who determines which dogs are eligible for which races, can manipulate this factor with a certain degree of latitude. Races may be either more or less closely-matched at one track than at another. (The races that are the "easiest" to handicap are those which are not closely matched, but these are the ones which pay the least when the handicapping does work!)

Different tracks also vary in course lengths, track surfaces, box placement, lure operation, and printed program format. The number and quality of kennels participating in a meet also contribute to the differences.

Your overall method will be almost the same at nearly every track, but the details and values that you plug into the method will need to be varied and tailored to each particular track, and then updated occasionally as the conditions at a given track change. This, of course, means that the more tracks you visit, the more homework you will need to do. This is a pretty good argument for sticking to one track and mastering your system for that track alone. But then again, it's fun to visit various tracks, and as long as you recognize that you must modify your system for each track, the dogs may very well pay for your travel expenses!

You can determine, with more accuracy than nearly anyone else who is present, just which dogs have the greatest, or the least, chance of being in the money. You will determine, for each dog entered, how to weigh each factor: the grade of race, the track, the course, the speed, post position, early speed, maneuvering skills, stretch gain, and class change.

If there is a "secret" in this book, it is that each of these factors *carry a different value in each grade of race,* even the post position factor! If you use a handicapping system that considers these comparative factors as being equal in different-quality races, you will quickly learn that this is an error. There are no "nevers" or "always" in dog racing. Once you begin your studies of the factors at a certain track, you will be astounded to discover the differences between grades. You may find, for example, that a seemingly obvious advantage, such as strong early speed, is of little or no consequence in certain grades or on certain courses; yet, in another grade, or on another course, it could be the *prime* factor.

Keep in mind that the major thrust of this book is to teach you how to select dogs *most likely to be in the money*—that is, dogs that are most likely to finish *in one of the first three places.* Your author is convinced that more profit is made betting on the trifecta, etc., than on betting to win, place or show. Therefore, this system is designed not so much to select the winner, but to select those dogs most likely to come in first, second or third. And different principles apply to this...

The chart in Figure 1 gives an example of the format which you will be striving for. Do not tear out the chart in Figure 1 and head for the races with it, figuring that it is better than whatever system you've been using. It is an example only, and very likely would not work well at any track.

The concept is that you will develop a similar, but accurate, formula

Figure 1

Track: Superdog Downs				Grade: A			Course: 3/8-mile
Date: February 1983							
Post position and order of factors	Value of post position	Early speed (jump)	Middle race gain	Late speed	Avg. speed, recent	% of recent money places (Form)	Grade change
1	+10	5	20	5	30	10	
2	+10	5	20		20	10	
3		5	10		10	10	
4		5			10		
5							
6							
7	-10						
8	+5		-20		-20		
UP							-5
DN							+10

54

for each track you attend. Naturally, I have current, well-tailored formulas for most of the tracks I currently attend. However, to publish any of these, in their current version, would be an extreme disservice to the reader, since their complexion is very likely to have changed vastly by the time this book reaches the reader's hands. And, believe me, working with a stale system which "used to work" is worse than working with no system at all! You must constantly tailor *your* system, once you have it developed. Even if there are six or eight other fans at your track who are working with this book, you will still have the edge on the others if you keep yours the freshest.

The development of your system will take a certain amount of time, and the smartest way to do it is by not betting the races during the period you're setting this up. You certainly do not need to bet $100 on a theory to find out if it works! The development of your system will involve figuring hundreds of races, but you need not bet on any of them. Simply lay out your factors and then use the result charts to measure their success. In other words, you do it all with "dry runs"—you "pretend" that you bet, but you don't. You don't even need to go to the track to do this, particularly if you can purchase programs off track, or have a fellow fan bring you his current used ones.

Again, I strongly suggest that you do not wager during this period. It is entirely probable that you will, early on, begin seeing some factors that really look exciting, and it will be tempting to try them out at the windows. However, as you gather more data, these factors may shrink back into a less exciting scale. So don't start prematurely experimenting with segments of your system until you have it all together.

If you've been going to the races for a while, and have some reasonably fresh programs in hand (*always* save your programs), you may use these to start working with. You should probably use a minimum of about 25 programs to formulate your basic method, and the fresher they are, the better. This is about three weeks-worth of programs, at most tracks, giving you about 50 races in each grade to evaluate.

If you can assemble this many fresh programs at once, you can look forward to the equivalent of about five to seven full days of work (or several evenings) to develop your system. That sounds like a lot of effort, and it is. But if you do it well, and use it wisely, it may well become the most profitable week that you have ever spent. If you can enlist some help, fine—it will get done that much sooner. If you are starting from scratch, and getting your programs one by one as the meet progresses, you will, of course, have many weeks of preparation before your system begins to take reliable form. If you are going to the races during this period, and picking your programs up there, it will take a lot of will-power to avoid betting. (Well, a couple of tiny, little bets couldn't hurt too much . . .)

If you don't have a quantity of current programs, perhaps a friend would loan you his. In any case, there is no way to learn what you must learn without studying the history of the factors which count at *your* track. This is where you're going to find out, for example, if that #1 box which is so hot in the Grade A races is going to prove ice-cold in the Grade D races.

The basic mechanics of developing your system involve taking a program, computing the relative advantages of each dog in each of the measurable factors, and then determining, by looking at the post-race results, which of those factors meant the most. For example, you will determine, by looking at the past performance lines, which dog in a given race has the seemingly fastest average speed; then, which dog has the second fastest, etc., right down to the slowest. Then, when the race is over, you record how the dogs finished in relationship to this speed factor. Let's suppose that the seventh-fastest dog won, the fourth-fastest placed, and the sixth-fastest showed. Looking at this one race, it would seem that speed shouldn't be considered as being much of a factor in that grade race. Obviously, we must look at *several* more races than this one, before any useful conclusions could/should be drawn. But, if after sampling and computing, say, 30 races in this grade, and coming up with a bottom line that indicates our example happened more often than not, we would have discovered that here is a potentially profitable piece of knowledge. Furthermore, this kind of knowledge will be shared only by those other fans who have bothered to dig this deep (or know how to) and we will have gained an edge over the vast majority of fans that we are betting with.

Early on, as you begin to accumulate this kind of information, you will notice some "handicappers" at the track who bought their program that evening on their way into the races, and after the fourth race, these experts will just begin their "handicapping" of the fifth. You'll hear them very seriously (and sometimes rather noisily) discussing factors which you have learned are absolutely irrelevant to the race at hand. They may be arguing about a given dog's lineage, or weight, or any of several other factors which you have long since learned simply do not apply. You'll hear no mention, in their discussion, of the two most important factors which you have learned do matter in this grade race, on this course. These types will often be absent for the last several races of the evening, because they've used up all their capital. As they leave the track, they'll be muttering about how they were ripped off, or how their luck was against them, or how they "should never have listened to Charley." They'll have learned nothing, while losing their money. Odds are that they'll pitch their program on their way out—probably torn to pieces, probably in the parking lot.

Once you're into this book, and the procedures outlined, you'll start learning some very valuable bits of knowledge. One more warning, though: Do not try to put a system into gear until you have the *whole* picture assembled. And, once you do have your system completed and functioning, don't discard it or turn it upside-down just because you experience an entire night with no wins, or even two nights in a row, because this will happen occasionally. Sorry. You must be able to accept it, without reacting with a major panic-driven revision of your system or a loss of faith in it. This may well be reason to ponder if the system is due for a freshening-up, but even the best and freshest system in the world is bound to suffer a *big skunk* now and then. You may be working with a fine system that has been producing a solid average of one trifecta win out of every four races bet for 10 nights in a row, and then suffer two nights without a single win. That hurts, for sure, but you must realize that it can happen.

In the chapters to come, we will be discussing and illustrating how to determine the value of each race factor which I have learned are of potential value. What we will be working toward is the compilation of a chart like the one in Figure 1. As simple as that chart may appear, it takes a good deal of study to arrive at just which digits go into which places.

You may wish to use the same formats, chart outlines, and forms as shown in this book, or develop your own. If you have access to a computer, you may want to store the forms and/or data in a computer program, to make it simpler and quicker to make future revisions. (However, the type of data which you are going to build your system with does not lend itself to be discovered and evaluated by a computer program itself. There is far too much "eyeball" evaluation and interpretation that only you can do. Believe it or not, computer-owner handicappers can get no better handle on the races than you can. In fact, your author has an $18,000 computer system, and is firmly convinced that the most it can do for handicapping is to help record some data, and make form revision a little quicker and handier.)

Chapter 9

Weighting the Various Handicapping Factors

Post Position

Since this book is primarily concerned with betting on the trifecta (and quiniela, perfecta, etc., in some cases), we are not too interested in which post position is the best box to *win* from. We need to learn, as well, if a certain post position, in a certain grade, also gives an advantage to the possibility of a *place* or *show* finish. If the box which produces the most winners, in all grades, was our only concern, most printed programs give us a pretty good look at that by means of publishing a history chart for this factor. Examples from two different tracks are shown in Figure 2. These charts show quite graphically that more races are *won* from certain boxes on each of the courses. Many fans use this, alone, as the basis of a "betting system."

The problem is that these charts do not indicate which post positions also favor a dog to have a chance at *place* or *show*. This is often a far different factor than the seemingly obvious sequence on the graphs. Then again, these charts give no indication of how the post position advantage applies in various *grades,* and, believe me, it does vary! Once a study is conducted, you will see quite plainly that a box that is extremely advantageous in one grade can be far poorer, or even a *dis*advantage, in another grade.

This was the initial discovery that brought me to dog racing from the horse tracks. At once, I had an edge on the fans who took the easy way, those who simply used the track's published charts to assign box values. Of those factors that we will be studying, this factor is the easiest to compute. You can begin to get a handle on your track by referring to past performance charts, recent programs, or current editions of the *Greyhound Racing Record*.

There are two methods of setting this up, and one or the other may be the more accurate for your track. The difference is that you either consider *all* dogs that were in the money; or you eliminate from your computations any dog that finished in the money that was the *favorite* in that

Figure 2

POST POSITION RESULTS

Box	PC	KC	BC	Other	Total
1	604	160	10	0	764
2	490	144	6	0	640
3	387	103	14	0	503
4	396	127	8	0	530
5	391	177	8	0	577
6	424	108	13	0	545
7	372	76	6	0	453
8	506	94	5	0	605

POST POSITION STATISTICS
(Thru November 5, 1982)

Box	3-16 990 Ft.	5-16 1650 Ft.	YC 2040 Ft.	CC 2310 Ft.	PC 2970 Ft.	Total
1	0	597	132	3	0	732
2	0	612	114	2	0	728
3	0	509	137	0	0	646
4	0	466	89	5	0	560
5	0	483	91	0	0	574
6	0	437	121	2	0	560
7	0	455	107	2	0	564
8	0	601	108	0	0	709

race, since he likely had more factors going for him that may well have outweighed a poor post position. Try both methods to determine which is the most accurate for your track.

List, grade by grade, the post positions that finished in the money in 20 to 25 recent races. (You may or may not wish to delete the favorite, as per the previous paragraph.) Your chart may look something like the one in Figure 3, for a certain grade and course:

Figure 3

| TRACK SAmpleDog PARK COURSE 3/8 mi |
| DATES RECORDED 10/6/82 thru 11/30/82 |

	AA	B	C
1	﹟﹟ ﹟ ﹟ ﹟ ﹟ ﹟ ﹟ (25)	﹟﹟ ﹟﹟ ﹟﹟ / (16)	﹟﹟ //// (9)
2	﹟﹟ ﹟﹟ ﹟﹟ ﹟﹟ /// (23)	﹟﹟ ﹟﹟ ﹟﹟ / (16)	﹟﹟ ﹟﹟ /// (12)
3	﹟﹟ ﹟﹟ ﹟﹟ (15)	﹟﹟ ﹟﹟ ﹟﹟ ﹟﹟ (20)	﹟﹟ ﹟﹟ //// (14)
4	﹟﹟ ﹟﹟ ﹟﹟ ﹟﹟ (20)	﹟﹟ // (7)	﹟﹟ ﹟﹟ ﹟﹟ ﹟﹟ (20)
5	﹟﹟ ﹟﹟ / (11)	﹟﹟ ﹟﹟ (10)	﹟﹟ / (6)
6	﹟﹟ ﹟﹟ ﹟﹟ ﹟﹟ ﹟﹟ // (27)	﹟﹟ ﹟﹟ ﹟﹟ (15)	﹟﹟ ﹟﹟ //// (14)
7	﹟﹟ ﹟﹟ // (12)	﹟﹟ ﹟﹟ (10)	﹟﹟ ﹟﹟ ﹟﹟ ﹟﹟ // (22)
8	﹟﹟ ﹟﹟ ﹟﹟ ﹟﹟ ﹟﹟ / (26)	﹟﹟ ﹟﹟ //// (14)	﹟﹟ ﹟﹟ / (11)

Remember to record not only wins, but place and show as well, since we are going for mutiple bets (i.e., trifectas, perfectas, quinielas, etc.).

The data recorded on the work-up chart in Figure 3 is from an actual sampling I recently did at a certain track. If one checked this against the post position charts published in that track's program, it would indicate that the #1 and #2 boxes were very hot on this course, and that the #8 box was very cold. This would cause a lot of fans to lay off of the #8 dog, in many cases. But note that in Figure 3, in Grade AA, #8 is a pretty hot box, at least for being in the money/trifecta. At this track, during the period of the sampling, notice that post position #5, at least in these three grades, is pretty cold, and this factor is also reflected in the track's program chart.

To translate the information that you have recorded into useable facts, you next need to break your data down into percentages. For example, looking at Grade B in Figure 3, the percentages would be as shown in Figure 4.

Figure 4

Post Position (Grade B)	Times in Money	% In Money
16	44%	
2	16	44%
3	20	55%
4	7	20%
5	10	27%
6	15	41%
7	10	27%
8	14	39%

(Thirty-six races total. Win, place, show recorded = 108 dogs in the money/trifecta.)

You must remember that this post position advantage changes from time to time at every track. Otherwise, we could provide you here with a work-up for every track. Once you have established the initial pattern for your track, be sure to re-test it periodically, for it may well go stale and start costing you money.

Now, let's look at the percentage chart in Figure 4 and interpret it for our purposes. A quick glance seems to indicate that post position #3 will be in the money *over half of the time!* Can this be true? Yes! But—and this is a very important factor to keep in mind throughout your handicapping—remember that by pure chance, *any* of the eight dogs will be in the money a full 37½% of the time! If, for example, we worked up a chart based on the letter of the alphabet that a dog's name starts with, the H's would be in the money 37½% of the time, the Z's 37½%, and so on.

Therefore, our #3 dog, which is in the money 55% of the time, *is* a pretty strong selection, but not stronger to the extent that we would keep him in our bet if he didn't have anything else going for him. Likewise, #1, #2, #6 and #8 are really not much above "average," at 39% to 44%.

However, post positions #5 and #7, at 27%, are pretty cool, and we likely will want to deduct something from their chances, though we won't make them automatic drops if they have other factors going for them. Post position #4, though, is in the money only 20% of the time; pure chance would get him there 37½% of the time, so there definitely must be something negative about the #4 box, *in this grade*. Ours is not to reason why, but you will see this factor appear often, and it can be a money maker for you. Now, this doesn't mean that we should *never* put a Grade B #4 dog in any of our bets; indeed, he *was* in the money/trifecta in seven of our 36 sampled races. If we had wiped him out because of post position alone, we would have lost a chance at those seven races. (But, we certainly need to still mark down his chances.)

This brings up the important point of determining exactly how each factor stacks up with the others. In other words, does the post position advantage, or disadvantage, that we just discussed outweigh considerations about speed, class, etc.? Well, that is the major point of this entire book, and there is no quick answer to it. You need to do some work to find out the answer, and not many are willing to do the amount of work that it takes. Once you have done your homework, though, you may well be one of a *very few* at your track who knows which factors are important, in each grade, on each course.

To bring this concept into focus, let us suppose that we devise a system which awards points to each dog in a race, based on his relationship to the comparative skills of the other dogs in the same race. Start with the assumption that a perfect dog, one that scores #1 in every category measured, will accumulate about 100 points. Now, let's say that we are going to measure five categories in this particular grade race. The question is, "Should we give 20 points for a #1 rating in each category?" The answer is an emphatic NO!, and the correct answer is exactly what you will be after in your research.

As an example, let's say we have determined *speed* to be the biggest single factor in a given grade race, on a given course, and that *manuevering ability* is the next biggest factor, and that *stretch gain* is a very small factor. We might therefore "weight" our point value of the various factors in the manner shown in Figure 5.

Figure 5

	#1 rating	#2 rating	#3 rating	#4 rating	#8 rating
Post	15	5	5		− 10
Speed	30	20	10	10	− 20
Mid-gain	15	10	10	10	− 10
Early speed	15	15			
Late speed	5				
% in money	20	20	10	10	

Figure 5 shows a very rough picture (which we'll be referring to later) but it does give you an idea of the kind of balance you will be striving for. In Figure 5, we see that *late speed* is a small factor in this particular type of race, and *speed* carries a great deal more weight. It is exactly this type of knowledge that will formulate your system and give you the *big edge*.

Referring to the post position example shown in Figures 3, 4 and 5, we might assign point values similar to these (all for Grade B, on a 3/8-mile course):

PP	#1	+ 5
PP	#2	+ 5
PP	#3	+ 15
PP	#4	− 10
PP	#5	− 5
PP	#6	
PP	#7	− 5
PP	#8	

The "point values" we are using for examples at this point are arbitrary, of course, and we will not be able to know exactly how to weight any given category until we have tested its pertinence to the track under study.

Back to those post position advantages again. The reasons why one post position is more desirable than another are difficult to explain. It may make sense that, at a given track, the lure is placed such, the track condition is such, and the starting box angled such, that a given box has a physical and "understandable" advantage or disadvantage over another.

What remains a puzzle, however, is why this very same factor may not apply equally in all grades run from that starting box, or why the factors strengthen or weaken in cycles.

In any case, the post position factor tends to change the most at any given track, and you must freshen up your system in this respect at least monthly, for you will find that it will vary. Do not, however, make a premature modification based on a certain box becoming hot or cold for two or three nights running. This happens, now and then, and it would be a great factor to use, *if* you could tell how long it was going to last. You can't, though, so don't be too quick to change your formula to accommodate, for example, a short-term hot box streak. Likewise, if you travel from track to track don't take a stale system with you that worked well at a particular track the last time; if it's too stale, it may well be worse than no system at all! If you are limited on time, at least check the current post position factors. If there isn't much difference between the hottest box and the coldest box in a given grade, don't assign any point value at all. To do otherwise would be grasping at straws, as well as a matter of over-handicapping, and may well cost you money in the end.

There, now . . . figuring the post position advantage wasn't too difficult at all, was it? This factor alone can give you an edge over most of the other fans, if you use it correctly. In fact, if you are able to determine that there are a few grades and courses at your track in which three boxes are quite a bit warmer than the other five, you could experiment with a *short-cut system* which may pay some small dividends. Simply box these three hot post positions with the crowd's favorite selection (or second-favorite, if the favorite is one of your hot boxes) for a four-dog trifecta box bet. If you avoid using this system on the grades which don't have enough post position difference to make it work, you may well make a modest profit. You won't be cashing as many tickets as with a complete system, but the ones that you do win will tend to be somewhat larger. If, at this point, you decide that what you really want is an "easy" system, this is far better than most others.

But, if you want to learn how to engineer a really good and profitable complete system, you need to study several other factors. Read on . . .

Speed Advantage

This one really isn't too hard to figure. It takes a little concentration, at first, but you'll find it gets easier and far faster with practice. Obviously, the dog that gets the fastest speed in a given race will be the winner. But what you are trying to do *before* the race is to determine, based on the recorded past performance, the *potentially* fastest dogs in the race.

In some ways, this is almost as much an art as it is a science. You'll find that recorded times often vary widely for a dog's recent races. Most track programs print the results of each dog's most recent six to eight races. You will need to train your eye to sort out what a dog's *average* speed is. You will normally look only at the dog's last two most recent races—how fast he ran last year, or even last month, doesn't count much toward what he may do tonight. However, if something about his time for the last two races doesn't seem to fit, you may need to look at earlier races. For this purpose, it doesn't matter at which grade these races were run.

Before you figure this factor, or *any* factor, and this is true with every program from every track, *cross out completely the record of every schooling race, or any race in which the dog collided, was bumped, or otherwise had problems!* (Ignore these races completely—which means, right off, that you won't have much left to handicap a maiden race with, so don't try.) Schooling races often don't have accurate times recorded; also, a schooling race may have been run against some truly garbage dogs, or some really classy dogs that were just recovering from an injury. You cannot use the data recorded from these types of circumstances, so just ignore it. Likewise, ignore all races in which the dog under considera- tion was interfered with in any way, or otherwise had it noted under the remarks that it was not a typical race for him. There is no way for you to know just how bad he was bumped in a given race, and just how much time that probably cost him.

Do not be too concerned about the track condition recorded for the races shown for the dogs under consideration. It does make some differ- ence, of course, but, unlike horses, dogs can often run as fast on a sloppy track as on a fast track. In fact, they usually do, and some even run a little faster. (Actually, you probably shouldn't be betting on a night when the track is slow, sloppy, or muddy, though it isn't quite the circus that the horse races are under similar conditions.)

So, your first move should be to scratch out all of the past performance races noted above. Then, average out each dog's time for his last two good races, and mark this on the program. Then, mark down the rank that the dogs fall into; that is, the fastest dog will be rated #1, the slowest dog #8, and so forth. A typical page in the program, when you have com- pleted these steps, might look like the example shown in Figure 6.

Figure 6

NINTH RACE(9)

TRACK RECORD—30.14
Jamie's Lane—10-24-81

5/16 MILE 1650 Feet

S.N.E.T. Co., Manchester, Conn.

QUINIELA AND TRIFECTA WAGERING

GRADE A

Post Pos.	Date	Dis.	Time	Wt.	PP. Off 1-8 Str. F.FW	ART	Odds	Gr.	Comment	Sts.	1st	2d	3d	4th	Order of Finish

1 RED — TM'S AMAZING 31.77 (72)

PLN 38 5 4 8 5
PLN 82 16 9 17 14

Brindle D., July 30, 1978. Share Profit*—Rushing Barbara

Owner—Teddy Meadows
Kennel—Teddy Meadows
Trainer—Otis Browning

11-13⁶	5-16	M 31.40	71½	1	6 7 7	7¹²	32.21	7.40 A Evenly	ChoiceAccont, SpareM, DBarClipprT
11- 9⁶	5-16	F 30.97	71½	4	4	5¹³	31.82	4.50 A Wide 1st tn	GoldenrodCt, RiverAngl, GllsAngl
11- 3⁹ˣ	5-16	F 31.26	71¼	4	1	1⁵	31.26	1.80 B All the way	BeauChien, IKidUNot, TourSand
10-28¹¹ˣ	5-16	F 31.12	71	1	•1	2⁹¼	31.75	2.50 B Offstr closing	RacingTheWind, AEsSuzyB, DrBosco
10-23⁶ˣ	5-16	F 31.12	72	2	1	8¹⁰	31.80	7.40 A Weakened	SuperRiver, Alvados, RsSpartan
10-17¹⁰ˣ	5-16	F 31.23	71½	6	2 2	3³	31.42	10.40 A Early threat	HardToHld, MOsBigPockt, BWGrouch

2 BLUE — GE'S DIXIE DOWNS 31.64 (56)

PLN 46 8 6 4 9
KW 9 1 1 1 0

Red Brindle B., March 6, 1980. G.E.'s Davaky—G.E.'s Falcon

Owner—David Wells
Kennel—John E. Currid, Jr.
Trainer—Cindy Currid

11-13⁶	5-16	F 31.21	56	5	5 7 2	3⁵	31.42	30.40 A Wide 1st tn	TnyBts, SugarWinWll, DFWhiteFthr
11- 9¹⁰ˣ	5-16	F 30.83	56½	5	7	7¹⁴	31.64	30.40 A Varied little	MeadowsWhiz, DonsIra, FirstWaltz
11- 4⁶ˣ	YC	M 40.03	56	1	6	1⁵	40.03	13.80 B Around leaders	Deportd, PrinterTim, PecosWranglr
10-29⁴	YC	F 39.91	56	4	6	4⁹½	40.33	6.20 TB Offstr bad tn	TBTllBrnd, PecsWrnglr, NoDwnPymnt
10-23⁸	YC	F 39.85	56	6	4 3	2²	40.00	13.20 TB Good effort	JudysChasr, RJsBrassRng, DutchKCl
10-17⁶ˣ	YC	F 39.66	57	8	6 7	6¹¹	40.39	4.40 TB Some gain	ChicagoKty, BoJonsJhnny, JimmysBab

3 WHITE — RIVER ANGELA 31.51 (60)

PLN 9 3 2 2 1

Fawn Brindle B., August 23, 1980. River Ben—River Princess

Owner—L.B. Kasberg
Kennel—British-Connecticut
Trainer—Joe Carreira

11-13⁶	5-16	F 31.21	60	6	7	7⁴	31.50	2.50 A Bumped early	TnyBts, SugarWinWll, DFWhiteFthr
11- 9⁶	5-16	F 30.97	60½	5	6 2 2	25¼	31.31	4.20 A Chased winner	GoldenrodCut, GullsAngl, DottieRx
11- 4⁴ˣ	5-16	M 31.28	61	6	3	4⁷	31.74	2.50 A Good effort	MOsBoldKng, GoldenrodCut, MagicLgs
10-29⁷	5-16	F 31.14	60	6	7	13¹	31.31	2.70 D With ease	PansyTwist, PasoZoro, AllensBozo
10-24¹²	5-16	F 31.51	59½	4	7	3³	31.70	2.40 B Good effort	Spirulina, GullsAngel, DutchBayou
10-20¹¹	5-16	F 31.54	59	7	2 3	3¹	31.62	3.60 B Good effort	LagunaSmoky, DutchDic, FinalStag

4 GREEN — LAMINE 31.40 (61)

PLN 30 5 5 1 2
GT 4 0 0 0

Brindle B., September 23, 1979. My Whitfield—Listed

Owner—Dayle Henry
Kennel—River Bend Farm
Trainer—Lawrence Henry

11-14⁹ˣ	5-16	F 31.06	61½	7	4 11 11	12	31.06	20.80 A Held firm	CheerflBll, RPSAmbrGrl, FlickFlk
11-10¹¹ˣ	5-16	F 31.30	61	4	4	5⁶⁷	31.77	18.20 A Varied little	DesertWtch, NorthEmbr, GingerQuen
11- 4⁹	5-16	F 31.51	62	7	6	6⁸	32.05	12.20 B Varied little	BobbyMA, MyPalWilly, JoMarMaggie
10-30⁵	5-16	F 31.23	61½	2	1 12 15	31.23	9.60 C Handily	GennysHowl, MeadowsMsk, BabyJanic
10-26¹²	5-16	M 31.65	60	4	2 5 6	6⁵	31.98	18.20 C Varied little	SassySherry, TurkeyCreek, ShurFred
10-20⁴ˣ	5-16	F 31.06	61	3	1	4⁶	32.18	Followed pace	DutchSnuggls, GingerSagHnds, BeATn⁷

5 BLACK — LARINDA 31.50 (59)

PLN 39 6 5 8 9

Red Brindle B., June 14, 1980. Big Ziggy—Adele

Owner—R.L. Block, Inc.
Kennel—D.K. Kennels, Inc.
Trainer—Patrick Gauthier

11-14¹⁰ˣ	5-16	F 30.83	59	4	8	6¹²	31.66	12.20 S Some gain	TedsGnny, PasoPetr, GoldenrodCut
11-10⁶ˣ	5-16	F 31.28	59	7	6	2¹	31.33	9.20 A Strong bid	PasoPeter, LoadedDice, MOsBossMan
11- 4⁶	5-16	F 31.43	59	2	6	2ⁿᵈ	31.45	3.50 A Strong drive ins	LoadedDc, HitNRunWbbt, LondonRbbr
10-30⁶	5-16	F 30.97	59	6	3	2³¼	31.19	6.20 A Stretch gain	MOsBigPckt, LondonRbbr, LoadedDc
10-26¹⁰ˣ	5-16	M 31.22	58	6	4	1¼	31.22	17.20 A Stretch drive	TedsGnny, ImpalaHeismn, LuckySlck
10-21⁶ˣ	5-16	F 31.01	59				32.17	30.60 A Offstr far tn	TMsCamelot, PasoPeter, LuckySlick

6 YELLOW — MO'S BOLD KING 31.27 (75)

PLN 28 5 6 2 7
HIN 38 9 2 7 3

Fawn Brindle D., March 26, 1980. King Hipockets—Barby Mo

Owner—Golden Mosier
Kennel—Frank Reid
Trainer—Herman Creagar

11-13⁶	5-16	F 31.21	73½	8	3	4¹¹	31.32	2.50 A Offstr early	TnyBts, SugarWinWll, DFWhiteFthr
11- 9⁶ˣ	5-16	F 30.92	74½	3	2	2²	31.22	13.40 A Forced erly pace	TMsDance, JetDancer, BluffYourWay
11- 4⁴ˣ	5-16	M 31.28	75	8	8	1⁴	31.28	11.00 A Easily	GoldenrodCut, MagicLgs, RiverAngel
10-30⁶	5-16	F 31.29	74	5	8	5⁵½	31.67	18.40 A Varied little	LittleCharli, Elkhrt⁶ᵗʰMesaWhispr
10-26¹¹ˣ	5-16	M 31.43	74	3	4	1½	31.43	4.50 B Up in stretch	TedsTony, TaxDollar, ValleyVarmit
10-20⁸ˣ	5-16	F 31.63	74	5	4	4⁷½	31.63	5.40 B Some gain	SpicyDish, DutchJimmyB, TamboBert

7 GREEN & WHITE — GOLDENROD CUTE 31.25 (56)

PLN 58 13 12 12 9
PLN 2 0 2 0 0

Fawn B., June 12, 1980. Merrin—Sandy's Pandy

Owner—D.Y. Kirkpatrick
Kennel—W.J. Wegrzyn
Trainer—Phil Maider

11-14¹⁰ˣ	5-16	F 30.83	54	2	7	3⁹¼	31.42	7.40 B Despite trouble	TedsGnny, PasoPeter, TMsDance
11- 9⁶	5-16	F 30.97	54½	2	1	15¼	30.97	1.50 A Easily	RiverAngela, GullsAngel, DottieRax
11- 4⁴ˣ	5-16	M 31.28	55	3	1	2⁴	31.56	3.50 A Closing wide	MOsBoldKng, MagicLgs, RiverAngel
10-30⁸	5-16	F 31.29	54½	2	5	4²¼	31.56	6.20 A Offstr gained	LittleCharli, Elkhrt⁶ᵗʰMesaWhispr
10-30⁶	5-16	F 30.94	54½	7	5 5	2ⁿˢ	30.95	13.20 A Just missed	MesaWhisper, PasoPeter, PattyMoss
10-21¹⁰ˣ	5-16	M 31.00	55½	7	3	8	31.43	3.60 A Blocked 1st tn	TedsGnny, ImpalaHeismn, LuAnnMur

8 BLACK & YELLOW — DF WHITE FEATHER 31.27 (64)

PLN 6 2 0 1 0
HIN 0 0 0 0 0

White and Black D., June 11, 1979. Lone Wolf Go—DF Black Diamond

Owner—Graydon Robtoy
Kennel—Wilton Corp.
Trainer—Graydon Robtoy

11-13⁶	5-16	F 31.21	64	7	3 4	3¹	31.30	8.40 A Hard try	TonyBts, SugarWinWll, MOsBldKng
11- 9¹⁰	5-16	F 31.12	64	4	7	7¹⁸	32.30	14.40 A Jammed 1st tn	MOsBigPckt, LondonRbbr, AllnsTby
11- 4⁶	5-16	F 31.12	64	7	6	5⁶	32.12	9.40 A Varied little	LoadedDice, Larinda, HitNRunWabbit
10-30⁹	5-16	F 31.23	62½	6	2	14¼	31.23	5.10 B Pulled away	GotTheWrd, ManhattanCoch, AlpineLe
10-26⁷ˣ	5-16	M 31.34	63	6	1	5⁶	31.96	7.20 B Forced wd 1st tn	DottieRx, DutchJRasco, BluffYourWy
10-21⁴	5-16	F 31.43	64	5	1	1¹	31.43	3.70 C Never headed	HomeGround, FirstMile, ZZTroubles

PROGRAM: 5—6—8

Note that in Figure 6 all the schooling races and troubled races are marked out. Look at the average times the author arrived at, and remember they were based on the last two good races only. You may not agree 100% with the author's interpretation. To some degree, one must be a bit arbitrary with this determination. In fact, if my wife and I score the same program, we sometimes come up with a little different ranking on a given race.

You will see that there is not much difference among the fastest three dogs. In fact, we have called it a three-way tie, in this example, between #6, #7 and #8. Likewise, note that even the *slowest* dog isn't that much slower. This is one reason why a system based on speed alone won't pay regular dividends. However, it *is* a factor (to at least some degree in most grades) of the chances the dogs have of being in the money/trifecta. Just how much of a factor is exactly what your research is going to help you discover.

You discover this via a rather specific and exact method. First, you must figure at least 20 or 30 races of a given grade. Rate the dogs in each race from #1 through #8 on a speed rating, as in the example shown. Then, mark the race results right on the program page. Next, record in which speed the dogs came in the money. For example, if your fourth fastest dog won the race, the "slowest" dog came in second (it happens!) and your "fastest" dog came in third, you would write the results as: 4 8   1. Enter these results of several races in a column, as follows (we will use only 10 races, to simplify the example):

4	8	1
1	4	3
3	7	1
4	2	3
1	5	8
6	2	1
2	1	4
2	4	5
3	1	5
1	3	7

Now, determine just what percentage of the time each speed rating was in the money. In our example, our slowest (#8) dog won none of these 10 races, but it *was* in the money in 20% (two) of the races. Your final tally, for this example, is shown in Figure 7.

Figure 7

		WIN	PLACE	SHOW	TOTAL
(Fastest)	#1	30%	20%	30%	80%
	#2	20%	20%	—	40%
	#3	20%	10%	20%	50%
	#4	20%	20%	10%	50%
	#5	—	10%	20%	30%
	#6	10%	—	—	10%
	#7	—	10%	10%	20%
(Slowest)	#8	—	10%	10%	20%

Obviously, in the Figure 7 example, speed does seem to carry some weight. We most definitely will want to give the fastest (#1) dog some extra points, since it was in the money 80% of the time. (This is somewhat unusual, but a pleasant discovery when you can document it.)

We will also note from the example in Figure 7 that, as a group, the fastest four dogs were in the money considerably more often than were the slowest four dogs. Therefore, we will give ratings #2, #3 and #4 some points, too, though not as many as #1. Should we then go on and *deduct* some points (minus points) for the slowest dogs? Probably not, because, in the example, the very slowest (#8) and next to slowest (#7) were actually in the money for four of the 10 races. If they have any other factors going for them, we had better not make them an automatic drop for this reason alone; by giving them so many negative points, nothing else could bring them back into our selection.

There may well be certain races and certain indications when logic says that you should automatically scratch the slowest dog from your list of selections. Even under these situations, though, you will still see the worst dog win a race now and then. Accept that this will happen occasionally, and if logic says "leave him out," then leave him out.

Using the example in Figure 7, we may wish to award points to speed in this manner:

(Fastest)	#1	+ 30
	#2	+ 10
	#3	+ 10
	#4	+ 10
	#4–#8	No points

69

Remember, though, that we can't decide exactly how many points to award for each factor until we can see how they all stack up with each other later. Remember, too, that you must have more races figured than just the 10 we have used in our example, or your factors will be most inaccurate.

Early Speed Advantage

Handicappers use a variety of methods to determine the early speed capability of a dog. Some look at only the first call column, to see how well the dog "jumped from the box." Others look at what the dog's position was at the 1/8 call. Your author finds that it works best at most tracks to look at the change in position between the first call (the break) and the 1/8 call. That is, no matter how well the dog broke from the box, did it gain or lose position on the way to the first turn?

Many handicappers place a lot of weight on this factor. While it may be an important consideration at some tracks, in some grades, and on some courses, at other tracks, and in other grades and courses, it appears to be absolutely no factor at all! Logically, it seems that a dog capable of being fast out of the box should be involved with far fewer collisions (and other casualties) and therefore be in the money more often, but other factors can more than neutralize this seeming advantage. Your author believes that this early speed is generally less of a factor than it is usually considered; dogs that are habitually slow out of the box are often quite strong finishers.

The ability to know when early speed counts and when it doesn't can be extremely valuable, and the only way to discover this is by testing and researching it, track by track, grade by grade, course by course. This isn't very difficult, as you will see, though it will take a little time. Again, as in the previous chapter, you will be working up the relative ranking of each dog in a race with respect to early speed, then documenting how these rankings fit into the actual finish.

I suggest you first use the method of comparing position loss or gain between the dog's first call and 1/8 call. (If you wish, you could also experiment with the other methods mentioned earlier.) First, as always, *cross out all the schooling races and troubled races.* Add up the dog's positions at the first call for the last three races; this will give you a total ranging from a possible low of three to a possible maximum of 24. Next, add up the dog's positions at the 1/8 call in those races; it likewise will be between three and 24. Then, write down, right on the program, by how much the second figure is higher or lower than the first figure. (If lost ground, mark with a minus sign; if gained ground, mark with a plus sign.) When a dog is in #1 position at both calls, count this as another one-place gain in position. Finally, rank the dogs in this particular race as to their apparent early speed capability.

In the marked program shown in Figure 8, we see that dog #3, though not always the fastest jumper from the box, in every race shown has picked up some positions by the 1/8 call. He gained from seventh to fifth in one race, fourth to first in the next one listed, and gets first and keeps it in the third race listed. (He gets an extra plus point for that.) In the other extreme, dog #5 quite consistently loses ground between these two calls, and is our #8 ranked dog. In this particular example, we had a three-way tie for the #4 ranking.

Notice that we ignored the schooling races and troubled races. Also notice that, to make this point, we have not computed the average speed of the dogs on this program page. We will do likewise with each example we make of the various factors, to keep from cluttering the pages. However, on your own program, when you are computing five or six factors on each dog, you will need to keep your figures, rankings, etc., smaller and marked in consistent places on the page so that you don't confuse them. A red-ink ballpoint works great for this.

To make this study valid, you will need to figure at least 20 or 30 races in each grade for this factor. Then, as you did for speed, write down in a column the order in which the dogs finished. Your results might look like this abbreviated sample:

4	3	6
1	3	6
6	2	5
2	3	8
1	4	2
3	7	2
2	4	1
5	8	2
1	7	4
4	6	2 (10 races shown)

Figure 8

GRADE B — **EIGHTH RACE — THIS IS A SELECT 6 LEG** — **TRACK RECORD**

Ark. Course 1748 ft.—532.8 M — QUINIELAS and PERFECTAS SOLD THIS RACE — 1981—Perceive—31.85

PP | Date | Dist | Tk | Time | Wt | PP | Off | 1-8 | Str | Fin | ART | Odds | Comment | Gr. | Order finish—Starts | 1st | 2d | 3d

No. 1 (Red) — RICH VAL 12/9 = +3 (62)

Owner—STEPHEN H. KARKLITZ; Kennel—JAYHAWK KENNELS, INC. — 27 5 3 2
Bdl. D., April 1979. Rocket Charge—Val Jenu — Trainer—TONDA WILLIAMS — HOL—22 3 4 8

Date	Dist	Tk	Time	Wt	PP	Off	1-8	Str	Fin	ART	Odds	Comment	Gr.	Order finish
10-23 8	AC	F	33.28	63	4	2	2	2	2^{nk}	33.31	8.50	Led in stretch ins	B	Baska, JoRascal, JenobarJet
10-18	AC	F	33.10	62	7	3	3	1^{hd}	1^{1}	33.10	5.10	Held gamely ins	C	LagRebel, NTSBarJean, Elmore
10-14	AC	F	33.02	62½	7	4	5	8	$6^{5½}$	33.40	4.40	Almost fell 1st tn	C	Bonico, Cujo, ShiftyJim
10-8 2	AC	F	32.72	62	2	7	4	2	6^{9}	33.36	13.80	Tired late inside	B	CGSandra, ChrylLon, SSndown
10-2	AC	F	32.62	62½	2	5	6	6	5^{6}	33.04	11.40	Steady effort ins	B	KayaMace, Content, CGandra
9-25 8	AC	F	32.59	62½	3	2	1	7	$8^{12½}$	33.47	7.10	Pinched bk 1st trn	B	WChase, Content, WCSpecial

2 (Blue) — FAMILY MATTER 8/7 = +1 (64)

Owner—ARVIN RANDLE; Kennel—DUANE RANDLE — 25 3 5 2
Bdl. B., July 1979. Kelly Jones—Mandy Lane — Trainer—JEFF LOVELY — HOL—28 5 2 6

Date	Dist	Tk	Time	Wt	PP	Off	1-8	Str	Fin	ART	Odds	Comment	Gr.	Order finish
10-23 10	AC	F	32.38	64½	3	3	4	8	$8^{20½}$	33.81	28.80	Flew 1st turn	A	Havencroft, PrmseAProfit, Hon
10-18	AC	F	32.95	64½	4	1	$1^{1½}$	$1^{1½}$	3^{2}	33.09		Set pace md-trk	4	StDestiny, CGSassy, MCLrAnn
10-14 9	AC	F	32.85	64½	5	6	5	6	5^{6}	33.29	4.10	Evenly outside	A	SkiBandit, LaguJewel, SpStart
10-7 9	AC	F	32.95	64	6	1	2	5	7^{4}	33.25	3.20	Early factor outs	S	TrFriend, MaStroder, WCSpecl
10-1	AC	F	32.76	63½	8	1	$1^{½}$	2	3^{2}	32.89	2.30	Good effort outs	A	ScDodger, MMxmillian, TFriend
9-24 12	AC	F	32.79	63	4	1	1^{1}	2	$3^{2½}$	32.96	9.10	Good effort outs	A	CDiplomat, Benatar, SolOrio

3 (White) — MAIN TOP 12/7 = +6 (72)

Owner—RAYMOND J. BARBER; Kennel—J. B. HARRIS — 6 1 3 0
Dk. Bdl. D., April 1979. Tank—*Handy Top — Trainer—B. E. LLOYD — DB—22 6 3 3

Date	Dist	Tk	Time	Wt	PP	Off	1-8	Str	Fin	ART	Odds	Comment	Gr.	Order finish
10-23 8	AC	F	33.28	71½	6	7	5	7	$8^{7½}$	33.81	7.30	Tiring inside	B	Baska, RichVal, JoRascal
10-18	AC	F	33.15	71½	4	4	1^{1}	1^{4}	$1^{3½}$	33.15	4.80	Early control ins	C	NTSLMary, IPass, KRenegade
10-14	AC	F	32.87	71½	5	1	1^{hd}	$1^{2½}$	$2^{3½}$	33.12	4.50	Outfinished ins	C	LoisMarie, Braid, MorngBeam
10-2 x	AC	F	33.02	71½	2	4	3	$1^{1½}$	2^{nk}	33.28	7.20	Outduelled inside	C	KitReilly, ShifJim, SoCHelicat
10-8	AC	F	33.25	71½	2	6	4	1^{1}	2^{1}	33.07	8.40	Outdueled ins	C	Hilarity, McGrnVixen, WisPam
9-25 6	AC	F	33.29	70½	1	4	3	5	5^{2}	33.44	4.60	Hard try ins	C	AskMe, ArizonaSadie, ShifJim

4 (Green) — STIVIK 22/21 = +1 (78)

Owner—KEITH DILLON; Kennel—KEITH DILLON — 31 6 0 7
Red D., Sept. 1980. Oversize—Tally Kay — Trainer—JIM SCHULTHESS — SP—6 1 1 0

Date	Dist	Tk	Time	Wt	PP	Off	1-8	Str	Fin	ART	Odds	Comment	Gr.	Order finish
10-23	AC	F	33.28	77	5	8	8	8	$6^{5½}$	33.67	10.10	Slight gain ins	B	Baska, RichVal, JoRascal
10-18	AC	F	33.00	77½	2	6	5	3	$1^{1½}$	33.00	5.70	Drawing clear m-t	C	Barto, TedsSilvie, SoCHellcat
10-14 1	AC	F	32.87	78	1	8	8	6	$5^{½}$	33.30	4.90	Outrun early ins	C	LoisMarie, MainTop, Braid
10-7 7	AC	F	33.03	77½	5	7	6	6	3^{6}	33.43	4.20	Late drive md-trk	C	DHeavenKnows, OHara, Wilde'
9-30	SC	F	42.01	77½	4	1	1^{ns}	2	6^{14}	42.99	5.30	Early lead md-trk	C	JHawk, KRenegade, CGGrcie
9-23 12	AC	F	32.70	77	8	7	7	5	4^{8}	33.24	26.20	Late gain md-trk	B	AlFrancis, McArgus, CGSandra

5 (Black) — MALOU MALADY 5/10 = -10 (58)

Owner—HIRAM N. SIMMONS; Kennel—H. N. SIMMONS — 25 4 3 4
Lt. Fwn. B., Jan. 1980. Half Mac—Malou Delite — Trainer—M. L. SIMMONS — GT—18 12 3 3

Date	Dist	Tk	Time	Wt	PP	Off	1-8	Str	Fin	ART	Odds	Comment	Gr.	Order finish
10-23 12	AC	F	33.28	58½	6	2	3	3	$2^{½}$	33.32	3.60	Good effort inside	B	MCMaxmillian, BlRed, CRiver
10-16	AC	F	33.28	57	7	1	3	4	6^{5}	33.62	3.00	Pinched bk 1st trn	B	RadSearch, ABlcndy, SSpecial
10-1	AC		32.17	56½	1	1	4	7	$7^{12½}$	33.05	64.40	Tiring md-trk	A	Havencroft, WlFriend, LnLake
10-7 10	AC	F	32.71	56½	8	2	3	4	4^{7}	33.18	13.60	Steady effort m-t	A	LandoLake, Dunrovin, SuffiSmi
10-1	AC	F	32.86	56½	2	2	8	6	$7^{6½}$	33.31	26.60	No room 1st trn	A	NugJohn, QueTrooper, ArToes
9-25 10x	AC	F	32.77	56	6	3	3	2	$1^{3½}$	32.77	17.00	Pulling away m-t	B	DrRowan, BlckyRed, GMMMas

6 (Yellow) — TED'S GIGI 5/5 = +2 (56)

Owner—B. H. COLE; Kennel—SHOCKLEY KENNELS, INC. — 26 ? 0 6
Wht. Tkd. & Fwn. Bdl. B., Mar '80. Shaggy Can I—Ted's Gala — Trainer—DONNIE SMITH — HOL—24 4 5 3

Date	Dist	Tk	Time	Wt	PP	Off	1-8	Str	Fin	ART	Odds	Comment	Gr.	Order finish
10-23	AC	F	33.28	54½	8	3	3	5	7^{7}	33.75	12.40	Early speed inside	B	Baska, RichVal, JoRascal
10-1 2	AC		32.91	54½	2	1	3	5	5^{6}	33.56	17.40	Crowded wd 1st t	B	ArzToes, DHevKnows, FletFame
10-1 7	AC	F	33.04	54½	4	1	1^{1}	$1^{2½}$	1^{1}	33.04	11.60	Safe margin inside	C	RRainbow, FErlanger, FAcpted
10-4 2	AC	F	33.09	55½	2	1	1^{hd}	$1^{1½}$	1^{1}	33.09	3.10	Held firmly inside	D	LFLucy, GunCry, BondersJan
9-30	AC	F	33.25	55	7	1	2	2	$4^{½}$	33.41	2.90*	Hard try inside	D	DntSeemFair, GunCry, Sumrfld
9-23 2	AC	F	33.15	55½	4	5	4	3	5^{8}	33.73	2.30*	Evenly inside	D	Casbah, Smerfield, BOperator

7 (Green White) — SUNMOSS GINGER 4/4 = +12 (54)

Owner—CARLYLE J. HALL; Kennel—DARBY HENRY — 24 5 1 1
Red Bdl. W. Aug. 1980. K's Clown—Sunbar Peggy — Trainer—BOBBY HENRY — SP—15 5 6 3

Date	Dist	Tk	Time	Wt	PP	Off	1-8	Str	Fin	ART	Odds	Comment	Gr.	Order finish
10-15 11	AC		32.90	54	1	2	2	3	7^{8}	33.45	13.10	Tired late inside	B	GMMnMan, RyLane, NTSREllis
10- x	AC		32.84	54½	5	1	1^{1}	4	$6^{6½}$	33.30	10.40	Early lead inside	B	LagJewel, MMagic, HiGJones
9-18	AC		33.15	54	6	1	1^{3}	1^{2}	$1^{1½}$	33.15	4.10	Safe margin m-t	C	AmbersAce, Bonico, Buckley
9-9 9	AC	F	33.18	53½	6	1	2	3	6^{6}	33.59	5.00	Early speed inside	S	KAGossip, RushOver, BreThru
9-4 8	AC	F	33.30	53	7	1	1^{2}	1^{1}	$4^{1½}$	33.40	11.20	Outfinished m-t	B	AnthFolly, WisPam, PCJyTime
8-31 11	AC	F	32.77	53	4	1	1^{2}	2	7^{2}	33.31	9.00	Tired late inside	B	FamlyMatter, Hon, AnothFolly

8 (Black Gold) — HON 14/16 = -4 (71)

Owner—DON BARTLEY; Kennel—CARROL C. BLAIR — 32 3 0 8
Red Bdl. D., March 1979. Streak—Go Pamela — Trainer—RANDLE BLAIR — SP—28 5 5 6

Date	Dist	Tk	Time	Wt	PP	Off	1-8	Str	Fin	ART	Odds	Comment	Gr.	Order finish
10-23	AC	F	32.38	69½	7	5	7	3	3^{10}	33.09	19.70	Good effort inside	A	Havencroft, PrAProfit, SDodger
10-1	AC	F	32.05	70½	6	5	6	5	3^{13}	32.94	15.20	Late drive inside	A	Havencroft, WilFriend, RuOver
10-1 9	AC	F	32.85	71½	6	5	6	7	7	oop	2.90	Fell 1st tur	A	SkiBandit, LaguJewel, SpStart
10- 10	AC	F	32.89	71	5	2	3	4	2^{1}	32.94	12.10	Hard drive rail	A	OhShAnn, LagJewel, NugJohn
10-2 x	AC	F	32.57	71½	6	8	5	4	4^{7}	32.72	10.00	Good effort ins	A	EarthGlow, SpiritStart, WThush
9-25 12	AC	F	32.99	70	3	6	8	8	5^{2}	33.12	5.60	Late drive ins	A	GoodJoe, KiwiChris, HstnGem

Please examine your tickets and change before leaving window

Handicapper's Choice: 8—2—1 — **Chartman's Choice: 8—5—1**

The results would then be translated to percentages, as in Figure 9.

Figure 9

		Win	Place	Show	Total
(Most gain)	#1	30%	—	10%	40%
	#2	20%	10%	40%	70%
	#3	10%	30%	—	40%
	#4	20%	20%	10%	50%
	#5	10%	—	10%	20%
	#6	10%	10%	20%	40%
	#7	—	20%	—	20%
(Most loss)	#8	—	10%	10%	20%

The result in Figure 9 is a good example of the arbitrary nature of interpreting this data. How would you assign points, in this case?

I suggest—since ratings #1 through #4 were in the money about 66% of the time, and ratings #5 through #8 were in for only 43% of the time— that *some* points be awarded. (Keep in mind that, because of ties for first, second, third or fourth, there are often no #5 or #6 rankings.) It would appear that our weighting shouldn't be too heavy for this particular grade. (Remember, you *must* figure this grade by grade. You will likely see a big difference between grades, and that is the whole purpose of this study.) Don't be swayed by the large percentage that came up for the #2 ranking in this example. Let this serve to illustrate how misleading too small of a sampling can be. Never draw any conclusions from a sampling of fewer than 20 races; 30, 40, or more would be far more accurate.

We might assign an arbitrary point scale similar to the one shown below, for this grade on this course:

(Most gain) #1	+5
#2	+5
#3	+5
#4	+5
#5 thru #8	No points

In general, you will probably find *early speed* to be more heavily weighted in the shorter and sprint courses than on the longer courses. In your study of this factor, you may uncover certain types of races in which this early speed seems almost to be a negative factor, not only worth no points at all, but seemingly worth some *negative* points for the dogs with the most early speed. That's nice information to have, especially when you hear two guys beside you at the races arguing over which dog "breaks out" the best in the coming race, while you have learned that it matters not!

Maneuvering Ability

Your author has found maneuvering ability to be quite a strong factor at most tracks. What we are speaking of here is the dog's ability to gain ground through the mid-portion of the race, including through the curves. We cannot measure this simply by the lack of accidents that he has, nor can we automatically down-grade a dog whose record shows several problems in recent races. (More on that later.)

Some greyhounds, finding themselves in the middle of the pack, tend to just stay there, and don't seem to want to fight for the lead. (Are they being social?) Others bore right up through the pack, because they have the heart or desire, or some sense of competitiveness. Sometimes this gets them into collisions or other accidents, but this *drive* is a strong factor in winning. In fact, in many cases it is more of a factor than potential power in the stretch.

On most tracks, we determine this quality by looking at each dog's last three (good) races. Note the position that the dog held at the 1/8 call, then the position held at the stretch call. Subtract one from the other to determine the total number of positions gained or lost. A dog holding the lead at both calls is given one point. An example is shown in Figure 10.

Figure 10

5-2	DARK FORCES	8/7 (+1) =+2	70	OWNER: Richard A. Nelson KENNEL: Double "A" Kennel TRAINER: Paul Petrone		1982 WD 39 6 8 5 RA 5 2 0 1	
4	Brindle D.; September 80 Share Profit, Imp. - Miss Calabash						
	10-27 4 PC	F 30.96 69	7 6 3 2¹	21	31.04 9.60 Steady drive, rail	A	DoItYourself,IslandDancer,DrDunk	8
	10-23 11x PC	F 31.01 70	2 1 12 14	1⁸	31.01 2.00* Box to wire	B	JREwing,TallNEven,RocosNorma	8
	10-19 4 PC	F 30.73 70½	4 5 4 4	4⁸	31.27 19.30 Followed pace, inside	A	IrMary,SamosSailor,Neno	8
	10-15 6 PC	F 30.97 70	1 5 4 3	3⁴	31.25 8.60 Steady gain, rail	A	Prospectus,JimTheGoalie,Pragmatic	8
	10-11 4x PC	F 30.97 70	5 5 5 5	7⁹	31.58 14.60 Stretch fade	A	DownMark,Pragmatic,GetawayVan	8
GREEN	10-6 9 PC	F 30.99 69	8 6 8 8	8⁴⁴	31.74 3.50 Went wide 1st turn	A	RiverAbba,Prospectus,DiamondChuvy	8

Compute the maneuvering ability factor for each dog in the race, then rate them in order, with the greatest mid-range gain being #1, and so forth. The program page, when completed for this factor, will look something like the one shown in Figure 12.

As with the previously discussed factors, you would next document the results of each of those races which you have computed, then list those results in numerical order, such as in the abbreviated sample which follows.

```
2   1   4
1   4   5
3   1   4
1   2   5
4   6   2
1   2   3
5   2   3
3   1   4
2   3   4
1   8   2
```

Translated to percentages, this sample would then look similar to the one in Figure 11.

Figure 11

		Win	Place	Show	Total
(Most gain)	#1	40%	30%	—	70%
	#2	20%	30%	20%	70%
	#3	20%	10%	20%	50%
	#4	10%	10%	40%	60%
	#5	10%	—	20%	30%
	#6	—	10%	—	10%
	#7	—	—	—	—
(Least gain)	#8	—	10%	—	10%

It should seem quite obvious that our sample in Figure 11 indicates that this mid-race gain deserves a pretty heavy weighting. (Remember, of course, that we won't have as many #5, #6 and #7 ratings, because of frequent ties for the #1, #2 and #3 rankings. And remember, too, that you will need to compute your study sample based on 25 or 30 races, instead of the abbreviated sample used here.)

Figure 12

CRITTENDEN COURSE ➤**SIXTH RACE—THIS IS A SELECT 6 LEG**➤ CRITTENDEN COURSE

1003 Ft.—305.7 M   Grade D   QUINIELAS and PERFECTAS SOLD THIS RACE   1976—Leadbelly—17.86

PP	Date	Dist Tk Time	Wt PP Off 1-8 Str Fin	ART	Odds	Comment	Gr. Order finish—Starts 1st 2d 3d

No. 1 — Red — KERRY GRACE 15/13(+1) = +3 **(64)**
Owner—JACK McAULIFFE   31 2 6 6
Kennel—MIKE CASTELLANI, INC.
Red Bdl. B., July 1978. Carry On—Sandy Cash   Trainer—BETH FOXWORTHY   SF—16 2 2 1

10-23	ACF 33.04 62½	8 8 8 8	7¹	33.69	5.10	Never close in	D SkiSnCap, NonTune, JustolDog
10-18	ACF 33.14 62½	4 1 1½ 1½	2¹	33.20	4.20	Caught late ins	D MrnBeam, KelTreat, SybleSims
10-14	ACF 33.01 63	5 8 8 8	8½	33.61	4.00	Shut off break	B QJoGabWang, Info, KelTreat
10-8	ACF 33.66 62	3 4 4	4²	33.82	5.70	Hard try inside	D Darley, OshkoshLamb, BrisUp
10-2 ⁷ˣ	ACF 32.54 63½	1 1 4	3¹¹	33.29	4.30	Steady effort ins	D Elmore, BrisieUp, HotTmeJean
9-25 ⁷ˣ	ACF 33.42 62½	5 8 7 7	4²	33.56	3.20*	Late drive ins	D ErlEEdge, NTSLtMary, BndDitty

No. 2 — Blue — MISTY WATERS 16/16 = 0 **(69)**
Owner—R. E. or CLARA G. THOMAS   18 2 2 3
Kennel—R. E. THOMAS
Bdl. D., March 1980. Kunta Kinte—Lilac Road   Trainer—WOODROW BLACKWELL   SF—25 1 4 4

10-23	ACF 33.04 69	3 5 6 4	8¹¹	33.75	3.00	Shuffled 1st turn	D SkiSnCap, NonTune, JustolDog
10-18	ACF 33.10 68½	1 6 6 6	6⁴	33.38	3.70	No room 1st turn	C RicVal, LagRebel, NTSBrbJean
10-14	ACF 33.02 63	3 3 3 3	5⁵	33.39	2.30*	Bumped wd 1st t	C Bonico, Cujo, ShiftyJim
10-8	ACF 32.95 62½	5 8 7 7	3²	33.07	7.60	Late drive inside	C CupBstShot, HDIvan, RbBBlake
10-4	ACF 32.76 68½	3 1 1 5	8¹¹	33.53	8.00	Brief lead ins	C SndySundown, OnJosie, Baska
9-25 ¹ˣ	ACF 33.02 69	1 5 3 2	2²	33.14	5.60	Good effort ins	C GoldenAl, Wilder, JenfrJones

No. 3 — White — PENNY BROKER 9/13 = -4 **(54)**
Owner—JACK A. HACK   17 3 6 0
Kennel—TODD & TRICE
Red Fwn. B., Sept. 1980. Five Card Stud—*Quarrymount Hase*   Trainer—MARK TWILLMAN

10-23	ACF 33.16 53½	1 4 3 3	2⁵	33.57	18.00	Good effort inside	D ArDesign, StCrab, RbsBBlake
10-18	ACF 33.14 54½	8 3 2 5	8¾	33.74	13.20	Tiring md-trk	D MornBeam, KerGrace, KelTreat
10-14	ACF 33.15 55½	1 5 4 4	4⁴	33.43	4.90	Steady effort ins	D SyCloneBabe, Laney, Oblique
10-8	ACF 33.34 55	5 4 1st 1¹	2⁴½	33.65	12.20	Outfinished ins	D TedSilvie, KellyTreat, Info
10-1	ACF 33.29 54½	4 2 2	1½ 1¹	33.29	12.70	Lasted on inside	E ChMark, JHPMLove, HHelga
9-23 ²	ACF 33.15 54	5 6 6 8	6³	33.42	15.00	No room blstr	D Casbah, Smerfield, BOperator

No. 4 — Green — JUSTANOLD DOG 13/6 = +6 **(75)**
Owner—D. Q. WILLIAMS   14 0 2 1
Kennel—H. B. & BILL WILLIAMS
Bdl. & Wht. D., Aug. 1980. Zam Zam—Shaggy Heather   Trainer—BUDDY POWERS   SM—10 2 1 2

10-23	ACF 33.04 73½	4 3 3 3	3¹½	33.50	7.10	Hard try inside	D SkhiSCap, NoTune, LotTomata
10-18	ACF 33.21 74	7 6 6 2	2¹	33.30	10.10	Challenged inside	D RJShutOut, KnBQuick, AmAce
10-14	ACF 33.32 74	3 2 5 5	8	33.45	1.70	Drifted wd str trn	D PindPay, LttaTomata, Wilder
10-8	ACF 33.31 75	4 5 3	1½	33.38	9.20	Caught late ins	D RoyRaquel, JxDillon, JenJones
9-30	ACF 33.18 73½	5 6	4¾½	33.64	12.70	Pinched bk 1st str	D Byword, OddKid, GitToGitten
9-25 ²	ACF 33.49 74	2 5 3 2	2³	33.81		Hard try inside	B Flplt, LucScott, VolupuousVal

No. 5 — Black — JW'S TAMMY 5/4(+1) = +2 **(58)**
Owner—JAMES R. FERGUSON   6 0 1 0
Kennel—MRS. ROBERT MARRIOTT
Blk. B., Oct. 1979. Alert's Ram Rod—*Fergusoni*   Trainer—ROBERT MARRIOTT, JR.   SAR—31 4 6 6

10-23	ACF 33.29 57½	3 1 1 1¹	2²	33.45	5.40	Outfinished inside	D BronzeStar, Info, DellaRiver
10-18	ACF 32.79 58½	3 2 2 1½	1²	33.29		Set pace inside	7 SkihiSnCap, ThnRoll, Rangoon
10-14	ACF 33.32 58	3 2 2 1¼	6²	33.47	12.90	No room str trn	D PindPay, LttaTomata, Wilder
10-7	ACF 33.62 58	7 3 3	6¹	34.04	7.20	Tired late ins	D NTSLitMary, KitSmoke, RJSOut
10-1	ACF 32.78 56½	5 2 3	7³	33.43	13.10	Early speed ins	C ButFlake, WylAlice, HDHpTop
9-24 ⁸	ACF 32.99 56½	2 2 1² 3	5⁵	33.36	14.00	Early lead ins	C OkThundarr, KeEnka, ScAGo

No. 6 — Yellow — STONE CRAB 6/13 = -7 **(57)**
Owner—J. N. or J. F. THAYER   25 3 4 4
Kennel—JAYHAWK KENNELS, INC.
Blk. B., Jan. 1981. Steel Cap—*Racing Fever*   Trainer—TONDA WILLIAMS

10-23	ACF 33.16 57½	2 1 1 2	3¹	33.64	6.80	Early lead m-t	D ArDesign, PenBroker, RBBlake
10-18	ACF 33.00 57½	3 4 4 5	6²	33.48	8.90	Evenly outside	C Stivik, Barto, TedsSilvie
10-14	ACF 32.84 56½	2 2 6	8⁹	33.45	13.70	Weakened md-trk	C OnJosie, SoCHellcat, RBBlake
10-8	ACF 33.44 56½	7 2 3	6⁴½	33.75	4.10	Steady effort m-t	C HDHpTop, NTSBaJean, OJosie
10-1	ACF 32.96 56	8 6 3 2	6⁵½	33.34	13.60	Tired late md-trk	B WCSpecial, HDJllyLady, Cast
9-25⁸	ACF 33.50 56½	4 1 1ʰᵈ 3	4²	33.39	31.10	Good effort m-t	B SnufmSi, LagJewel, McGrAura

No. 7 — Green White — HD'S ALTOONA 22/13 = +9 **(67)**
Owner—H. D. BECKNER   11 0 1
Kennel—H. D. BECKNER
Bdl. B., Jan. 1981. H.D.'s Rooster—*D's Wilma*   Trainer—ROBERT THORNE

10-23	ACF 33.16 66½	4 5 4 4	4½	33.46	18.10	No room 1st turn	D ArDesign, PenBroker, StnCrab
10-16	ACF 32.93 66½	4 8 5 5	4¹¹	33.63	19.60	Slight gain md-trk	D CDSummer, TTooth, MMMary
10-11	ACF 33.44 66½	6 8 6 3	1¹	33.54	11.10	Drawing clear ms-t	M JoByeGun, SheerSilk, A'sTecln
10-4 ³	ACF 33.36 66½	8 8 8	3¹	33.93	17.00	Crowded wd 1st t	M Kuralt, YourDeal, ProGrandma
9-27 ³	ACF 33.25 66	5 3 8 5	3¹	33.61	33.10	Late gain md-trk	M JoZFabber, YurDeal, FletMike
9-20 ³	ACF 33.46 66	6 6 8	7¹¹	34.16	14.90	No room 1st turn	M RshAbby, Spago, ATumblweed

No. 8 — Black Gold — DELLA RIVER 11/13 = -2 **(57)**
Owner—L. B. KASBERG   5 0 0 0
Kennel—J. B. HARRIS
Red Bdl. B., Feb. 1980. Sandy Printer—*Flying River*   Trainer—B. E. LLOYD   DB-28 7 4 1

10-23	ACF 33.29 56½	2 6 3 4	4¹	33.63	13.90	Steady effort m-t	D BronzeStar, JWsTammy, Info
10-18	ACF 32.96 57	4 4 4 4	5³	33.61	10.30	Evenly inside	D FrelyAccepted, MStruffer, Sum
10-14	ACF 33.21 57	5 2 4 5	6¹	33.50	12.30	Hard try inside	C JAFunnyBaby, IdlIdol, Baska
10-2	ACF 32.74 56½	4 4 7½ 7	7¹½	33.89	14.10	Jammed far trn	C MakRoom, EurBabe, BluWater
9-27 ⁸	ACF 33.18 55½	4 7 5 6	5³¹	33.43	14.90	Closed good m-t	C MsSuperSpy, Casbah, BrnzStar
9-20 ¹ˢ	ACF 32.84 56	5 3 3	4¹	33.67		Evenly md-trk	J SnpeeSue, MoinTop, SkihiNobs

Please examine your tickets and change before leaving window

Handicapper's Choice: 6—5—3   Chartman's Choice: 5—6—1

76

From our sample, we can see that the #8 ranked dog finished in the money only once out of the 10 races. Considering that at least one race out of every 10 will be a "fluke race," we should strongly consider dropping any dog ranked #8 (from any race on this course, at this grade) from our selection. We can accomplish this by giving #8 a substantial number of minus points.

Also, in our sample, the #1 and #2 rankings were both in the money in seven of the 10 races, and deserve some pretty heavy points; #3 and #4 were pretty strong, too. Our point award table for this grade and course, based on this example, might look like this:

(Most gain)	#1	+ 25
	#2	+ 25
	#3	+ 15
	#4	+ 15
	#5	
	#6	
	#7	− 15
(Least gain)	#8	− 25

Obviously, maneuvering ability is a pretty important factor in our handicapping, and one not discovered by many others. This leaves only three more grading factors to be covered.

Stretch Gain, or Late Speed

Whether you call it "kick," strong finish, late speed, drive, or stretch gain, this is the ingredient that tells us which dogs close the best coming down to the wire. More importantly, our study will tell us in which types of races this counts, and in which ones it does not. Odds are that you will discover this strength is a far smaller factor than is commonly thought, in several grades. Or, to put it another way, though the factor itself may be somewhat important, we do not have the information available to us to be able to determine it well enough. The problem is that most programs do not show us how many lengths off the leader any of the other dogs are, at the various calls. So, if we try to determine how well any dog other than the leader is doing in the stretch, we have only his position to go by. This is simply not as accurate.

It is possible, for example, for a dog to pick up three positions in the stretch, but still lose ground to the leader, due to three other dogs losing even more ground, or bumping. Horse race past performance charts give us this information, but for the dogs, we just have to use what we have at hand. In some cases, it is useful, even if not completely accurate. In other cases, you may find that it has zero value. Don't try to make more of it than your study indicates.

You will compute this factor in a similar manner that you figured the factors for early speed and maneuvering ability. *Scratch out the schooling races and troubled races* before you begin. Total the stretch call position for the last three good races. Then total the finish position for these races. Subtract one from the other for the positions gained (plus), or lost (minus). Then rank the dogs on the page in order. The page completed, for this factor, would look like the sample in Figure 13.

Notice that on the example program page in Figure 13 only one dog averaged a position *loss* in its last three races. This is rather unusual, since you will often find two or three dogs in a race which have this weakness. Furthermore, the one dog which does have this minus rating (#5, *So C Wink*) obviously doesn't have, at least in the six races shown, a real habit of losing ground. In fact, this dog *won* three of its last six races! There will be times when a numerical system of rating needs a little human interpretation, and your good sense might tell you, in this example, that this dog doesn't really seem to be a "stretch fader," and that perhaps the person who wrote the remarks on the past races missed noting a bump or collision that *So C Wink* suffered in that 11/6 race.

On the other end of the scale, it certainly appears that #7 in this example race is the strongest stretch-gainer in this group. Notice that he also closed well in *stakes* (S) races, so we can rank him pretty high. We also had three dogs which scored "0", neither gaining or losing ground in their last three races. This created a three-way tie for fourth, so we had no fifth- or sixth-rated dogs. We had no eighth-rated dog either, because of a scratch.

In any case, once you have scored 25 to 30 races in this respect, and documented how they actually finished in their races, record those results just as you did for the factors discussed in previous chapters, and list them in order as shown in the (abbreviated) example here:

4	7	2	2	3	6
4	1	5	2	1	4
8	2	4	2	8	6
6	4	1	5	1	8
1	2	7	1	5	8

Figure 13

TENTH RACE(10)

Travel Time Bus Company. Worcester. Mass.

TRACK RECORD—38.32
CM's Happy Son 5-27-82

YANKEE COURSE

2040 Feet **QUINIELA AND TRIFECTA WAGERING**

3rd Round Grand Prix Qualifying

GRADE S

Post Pos.	Date	Dis.	Time	Wt. PP. Off 1-8 Str. F.FW	ART	Odds	Gr. Comment Sts. 1st 2d 3d 4th	Order of Finish

1 RED — GH'S MELISSA(WL) 7/7(+1) = +/ (64)

Black B., June 15, 1979. Downing—Quare Lass*

PLN 23 8 2 3 4
WON 12 1 0 0 2

Owner—Antonio Arria
Kennel—D.K. Kennels, Inc.
Trainer—Patrick Gauthier

11-14⁸x YC	F 39.27	62½ 1	3	2	2	2¹	39.34	*2.20 S Closing wide	SoCSprite,TammeyImage,RJPsTony⁷
11-10¹⁰xYC	F 39.38	63½ 4	5	8	8	7¹¹	40.16	7.40 S Shuffled early	WinlDo,DutchKCal,BetterMoney
11- 3⁸x YC	F 39.43	62½		5		3⁵	38.70	2.30 TA Shuffled far tn	ChefDomsDuk,FirstWltz,JudysChasr
10-28⁵x YC	F 38.76	63 5	2	11	16	19¹	38.76	*1.00 B Going away	RJsBrassRing,CozyScott,Chuckling
10-23¹⁰ YC	F 40.05	63 3	5	4	4i	4⁹	40.09	4.20 TA Hard try	GLsPup,MissRosalee,TammeyImage
10-20¹⁰xYC	F 39.49		5	fl		OOP	2.60 A Fell 1st tn	MissRosale,LCsFirFly,PrinterTim

2 BLUE — LC'S FIRE FLY 19/14 = +5 (56)

Dark Brindle B., November 10, 1978. Surefire Glennn—L.C.'s Faye

PLN 18 8 6 4 5
WON 3 0 0 0 0

Owner—Luther Ray Carter
Kennel—River Bend Farm
Trainer—Lawrence Henry

11-14⁶x YC	F 39.54	55	1	1	5	6⁴	39.54	12.20 S Followed wd pace	TMsStarChsr,ChefDomsDk,DtchKCl
11-10¹⁰xYC	F 39.55	55	1	3	7	6⁴	39.85	30.20 S Stretch gain	WinlDo,DutchKCal,BetterMoney
11- 5¹⁰ YC	F 39.55½	4	8	7	5	4¹⁰	39.53	40.40 TA Stretch gain	WinlDo,MissRosalee,SoCSprite
10-30¹⁰ YC	F 39.16		6	8	8	8¹²	41.17	20.20 A Fell 1st tn	PecosVinc,MissRosalee,TammeyImag
10-23¹⁰ YC	F 40.05	55	8	8	8	5⁵	40.36	9.40 TA Late gain	GLsPup,MissRosalee,TammeyImage
10-20¹⁰xYC	F 39.62	55½ 1	3	5	5	2²	39.62	8.20 S Showed	MissRosale,PrinterTim,StartHom

3 WHITE — TAMMEY IMAGE 12/12 = 0 (51)

White Ticked and Brindle B., April 10, 1979. Streak—Judy's Image

PLN 27 5 4 5 2
NFM 0 0 0 0 0

Owner—D.Q. or Sharon Williams
Kennel—Teddy Meadows
Trainer—Otis Browning

11-14⁸x YC	F 39.27	51	2	1	3	3⁹	39.86	8.40 S Distant show	SoCSprite,GHsMelissa,RJPsTony⁷
11-10¹²xYC	F 39.80	50½ 8	7	7	7	7⁰	40.07	14.40 S Shuffled early	BigMacSnkr,GllsInky,JBSTennrTnr
11- 5¹⁰ YC	F 38.90	50½ 8	3	6	6	6¹¹	39.61	30.20 TA Followed pace	WinlDo,MissRosalee,SoCSprite
10-30¹⁰ YC	F 39.16	50	2	1	3	3³	39.41	14.20 A Good effort	PecosVinc,MissRosale,SandRousr
10-23¹⁰ YC	F 40.05	50½ 3	2	3		3¹⁵	40.07	25.40 TA Nearly up	GLsPup,MissRosalee,GHsMelissa
10-16¹⁰ YC	F 39.15	50	4	7	6	6⁸¹	39.71	24.40 A Some gain	ChefDomsDk,SoCSprt,JBSTennerTnr

4 GREEN — GULL'S INKY 8/8 = 0 (65)

Black D., December 19, 1980. Derek's Cadillac—Angel Shade

PLN 7 2 4 0 1
BIS 9 1 0 1

Owner—Gull Haven Kennel, Inc.
Kennel—Wilton Corp.
Trainer—Graydon Robtoy

11-14⁸x YC	F 39.15	64	5	4	4	4⁴	39.41	2.40 S Fine try wide	TMsStarChsr,ChefDomsDk,DtchKCl
11-10¹²xYC	F 39.80	64½ 5	2	2	2	2²	39.93	9.20 S Chased winner	BigMacSnkr,JBSTennrTnr,WarriorQn
11- 6⁸x YC	F 38.89	64	4	2	2	2¹	38.96	10.40 A Hard try inside	OverTher,FearThePric,WarriorQuen
11- 2⁸x YC	F 39.46	64	4	3	2	1³	39.46	2.50 TB Closing wide	BetterMny,BuckJrdn,FatBottmGrl
10-27⁸x YC	F 39.22	63	2	3		19	39.52	*3.40 B Shuffled far tn	RynsWhz,JamsBigPrl,RocksprngFlyr⁷
10-22⁵ YC	F 39.72	65	6	1	3	13	39.72	.90 C Handily ins	GlamorsMrcn,FtBttmGrl,ChmpsLttr

5 BLACK — SO C WINK 9/11 (+1) = -/ (53)

Red Brindle B., June 16, 1980. Highway Robber—Sparkle Flossie

PLN 15 5 5 0 1

Owner—APS Kennel
Kennel—A.J. Meyer
Trainer—Helen Gauvin

11-14¹²xYC	F 39.43	53	5	7	2	2⁴	40.25	6.20 S Blkd 1st tn	WinlDo,PecosVince,JBSTennerTuner
11-10⁸x YC	F 39.44	53	3	11	10	14¹	39.44	3.70 S Easily	PecosVnc,ChefDomsDk,JamsBigPrl
11- 6⁸x YC	F 38.89	53	6	7	3	8¹⁴	39.80	3.40 A Never prominent	OverThere,GullsInky,FearThePrice
11- 2¹⁰ YC	F 39.57	52½ 3	7	2	3	2¹¹	39.65	*2.20 TA Hard try	OverTher,FearThePric,WarriorQuen
10-28¹⁰ 5-16	F 30.66	52½ 4	2	12	13	11	30.66	5.40 A Going away	JoeKent,TMsTorch,BlackyHawk
10-16⁸x YC	F 39.37	14	8	8	13	11i	39.37	8.40 B Easily	DarkWish,LTsRunner,RJPsTony

6 YELLOW — DUTCH K CAL 11/11 = 0 (55)

Red B., February 11, 1981. Sod Buster—Dutch Cappy Ann

PLN 15 3 3 3
PUE 8 1 1 1 2

Owner—Herb Koerner
Kennel—Herb Koerner
Trainer—Kim Maher

11-14⁸x YC	F 39.15	54	3	3	3	3⁴	39.38	7.20 S Good effort	TMsStarChsr,ChefDomsDk,GllsInky
11-10¹⁰xYC	F 39.38	54½ 6	4	2	2	2⁶	39.74	25.20 S Closing wide	WinlDo,BetterMoney,LCsFireFly
11- 6⁵x YC	F 39.14	54½ 6	5	6	6	6¹⁰	39.79	5.20 B Followed pace	RocksprngFlyr,CDsGl,MistyPrntr
10-30⁸x YC	F 39.39	54½ 6	2	5	4	4⁷	39.39	2.30 C Strong finish	ChampsLttr,SSPatric,LeChampgnn
10-23⁸ YC	F 39.85	54½ 6	8	5	4	4⁷	40.33	10.20 TB Sl brk, gained	JudysChsr,GEsDixiDwns,RJsBrssRng
10-17⁷x 5-16	F 31.63	54½ 6	4	4	4	32.11	4.40 B Bumped 1st tn	HelenG,MrZigMo,JonOne

7 GREEN & WHITE — JBS TENNER TUNER 14/8 = +6 (59)

Brindle B., September 16, 1979. Step Proudly—JB's Six Five

PLN 14 8 8 9 3
LGP 2 0 0 0 0

Owner—Johnnie B. Lewis
Kennel—British-Connecticut
Trainer—Joe Carreira

11-14¹²xYC	F 39.43	59	5	4	4	3²	39.58	17.40 S Hard try wide	WinlDo,PecosVince,BigMacSneaker
11-10¹²xYC	F 39.80	58	7	6	3	3²	39.94	4.40 S Blkd closing	BigMacSnekr,GllsInky,WarriorQun
11- 3⁸x YC	F 39.43	58½		6	5	4⁵	39.81	2.40 TA Stumbled break	ChefDomsDuk,FirstWltz,GHsMeliss
10-29¹⁰ YC	F 39.28	58	8	6	6	4⁵	39.64	7.40 A Bmpd closing	WinlDo,ChicagoKaty,JudysChaser
10-22¹⁰ YC	F 39.38	59	8	7	6	2¹⁰	40.03	8.20 A Str gain	WinlDo,CDsGail,SunbeltAaron
10-16¹⁰ YC	F 39.15	57	6	4	4	3²	39.28	6.40 A Good effort	ChefDomsDuke,SoCSprite,GirlJerri

8 BLACK & YELLOW

(SCRATCH)

These examples happen to be taken directly from a recent test which I ran at one of my favorite tracks. It was from a Grade C race on the short sprint course. You will see that this is not a factor which deserves much weight at *this* track, in *this* grade, on *this* course—especially when we translate the above column to percentages, as in Figure 14.

Figure 14

		Win	Place	Show	Total
(Best stretch gain)	#1	20%	30%	10%	60%
	#2	30%	20%	10%	60%
	#3	—	10%	—	10%
	#4	20%	10%	20%	50%
	#5	10%	10%	10%	30%
	#6	10%	—	20%	30%
	#7	—	10%	10%	20%
(Least gain)	#8	10%	10%	20%	40%

You can see that dogs rated #4 through #8 were in the money/trifecta far more often than dogs rated #1 through #3. Obviously, this factor doesn't count for much here, so we will give it a pretty low point weighting, perhaps something like the following:

$$#1 + 10$$
$$#2 + 10$$
$$#3 \text{ through } #8 = \text{No points}$$

Once again, realize that our abbreviated sample can easily give us misleading information, and you must be sure to test more races than this in each grade, on each course.

Notice that we didn't give any points to the #3 or #4 ratings here, as we did in some of the previous factors. In this case, the #3 and #4 ratings just didn't look strong enough; in fact, the #3 rating was the weakest of all. Logic says, though, that a dog which is the third best at *any*thing isn't likely to lose *because* of it! Instead, our short sample simply gave us some illogical information. If, however, you come up with something like this in a sufficiently large sample, give or take points accordingly, logic be damned! There may well be some weird reason for it.

You will discover that in nearly every case this stretch-gain factor (or late speed, as most handicappers call it) is far less of a factor on sprint courses than it is on longer courses. In fact, there are tracks at which I consider it to be no factor at all in any sprint race, any grade. If you come up with a determination like this for your track, then you need not even compute this factor for those races, except for now and then to make sure something hasn't changed. Discovering something like this can save time in your program scoring.

At some point in building your system, especially after discovering that a given factor is of little real consequence, you may say to yourself, "Wow, that was a lot of work just to find out that all of this scoring on this factor is really of no handicapping value!" That, Mr. Handicapper, is exactly the point of all this engineering—to find out not only what *does* count in a given race, but also what *doesn't*. Someday, after having done your homework, you will find yourself at the track, knowing, through your studies, that a given factor isn't worth even looking at in a particular race. You've done your homework, you've scored your program, and you've pretty well determined how you will be betting. You have made your selections based on the factors that you *know* are important in this race. Seated behind you are three guys who consider themselves "serious players." They are just now, with only four minutes till post time, having a heated discussion about their intended picks, and their loudest disagreement is on the one factor which you know to be the least important. It was important for the last race, but not for this one! Now, you may not win that particular race—in fact, maybe one of *them* will. But eventually you will see it happen to your advantage so often that you will indulge yourself in a little smugness when situations like this occur. It's a nice feeling, and your homework will pay. It certainly won't win every race for you, but it *will* pay.

And those other fellows, no matter how professional they think they are, will usually not have the patience or the determination to benefit from the knowledge you are gaining here. Beating the dog races isn't easy, and one has to be satisfied with fewer wins. But, if engineered and wagered intelligently, you can have a system that will let the doggies buy just about anything that you might want! (But, of course, it won't be the doggies that buy it for you—it will be those guys who were sitting behind you!)

Percentage of Recent Finishes in the Money

The last charted category we will discuss is the recent accomplishments of each dog, in relationship to each other in the current race. In other words, how has each dog been doing lately, as far as finishing in the money? For this, we again look at the last six or so races reported on the program. We could instead look at the dog's performance for the year to date, but this won't give you as accurate a picture as will the most current data. It is even more true for dogs than for horses that what the critter did last month doesn't mean nearly as much as what it has done lately.

What this factor is doing, in a way, is determining in a meaningful manner just what class the dog is currently performing in. Disregarding what grade the recent races have been, any dog that has been in the money in three or four of its last six races is running like a top-grade dog. In fact, top-grade dogs tend to average in-the-money finishes in about 50% to 55% of their races. Dogs which can't average about 33% often work down through the grades and will eventually get graded out of the meet. So, if you have some dogs in the race at hand which have been in the money 66% of the time (four out of six races), and others that have been in the money only 16% of the time (one out of six races), this is very often a telling factor, and is nearly always worthy of some weight in your point system.

However, if you would feel more comfortable knowing more about a dog's background than just the six races listed in the program, you can purchase "past performance charts" at most tracks, which list each dog's performance through the last several months. Frankly, though, I don't find this useful for the purpose being discussed here.

To document this factor, simply look at all of the "good" races shown for each dog on the program. If, as an example, six races are recorded for each dog, but a particular dog was troubled in two of his last six races, but finished in first, second, or third in three of those four good races, you would score him as a "75% dog." A dog with five good races to look at, but which finished in the money for only one of those five races, would be a 20% dog, and so forth. Again, as with the other categories, you first cross out all schooling or troubled races for each entry. Two sample entries are shown in Figure 15.

The program used in Figure 15 (Biscayne) lists nine or 10 past races, but this is a rare exception, because nearly all other tracks list only six. Just as a point of curiosity, note that one of our example dogs was in the money 75% of the time, recently, and the other was in 62%, yet between them, only one race was won! (This is of no particular interest to this system.)

Figure 15

Post Pos.	Date	Dist.	Time	Wt.	P.P.	Off	½	Str.	F.FW	ART	Odds	Comment and Grade		Order of Finish	Starts	1st	2d	3d
														Kennel—Kerry Patch 145	BIS	2	0	0	2
VITO RILLA $75^{5}/_{0}$ (74)														Owner—Lakeside Kennel	FLA	13	1	3	4
	White Red D. Dec. 1979 Sandy Printer—Lakeside Pat													Trainer—Grace Browning					
11-11¹	5-16	30.86	75	3	6	3	3	3⁵	31.19	3.90	Early gain. inside	B	Kim'sBilly.OutsideChance.ApacheStar				
x11- 4¹⁰	5-16	30.84	73+	1	3	2	3	3⁶	31.26	4.00	Good effort. inside	B	ForgedAlloy.SwaneesCosmos.HelperMchal				
								(Races below were run at Flagler Kennel Club)									
10-29⁵	5-16	31.73	73	7	4	2¹	2	3²	31.86	4.50	Good effort. inside	B	SumguySam.Gull'sYakki.Kim'sBilly				
10-26⁷	5-16	31.69	73	1	2	3²	3	4⁵	32.01	6.00	Outfinished. ins.	A	JillGin.SC'sJr.Underoo				
10-22⁷	5-16	31.86	74	4	4	3¹	3	5¹+	31.96	5.00	Outfinished. ins.	A	MyVedaJ.Ted'sGus.MC'sBayouAbbey				
10-18⁸	5-16	31.49	74	4	3	3⁴	3	3⁹	32.10	8.00	Best of rest. inside	A	SC'sJr.Arista'sFujiko.MC'sEleanor				
10- 9⁹	5-16	31.67	74	7	4	R	8	8	oop	17.90	First turn	A	JoeyJones.LantanaReporter.SandyShaw				
10- 6⁸	5-16	31.64	74	8	8	6⁶	5	3⁴	31.90	15.30	Steady drive. inside	A	LantanaReporter.BorneGambler.RadarWav				
10- 2⁴	5-16	31.90	74	1	6	2²	3	3²	32.01	*2.50	Good effort. inside	A	RadarWave.MarKirLance.OneThinDime				
														Kennel—Rushaway 253	BIS	1	0	1	0
OUTSIDE CHANCE $62^{2}/_{0}$ (69)														Owner—J. P. Richardson	JAX	11	2	1	2
	Light Brindle D.. July 1980. K's Clown—Ladette													Trainer—Harold Roderick					
11-11¹	5-16	30.86	69	5	4	2	2	2⁴	31.15	9.50	Followed pace. inside	B	Kim'sBilly.VitoRilla.ApacheStar				
11- 3¹⁵	BC	33.97	69	5	4	5	5	5¹+	34.87		Bumped-1st tn		SpeedyMontana.JR'sSpeck.JimmyGin⁶				
								(Races below were run at Jacksonville. Florida)									
10-28⁸	5-16	31.14	70+	5	3	4	3	2¹+	31.26	3.40	Good effort	B	SpotCat.JamsAlibeth.CashTaker				
x10-23¹⁰	5-16	31.52	71	3	4	2	2	3¹	31.58	3.70	Good show	B	KuntreeKyle.ShebaHipckts.MTsBustr				
10-16⁷	5-16	30.97	71	8	3	2	2	3²	31.11	11.60	Faded to show	SB	JcksMagnum.KIsosPrince.BJsNight				
10-13¹⁰	5-16	31.81	71	5	8	5	5	5¹⁰	31.54	48.50	Steady bid	SA	MProblm.ElctrcStuf.JhnieGren				
10- 9⁶	5-16	31.00	71	6	8	8	8	8¹²	31.85	16.00	Always last	SA	JcksMgnum.ChnswRed.BngoNut				
10- 4¹¹	5-16	30.84	71	2	3	3	7	7¹³	31.73	7.70	Early factor	A	DebonairDate.TmothyCrttr.CllMeKmi				
9-29⁶	5-16	31.49	71	3	4	1²	1⁴	1³+	31.49	5.90	Quickly on top	B	JhnieGren.Whalr.PddyWagn				

After you have scored 20 to 40 races on this factor (in each grade), you would then record the finish order for each of those races and list the results in sequence, as you have done for the other categories. Again, for the sake of demonstration, we will concern ourselves with 10 races for an example:

1	4	3
4	2	1
1	3	6
3	2	4
3	1	8
5	2	1
5	3	2
1	2	4
3	1	6
7	2	1

The percentages, then, on this sample, would work out as shown in Figure 16.

Figure 16

		Win	Place	Show	Total
(Highest % rating)	#1	30%	20%	30%	80%
	#2	—	50%	10%	60%
	#3	30%	20%	10%	60%
	#4	10%	10%	20%	40%
	#5	20%	—	—	20%
	#6	—	—	20%	20%
	#7	10%	—	—	10%
(Lowest % rating)	#8	—	—	10%	10%

Now, if you come up with a percentage table similar to the one shown in Figure 16, after working up an adequate number of sample races, you will really have something to sink your teeth into! Even when we realize that we will probably not have as many #4, #5 and #6 ratings, because of some ties for the first three ratings, we still see that, *in this grade, on this course,* our top three rated dogs do extremely well. And also that our #6, #7 and #8 dogs do lousy.

In fact, in this example, our #8-rated dog finished in the money in only one of the 10 races, and then only for show. We can consider this a fluke, easily enough, and all but give that #8-rated dog an automatic scratch by assigning that rating a substantial number of minus points. He would really have to have a number of other positive things going for him before we would want him in our selection. If, in a given race, we find him to also be starting from a "cold" box, we could pretty well figure that we had just eliminated a dog from the race.

For this example, we would probably assign our points somewhat like this:

(Highest % rating)	#1	+ 30
	#2	+ 30
	#3	+ 20
	#4	+ 10
	#5	
	#6	
	#7	− 20
	#8	− 25

It would be tempting, upon discovering a factor this strong, to start using it for all grades. Wrong! You will probably find that it is a far weaker factor—maybe not one at all—in another grade.

Remember that you also need to compute the outcome of more races than the 10 we are using here as an example. Do your homework adequately and accurately, and your "salary" will be handsome indeed.

Keep in mind that you must avoid assuming that some of the conclusions we seem to be reaching here are going to be valid at any track. In the previous chapter, for example, I mentioned that I have found late speed to be a very small factor on sprint courses at most tracks. In fact, I no longer even compute it for sprint races at my favorite track. But do not consider that this is the case at most tracks—make your own study for your own track. You may very well find the case to be an absolute reverse.

Furthermore, when I state that I no longer compute this factor for certain races, I am not being entirely accurate. I currently do not *use* the late speed factor on the short course at this one track, but I still occasionally *compute* it just the same, to see if this factor has changed. And indeed, for a period of about two months a year ago, it did. That's a very strong argument for keeping your system freshened up.

Grade Change

Now we come to the final numerical determination in this system. Here, we will determine if a dog moving up or down in class should be down-rated or up-rated for our selection. Most handicappers would say "Why waste a chapter on this? Any dog moving up in class has less of a chance of being in the money, and any dog moving down in class has to have a better chance of being in the money." Well, that blanket assumption is often wrong, and you can prove it to yourself.

Remember, most handicapping is based on the selection of the most logical *winner*. The assumption is that the strongest three dogs in a race, with everything else being equal, are the ones that have the best chance to also place and show, as well as win. But that is often not the case—there are many dogs (and horses) who must *win* or nothing. They will go all out to win, and either win or blow the race, seldom coming in second or third. Likewise, there are dogs in most races which have very little chance to win (because of post position, etc.), but may have a better chance to show than does the mutuel favorite!

The mutuel favorite, by the way, actually wins only about 30% of the time, at most tracks, and your strongest selection by this numerical system will likely not do a good deal better. (Though if you give adequate time to building your system, it is almost sure to do better than the crowd does, as far as picking winners.) The catch is that it is nearly impossible to make a profit betting win, place or show at the dog track. Your system, built from this book and your work, will do a good job of picking not only winners, but—more importantly—of selecting the dogs most likely to place and show—in other words, to be in the quinielas, perfectas and trifectas, where the profit is.

Now, back to the matter of grade change. This is definitely worth studying; it is not as automatic or as simple as most fans and handicappers think it is. You are very likely to find instances in which a dog moving down from a certain grade to a certain grade, on a certain course, at a certain track, should have points *deducted* from his chances. You are almost certain to also find other circumstances in which it has no meaning at all. And, of course, you will also find that, in some cases, it *is* as per the common assumption.

This is one of the easier factors to compute, in that you need not score any programs and compare the results. Simply get a fistful of programs from the track under study, and look through the past performances. There, you will see many instances, in each grade, of dogs moving up or down in grade, and the results of that grade change are recorded right there. Figure 17 shows some examples of how to locate and isolate this factor.

After marking several programs in this manner, record your findings in the manner shown in Figure 18.

You may, of course, design your own version of this form, probably much abbreviated from this example, or simply do the job on scratch paper. You can get a pretty good handle on this factor at your track in just a few hours of study.

The segment example illustrated in Figure 18 is based on an actual sampling which your author recently did at a certain track. Do not use it as a general rule at any track. It not only will not apply at any and all tracks, it may well not even apply at the very track where this study was made, a few months later.

As you interpret these findings, again keep in mind that any purely *random* sampling of dogs will show up in the money an average 37½% of the time, so don't draw any premature conclusions from your findings without considering this.

In the samples illustrated in Figure 18, we can see that, on this course,

Figure 17

6-1 | **6** | YELLOW

HILTON HEAD — 71

OWNER E J Alderson
KENNEL E J Alderson Kennel
TRAINER Tim Andrews

1982 WD 49 5 12 6
1981 WD 6 1 1 0

Fawn D . March 80 K s Flak Flamingo Eve Imp

10 26	1	PC	F	31 41	70½	6	7	7	7	$8^{[illegible]}$	31 89	22 80	Bumped 1st turn	C	ClassySnowflake.CountryPath.Bleason
10 21	2	KC	F	39 41	71	4	1	7	5	4^{13}	40 31	6 80	Bumped up some	C	EzBoldRed.JodieL PecosBobKat
10 18	2	KC	F	39 60	70½	5	8	7	6	6^{11}	40 36	6 10	Bumped 1st turn	C	CdDawn.WyldeBlackberry.PecosBobKat
10 13	2	KC	F	39 34	71	8	5	2	3	3^{6}	39 78	2 50	Weakened inside	C	BanjoStrings.PrettyPollard.BlueTequilla
10 9	2	PC	F	31 56	70	2	1	8	8	6^{5}	31 90	6 40	Always back	B	BettysDouble.LilHeartbreaker.RcDeckMate
10 6	2	PC	F	30 68	71	4	4	6	6	5^{15}	31 71	13 60	No threat	B	RipSnorter.PamersPacman.HonestCandidate

12-1 | **7** | GREEN & WHITE

TERBO APPLE JACK — 65

OWNER D Andrews or D F Cahill
KENNEL Dick Andrews
TRAINER F Calvin Fillmore, Jr

1982 WD 8 0 0 0
DB 2 0 0 0

Brindle D March 81 Demon Jones Inkan Kuddles

10 26	3	PC	F	31 49	65½	2	1	3	3	$4^{4½}$	31 80	17 60	Outfinished, inside	D	CeeJenni.IrsSmuggler.JustAFantasy
10 20	3	PC	F	31 47	65½	3	5	7	7	$7^{14½}$	32 49	22 60	Bumped 1st turn	D	RustyBoots.SalemWitch AdamsCadillac
10 16	1x	PC	F	31 41	65½	6	4	3	3	6^{6}	31 81	9 20	Speed to stretch	D	ExpandedRole.SalemWitch.WindCurrent
10 11	9x	PC	F	31 17	65	1	1	6	6	6^{17}	32 33	14 40	Followed pace, rail	C	CajunBeth.JvsBlueBell.HesASholn
10 6	8x	PC	F	31 09	65	7	5	2	2	4^{9}	31 70	26 60	Speed to stretch	C	DarbyJoe.MarKirCloud.BurrBets
10 2	6	PC	F	31 05	65	4	8	4	5	7^{13}	31 95	14 90	Faded, inside	C	AnnieJune.GoodRisk.LittleMischief

9-2 | **8** | YELLOW & BLACK

JUST A FANTASY — 64

OWNER Jay R Rauen
KENNEL Double "A" Kennel
TRAINER Paul Petrone

1982 WD 9 1 0 2

Red Brindle B . April 81 Demon Jones Tuf Lou Ekko

10 26	3	PC	F	31 49	63	7	4	5	5	3^{4}	31 76	10 80	Late effort, midtrack	D	CeeJenni.IrsSmuggler.TerboAppleJack
10 20	5x	PC	Sl	31 36	64	5	3	4	5	$6^{6½}$	31 82	9 60	Weakened, midtrack	D	SoGoAmber.CousinsMoose.ChubsDolly
10 9	5	PC	F	31 21	64	8	5	7	7	8^{11}	32 00	7 20	Always back	C	XsLongNLean.CoverLook.BamasUranus
10 6	11x	PC	F	30 91	65	8	4	3	3	5^{7}	31 39	6 40	Speed to stretch	C	XtraExpress.OddFontella.PyrmidKapOn
10 2	11x	PC	F	30 78	64	5	2	6	7	$7^{8½}$	31 38	8 30	No threat	C	DirectControl.XtraExpress.RoseOfPdl

Figure 18

3/8-mile course:

Grade AA

Of this many instances of change: 〜〜〜〜〜〜〜〜 I
This many dogs who moved up from Grade A finished in
the money: 〜〜 I (30%)

Grade A

Of this many instances of change: 〜〜〜〜〜〜〜〜 I
This many dogs who moved up from Grade B finished in
the money: 〜 IIII (9) (22%)
This many dogs who moved down from Grade AA finished in
the money: 〜〜〜〜 I (21) (51%)

Grade B

Of this many instances of change: 〜〜〜〜〜〜〜〜
This many dogs who moved up from Grade C finished in
the money: 〜〜 IIII (14) (31%)
This many dogs who moved down from Grade A finished in
the money: 〜〜〜 II (17) (43%)

dogs moving up from Grade B to A certainly do seem to suffer a disadvantage. Only 22% of them end up in the money, while about 51% of
the dogs moving down from Grade AA to A finish in the money. We will
definitely want to deduct some points from the dogs which are jumping
up from Grade B to Grade A, though we will probably not want to automatically remove them completely from our selection. (After all, they
were in the money in nine of the 41 examples.) Of course, we will want to
give some plus points to the dogs moving down from a Grade AA to a
Grade A race. (But probably not so many points so as to make *them* an
automatic selection, either.)

Realistically, one must also temper this numerical system with some
arbitrary interpretation. There are times when it is obvious, from the past
performance record, that a given dog is moving down in grade not just
because of poor performance, but because of a streak of "bad luck,"

such as bumps, collisions, being "forced wide," etc., in a number of successive races. This is one of the instances in which the chartwriter's comments can be helpful in identifying such a situation. In a case like this, the dog would deserve some plus points regardless of an indication otherwise from your numerical system.

After studying this factor at a given track, you would set up a table similar to the one illustrated in Figure 19, then translate these plus and minus points over to your final "scoring sheet." We will later refer to this scoring sheet as our *"factor weighting"* form, on which you bring all your learned factors together to use in scoring the race program.

Figure 19

3/8-mile course

From A to AA	– 10
From AA to A	+ 10
From B to A	– 10
From A to B	No points
From C to B	– 5
From B to C	No points
From D to C	+ 10
From C to D	– 5
From M to D	No points

5/16-mile course

From A to AA	– 15
From AA to A	+ 5
From B to A	– 5
From A to B	+ 10
From C to B	No points
From B to C	No points
From D to C	+ 10
From C to D	No points
From M to D	+ 10

In looking at this grade change factor, you will want to compare the percentages with that norm of 37½%. Any percentage less than about 32% deserves some minus points. Any percentage of about 44% or more should get some plus points.

You will probably discover that this grade change factor by itself will rarely indicate a "lock-in" or "lock-out" situation. In general, it tends to be less of a factor than most handicappers believe. (And usually far less, too, than most "morning odds" writers believe.) When you can determine in which cases, on which courses, this is the case, you will be one more step smarter than the average fan . . . and probably several steps richer, too, if you mind your betting!

It is entirely possible—in fact, probable—that you will discover one or more instances where moving up a grade is a plus-point situation—the exact reverse of what logic would seem to indicate. Likewise, you may well uncover certain cases when moving down is a disadvantage. This is valuable knowledge! It's the kind of discovery that's the next thing to automatic profit. Don't worry about the logic of the contradiction; if you can prove it on paper from actual documented past performances, it is concrete enough to accept as a weighting factor.

As a point of curiosity, how can this happen? There are a couple of possible explanations. For instance, the Racing Secretary at any track has a certain amount of latitude in the mix of the dogs he selects for most races, and at times, his purposes, which are not visible themselves for handicapping, may outweigh the logic of normal grade changes. Another (more common) factor is that often a dog moving up is on a hot streak that will carry it at least into the money, if not the lead, in the next higher grade. Older dogs also have these streaks. Likewise, a dog moving down in grade, especially if the down move is not due to innocent bad luck, may well be unhealthy, injured, depressed or, for whatever reason, off form, and perhaps on its way to moving right down through the grades and out of the meet. A dog in this situation might not manage to get in the money if it was dropping *two* grades at once. The fan who adds points to this dog is in for a loss. Of course, *you* can't positively identify him either, but you are far more likely to learn the truth by applying the other factors learned in this book.

All in all, this grade change factor is well worth working out for your track. Don't take the easy way out by just using the general rule of thumb that "Down is good, up is bad."

Chapter 10
Putting It All Together

Later in this book is a brief discussion of some other handicapping factors which are often discussed and used by others. There are many, and some have pretty vigorous proponents. My studies have shown most of these factors to be too small to spend time on. There are those, however, who will base their entire "system" solely on the dog's weight, or on the dog's parentage, or such. Many have never really tested their theory other than the hard way—by losing money using it, which they usually blame on bad luck.

By using the principles in this book, *you* will test all of these theories, including this author's or any others that you or someone else discovers, by working it out *on paper,* not at the mutuel windows. Everything you need to learn for intelligent betting is already history, well documented in past programs and past performance charts. Is it true that dogs born between March and June tend to do better than dogs born at other times? You don't have to bet $1287 to find out—just run a study on it from material at hand. (Let me know the outcome, if you find there's something to this. . .)

The factors brought forward in this book are the ones that this author has found, after much study, to be most pertinent to the selection of win, place and show finishes. You could add other factors to these, if you wish, but if you do you may discover that there is a point where you can over-handicap.

To cash in on your studies, you'll need to get all your intelligence together on one sheet. You may want to use a format like the one illustrated in Figure 20 (Chart FW-1).

A blank version of Chart FW-1 is printed near the back of this book. You may duplicate this for your own use, if you wish, (but not for public distribution, or for sale), or you may prefer to develop a format for yourself.

Once you have developed your form, or adopted this one, you simply plug all your information into it. Here is where you first see how each

Factor Weighting   Figure 20   Chart FW-1

TRACK *PUPPY PARK* COURSE *MARATHON* DATE *12/82*

GRADE AA / GRADE A / GRADE B

	GRADE AA							GRADE A							GRADE B						
	PP	EG	AS	MA	SG	PM	GC	PP	EG	AS	MA	SG	PM	GC	PP	EG	AS	MA	SG	PM	GC
1	5	10	10	20		10	-	10	10	20	30		10	-		5	10	25	10	10	-
2	5		10	20		10	-	5	10	15	20		10	-		5	10	25		10	-
3			10	10		10	-			5	10	10	5	-			5	15		10	-
4			5	10		5	-			5	10		5	-			5			10	-
5	-10						-							-	-5		5				-
6							-							-							-
7							-	-10						-	-10						-
8	5		-5	-10			-					20	70	-	10						-
U	-	-	-	-	-	-	-10	-	-	-	-	-	-	70	-	-	-	-	-	-	-
D	-	-	-	-	-	-		-	-	-	-	-	-	+5	-	-	-	-	-	-	+5

GRADE C / GRADE D / GRADE ___

	GRADE C							GRADE D							GRADE						
	PP	EG	AS	MA	SG	PM	GC	PP	EG	AS	MA	SG	PM	GC	PP	EG	AS	MA	SG	PM	GC
1	10	5	15	15		10	-	5		20	20		10	-							-
2	10	5	15	5		10	-			20	20		5	-							-
3		5	10	5			-						5	-							-
4	10		10	5			-							-							-
5							-							-							-
6							-							-							-
7	-15						-	-5						-							-
8	5						-							-							-
U	-	-	-	-	-	-	+10	-	-	-	-	-	-	+5	-	-	-	-	-	-	
D	-	-	-	-	-	-	-5	-	-	-	-	-	-	-5	-	-	-	-	-	-	

PP = Post position advantage
EG = Early gain, or jump
AS = Average speed, recent
MA = Maneuvering ability
SG = Stretch gain, late speed
PM = Percentage races in money
GC = Grade change
U = Up in grade
D = Down in grade

category is going to mesh with the others. You may decide to take another look at some of the weighting again, before adopting it as your system, once you see how it comes together with everything else. In any case, few factors should be so strong, in themselves, that they by themselves make any dog a lock-in or a lock-out. You may discover some factors deserving of this kind of weighting, and that would be great, but this is, frankly, rather rare.

You will need an FW-1 sheet for each course at your track, and several other sheets if you should frequent more than one track. You may be able to devise a single sheet on which are listed all of the courses at a given track (most have only three). All of this will take a good deal of time. If you have followed my advice, you will have been doing little or no betting during this system development period. Unless you had been previously using an even better system (and I humbly doubt that), this break very likely will have saved you some money. That's good, because you will need to build up a stake to make this (or any) system work for you.

The chart reproduced in Figure 20 is filled in for demonstration purposes only. It is not a valid system, so don't tear it out and head for the track with it!

Note that on the Figure 20 sample chart a dog earning top points in each category could be awarded as many as 75 to 80 points. A top figure of between 70 and 100 points is a good chart balance. Of course, in the grades in which you determine not to score all categories, the top score will be somewhat lower. In the sample chart illustrated, for example, we are not using *stretch gain* in many of the grades, on this course, at this track.

To the uninitiated person, this chart may look like it could have been whipped out in short order. But, by now, *you* realize that it takes hours of homework to work it out. For that reason, along with the financial edge the chart will afford you, I suggest you do not make copies of it to distribute to your friends! (It may be wise to make a back-up copy for your own files, however.) On the other hand, if you wait until the current version of your chart begins to get stale, and then pass out *some* copies, you won't be diluting your own winnings as much (as long as you don't freshen up their copies when you do your own). I certainly couldn't recommend this practice, however. Not only would it be a dirty trick on your friends, but they would become fewer and fewer, and poorer and poorer!

Likewise, you shouldn't *sell* current versions of your chart, even with a "freshen-up, follow-up service." The more people at a given track using your system, the smaller your share of the payoffs will be. And with some of the larger trifecta payoffs, particularly, one additional winning ticket holder can lower the payoff by several hundred dollars.

In a later chapter, we will discuss how to *bet* with your chart. Before you get your bankroll out, though, you should make several dry runs with your fresh chart to make sure it works—that is, that it will produce a profit for you.

Remember, too, that you will need to double-check each of the categories occasionally to keep your chart up to date. A chart which is red-hot for you today could be a loser a few months later, at the very same track, if you don't keep it fresh. It is difficult to recommend a specific time interval to check this. In general, you probably should go "back to the drawing board" if you suffer as many as three losing nights in a row. However, because of the importance of intelligent wagering, it *is* possible to lose money with the world's *best* chart, if one doesn't use it properly. (In other words, you can *make* money with a good chart and intelligent betting, or you can *lose* money with a good chart and poor betting. But you *can't* make money with a *bad* chart, or no chart, no matter how intelligently you think you are betting.)

You're more likely to find that one or a couple of grades which were producing for you suddenly no longer do. While it isn't very likely that your whole chart will go sour at once, you will see parts of it which obviously need modification. It's most important to *record* your results of every race, so that you will be able to see how the various parts of your system are doing. In the practice of doing this, preferably in the dry runs, you will see that certain grade races, on certain courses, simply cannot be handicapped with enough reliability to produce a profit. That means, of course, that you will be able to see which races you do not want to bet on. That might seem like a shame, since it will have taken quite a bit of work to discover this, and it may seem at first that this work was wasted if it doesn't result in a wagering opportunity. But think what a tremendous advantage it is to know which kinds/types of races afford a profit and which ones create a loss. Ask the average intelligent fan which grades and courses he has made his last few wins on, and if he avoids betting on any particular grade or course, and he probably won't be able to give you an answer. What a disadvantage! You will have your answer, and have it recorded plainly. You will probably never get so good at handicapping that you can make *every* grade/course pay, so you had better study which ones do and which ones don't.

Here's how you keep track. Later, we will discuss methods of "scoring" your program, using the information on our FW-1 chart. For now, simply realize that the end result will be that, in each race, you will have placed the dogs, via your system, in a numerical order of selection. In other words, you will have awarded points, based on your studied criteria, to each dog. One dog will end up with the most points, and be your top selection; another will have the fewest points, or maybe even some minus points, and be your bottom dog, or your last (#8) selection. For each race, you will have your order of choices lined up from one through eight (less any scratches, of course). When the race is over, you simply record how your selections finished. If, for example, your third choice won, your first choice placed, and your sixth choice showed, you would record the results thusly, using zeros for your selections that weren't in the money: 2 0 1 0 0 3 0 0. If there had been one scratch, simply place a dash in the eighth slot. If your selections had come in 1, 2, 3, your results would be recorded as: 1 2 3 0 0 0 0 0. And so forth. You would then keep track of *all* your results on a master form, as illustrated in Figure 21.

We've called the chart in Figure 21 our RT-1 form—*Results Tabulation*. A blank form for your use is reproduced in the back of this book.

The sample entries made on the Figure 21 chart are actual, and recent. We will be returning to this chart several times as we later discuss wagering. At a glance, however, you can see how immensely important this chart is to our system. Not only does it show us how our system is performing, but it shows how we can profitably wager, (or profitably not wager, as the case may be).

The chart also lets us apply dry run betting systems, with instant test results. Will we make money betting our top choice to win, in class A races? Obviously not! Is there any grade on which our system works extremely well? Very poorly? Here is where you see it all come together. This is the second of the three major steps of profitable handicapping. First, you will have built a system of handicapping, and used this to score your program and make your selections. Second, you will have recorded the performance of your system on a reference record, like our RT-1. All of this can be in your hand and ready for your use, without your having risked any wagers, by using dry run tabulation. Then, with all this intelligence at hand, and a wagering method (money management system) worked out, you should be able to build a nice profit for yourself. You certainly will be a thousand times better prepared to do so than at least

Figure 21

Chart RT-1: *Results tabulation, by overall ranking sequence.*

TRACK __Doggy Downs__   COURSE __SPRINT__

GRADE	DATE	1	2	3	4	5	6	7	8	BOX TRI $	PER $	QUIN.$
A	11-23	0	0	2	1	0	3	0	0	4/2	1/2	41
	11-23	3	1	0	2	0	0	0	0	156	61	19
	11-29	0	2	1	0	3	0	0	0	210	54	16
	11-29	1	0	0	2	0	0	3	0	91	36	11
	12-7	0	3	2	0	1	0	0	0	418	170	62
	12-7	2	0	3	1	0	0	0	0	219	104	49
	12-9	2	1	0	3	0	0	0	-	86	34	9
B	11-23	0	1	2	0	0	0	0	3	194	41	18
	11-23	1	0	3	0	0	2	0	0	240	110	49
	11-27	2	3	0	0	1	0	0	0	509	210	90
	11-27	0	2	1	3	0	0	0	0	218	78	29
	12-6	0	0	0	1	0	0	3	2	1748	340	129
	12-6	1	3	0	2	0	0	0	-	107	69	21
	12-7	3	0	0	1	2	0	0	0	540	126	74
	12-14	0	2	0	1	0	3	0	-	604	181	44
	12-14	3	0	2	1	0	0	0	0	257	141	39
	12-17	0	0	0	1	2	3	0	0	490	102	57
C	11-23	0	1	0	0	3	2	0	-	394	210	64
	11-27	1	3	0	2	0	0	0	0	292	80	36
	12-6	1	3	0	0	0	0	2	0	63	42	10
	12-6	2	0	3	1	0	0	0	0	370	143	67
	12-7	3	1	2	0	0	0	-	-	69	28	16
	12-14	0	0	1	0	2	3	0	0	1110	224	100
	12-14	0	1	3	2	0	0	0	0	189	89	34
	12-17	2	0	3	0	1	0	0	0	372	194	86
D	11-23	0	0	1	0	0	3	0	2	1974	408	161
	11-25	0	2	0	1	0	3	0	0	209	104	30
	11-30	3	0	2	1	0	0	-	-	46	40	31
	12-6	0	1	0	3	0	0	2	0	319	106	109
	12-14	0	3	2	0	1	0	0	0	166	84	33

99% of the other people in attendance.

Naturally, we'd like to perfect our system well enough so that all our results columns have zeros in the last five slots. Sorry, but you'll never get that good—at least I never have—but that's what you keep working toward, just the same!

Notice that in the Figure 21 chart we have recorded the box trifecta payoff—usually one-half the straight ticket payoff, though at a few tracks it is one-third. Notice also that the payoffs are rounded to the nearest dollar.

The form used at this point, the one we're calling RT-1, is the bottom line. This is where it all comes together, and this is where we first see which grades, etc., we have a good handle on, and which ones we don't. This is also where you can see if your system needs work in any of the various grades or other factors.

Everybody at the races, of course, feels that they are using some kind of a system, even if it only involves betting on the daily lottery number, the day of the month, a combination of the #1 box with the mutuel favorite, the lightest weight dog, or whatever. Some people stick with such "systems" for long periods, and some even cash a ticket now and then. But whatever logic they use, they would be much better off if they simply kept track of which types of races their "system" works on, and which ones it doesn't. This they could do on a scratch pad, or even right on their programs, and then save and check the programs now and then. To the serious handicapper's advantage, however, is the fact that it seems to be human nature for most fans to avoid anything that might cause someone to think they are taking the races "seriously." Some seem embarrassed to even make notes in their program, let alone show up with a clipboard, forms, notes, or anything that somebody might think is a sign of a handicapper.

It may well be that you, too, would rather not draw attention to yourself at the track. It certainly is not necessary to haul a briefcase, a stack of old programs, or even a clipboard to the races. In fact, *at* the races is not the place to be working on your system; better that you have done this at home, in advance. The information you are going to be betting with can be easily condensed to a few pages, perhaps only one or two, or can even have been transcribed over to your program, if you obtained it in time to score it before going to the races.

All your efforts in developing your system are spent in trying to get more zeros in the right-hand columns of form RT-1 (or whatever form you devise to keep track of your success on). In other words, you want your selection process to be accurate enough to avoid having many of your #5, #6, #7 or #8 dogs come in the money. Of course, flukes occur, bad crashes happen, long shots get hot, etc., so it is impossible to devise a system that is perfect. But it is when you can look at this results form, and see how your system is doing, that you will be able to see what works, what doesn't work, what kinds of races to bet, which ones not to bet, and exactly how *your* system is faring in all respects. *The best of systems could not function well or produce a consistent profit without this particular step of recording its results.* Even if you develop your own system, entirely different from the one in this book, or if you adopt a system from another author/handicapper, don't fail to use at least this step. It is virtually your road map to success and/or your early warning signal for catastrophe.

Now we're getting down to some of the most basic steps of applying the system which you are developing. The next chapter will discuss the *scoring* of the program, with the use of the factor-weighting methods that you have determined.

Chapter 11

How to Score the Printed Program

Your system is together, you've done your research, and you're ready for a trial flight. The next step is applying all you have learned to the scoring of the race program, to develop your sequence of selection for each race.

It is important that you realize, right from the start, that applying this quantity of knowledge is going to take some time. It is highly unlikely that you will be able to refine your methods to the point where you can score races between races (in other words, figure one race at a time, bet it, and then figure the next); not impossible, perhaps, but pretty difficult, and hurrying can lead to expensive errors. One should plan for at least an hour, perhaps as much as two or two-and-a-half hours, to accurately score a program. It's best to obtain a program in advance and do your scoring away from the track. If you can't do this, plan to get to the track early enough to get at least a substantial head start on it. You definitely don't want to feel rushed, and you don't want to be interrupted, because doing it right does take a degree of concentration. If you can't get a program in advance, get to the races an hour or so early. If this isn't possible, simply ignore the first several races, and start scoring the last half of the evening's program, taking your time to do it correctly. (You should mark down the results of the early races, though, so that you can dry-run score them later, for information.)

In any case, you will want some undistracted time alone with the program. The information printed there, interpreted and digested by means of the intelligence you have gathered, is what will give you the handle on each race. What you are going to be working toward is lining up those eight dogs in the sequence which your system indicates is the order in which they are most likely to finish. Your sequence may or may not agree with the selection of the morning oddsmaker, the resident track handicapper, or the various tip sheets that are available. You are going to put those dogs into the order that *you* think is correct, and you are going to do it by using the "secret information" you have so carefully assembled.

Your author likes to mark right on the program pages, and usually with a red-ink ball-point pen so that the notes stand out well. It is also possible to devise forms on which to record all the pertinent information without writing on the program, if you prefer.

Your first move should be to go completely through the program and cross out, nearly clear across the page, all races in the past performance charts of those dogs *which were in schooling races, or in races where the dog experienced trouble of any kind, according to the chartmaker's comments.* Don't put off this step. Such races are not pertinent to the information you need. Schooling races, particularly, are races in which the dog has been entered for any one of a number of reasons, some of which are bad news. The dog listed in your program obviously was considered to have done well enough in the schooling race to be entered in a "real" race now. Some of the other dogs in that schooling race, however, may have been ill or injured, so the typical schooling race, some of which have only five or six entries, is no real measure of a dog's performance. Furthermore, this author is convinced that, at most tracks, the times recorded for the schooling races are often inaccurate and/or misleading. Ignore them!

You should also cross out any race that was not a normal race for that dog. There is no way for you to judge whose fault the collision was, or to estimate how much speed that bump should be figured to have cost. Ignore these races, as far as gleaning data from them concerning early speed, late speed, etc. Obviously, a dog moving down in class because he has been bumped in his last three races, in the former grade, needs to be noted. Your scratch-out marks will help call your attention to a situation like this. Do not cross out these races with a felt-tip pen so wide that it will completely obstruct the information. Though you must cross out these races, some bits of information contained there may be of some use, so let it remain visible through your line.

Next, you should note what *grade,* and on what *course,* the race is going to be. This is extremely important, and the fact that each type of race needs to be scored differently is the heart of the theory of this system. Don't make an error right here at the start!

Then, all that remains is to score each factor you will be considering for this race, such as average speed, late gain, post position, etc. You are doing this with a numerical system, so that you can see the advantages or disadvantages of each dog *in relationship to the other dogs in that par-*

ticular race.

How you mark the page or score the factors is up to you. Devise a method that enables you easily to keep the factors separate and scored. Again, this takes some concentration, so remove all possible distractions while you are doing this. A sample program page, scored and marked, is illustrated in Figure 22. You may or may not wish to use a method like this. (Do use colored ink, though, which cannot be shown in this illustration.)

To the uninitiated, the Figure 22 program page would appear to be a marked-up mess. To the author, though, each mark has a meaning. If you are with us so far, you could probably figure out what has been noted where. It is not important that you adopt this particular marking method. It is important, however, that you are *consistent* in whatever marking method you devise. Mark the same factors in the same places each time. You will see that in this example, the *rating* in each factor is circled. Also, the total number of points awarded to each entry is noted in large digits to the right, and circled, and then recorded in sequence in the right margin. This sequence, and the differences in the numbers of points for each dog, are the basis of all the betting and money control systems that we will be discussing in later chapters.

Some other comments on our example in Figure 22 follow:

Once we have crossed out all the schooling and troubled races, we are left with fewer than three lines on some of the dogs. In this case, when figuring a factor for which you have determined to average out *three* recent races, you have no choice but to look at the one or two that are available, and project this out to the three. In other words, if you wanted to average out the early speed of a dog in the last three races, but only had two good races to look at, and the dog had gained a total of four places in those two races, you would extend this to a supposed total of six places, (since you are looking at three races for most of the other dogs, and recording that total for them).

Occasionally, some dogs have *no* untroubled past races to judge by. This is nearly the case with dog #7 and dog #8 in our example. The only races you can look at that were not schooling races are from other tracks, and from more than a month ago. In this case, you can only do the best with what you have, and try to estimate from what you *can* see what you *think* the dog can do. Better yet, when you have entries like this in a race, you can simply skip the race. Too often, those dogs on which you can't dig out enough meaningful data are the ones that make a surprise finish,

Figure 22

SECOND RACE(2)

TRACK RECORD—30.14
Jamie's Lane—10-24-81

1/16 MILE

1650 Feet

QUINIELA AND TRIFECTA WAGERING
SECOND HALF DAILY DOUBLE

GRADE **D**

Post Pos.	Date	Dis.	Time	Wt.	RP	Off 1-8	Str.	F.	FW	ART	Odds	Gr.	Comment	Sts.	1st	2d	3d	4th	Order of Finish

1 RED — **SALLISAW JOE** (67)
Black D., September 19, 1980. Sand Cut—Misty Glow

PLN 4 0 0 0 0%
PEN 21 4 5 1

Owner—Carol J. Parris
Kennel—River Bend Farm
Trainer—Lawrence Henry

11- 6²	5-16	F	31.36	67	1	5	4	4	6⁶		31.75	5.20	D	Followed pace	TimePatch,JetPower,RaiderBruiser
10-31¹³x	5-16	F	31.24	67	4⁷	5		8¹⁹		31.96	4.80	C	Shuffled far tn	MissSabyn,MasterKely,DKsFormul
10-26⁷	5-16	F	30.92	67	6	8	8	8¹⁹		32.20	15.20	C	Forced wide 1st	SweetConni,GennysHowi,HomeGrond
10-21⁴	5-16	F	31.43	67	4	5¹⁰		32.09		8.40	C	Early factor	DFWhiteFeathr,HomeGrond,FirstMil
10-16³⁵	5-16	F	31.17	66½		6¹⁴		32.26			No factor	DKsFormula,DFWhiteFeather,HiBlue⁶

2 BLUE — **LIBERTY MS** (56)
Dark Brindle B., January 11, 1980. K's Magellan—Emily's Pick

PLN 44 7 6 4 0%
SO 3 0 1 0 0

Owner—Richard Carlson
Kennel—John E. Currid, Jr.
Trainer—Cindy Currid

10-30¹²	5-16	F	31.36	55½	7	3	11	2	4⁴	31.65	2.50	D	Wide costly	TimePatch,JetPower,RaiderBruiser
10-23¹⁰	5-16	F	31.75	56½	4	2	12	18	19	31.75			All alone	ChicBasbar,DoughTuftn,DownSwng⁶
10-19¹ⁿ	5-16	F	31.91	57			2	2	22½	32.06			Good effort	Wishy Jack,CheckPlease,IfAtFirst⁶
10-14¹²	5-16	F	31.57	57	1	1¹	2	4²	31.70	4.50	C	Early leader	DrBox,GoldTrinie,AskSue⁷
10- 7⁵	5-16	F	31.56	56		4	4	2⁷	32.01	4.40	C	Slight fade	VadeyChf,BenellFlk,ClipperPit
10- 7⁵	5-16	F	31.63	56		2	3	6¹³	32.15	3.20	C	Slight fade	MyPalWilly,PeppersDan,Leiria⁷

3 WHITE — **LORD FANTASTIC** (67)
White and Blue Brindle D., July 31, 1979. Big Boy Billy—Nipa Fan*

PLN 37 3 4 10 0
PLN 17 1 4 2 7

50% (2)

Owner—Mark Haber
Kennel—Whirlwind
Trainer—Sy Heller

11- 6³	5-16	F	31.42	67	2	12	13	2¹	31.49	6.20	D	Nearly lasted	MeadowsMomnt,JodenPatt,PeskyBrod
11- 2⁴	5-16	F	31.52	67	4	7	2¹¹	2⁵	31.62	15.20	D	Brief leader	WishyJack,FastBlend,RockRainey
10-28⁴	5-16	F	31.40	67	4	7	11	2	5⁷	32.01	15.20	C	Gaveway stretch	RoyalBanuret,FastBlind,DutchDinh
10-21⁵x	5-16	F	31.60	67	4	2	2	32.15	15.20	C	Tired stretch	ZanyMomnt,GennysHowie,Lorita
10-16²⁵	5-16	F	31.60	66	5	2	3⁸	31.78			Led to stretch	MilfodBatr,CopaCabnn,ZanyMmnt⁵
10-10³⁵	5-16	F	31.38	66	5	2	2	5⁷	31.86			Steady fade	DebsDimndstd,DFWhiteFthr,LovFlk

4 GREEN — **LITTLE MAUDE** (56)
Dark Brindle B., July 18, 1980. Merrin—Beach Bunny

PLN 6 0 1 2 1 100% (1)
DB 1 0 1 0

Owner—J.N. Clack
Kennel—W.J. Wegzryn
Trainer—Phil Maider

11- 6²	5-16	F	31.36	55	7	8	6	6⁶	31.73	4.50	D	Forced wd 1st	TimePatch,JetPower,RaiderBruiser
10-31²	5-16	F	31.47	56	1	2	3	3	2¹	31.61	6.20	D	Hard try	MasterKly,RegalLine,TriMeBruce
10-27²	5-16	F	31.43	56	5	3	3²	31.65	6.20	D	Shutoff break	GHsLynd,TriMeBruce,JBsSnowman⁷
10-21⁴	5-16	F	31.50	56½	1	2	3²⁰	32.08	4.20	D	Stretch gain	DKsFormula,JBsSnowman,JetPower
10-16⁸	5-16	F	31.54	54½	4	1	2	31.54			Det. winner	Cushidown,TriMeHattie,FurFiber⁷
10-10⁶⁵	5-16	F	31.74	55		2	3	1ⁿᵈ	31.74			Drew clear str	SoloMo,RodeoDream,BillyDay⁷

5 BLACK — **JET POWER** (72)
Black D., July 10, 1979. Shaggy Can I—No More Tears*

PLN 47 1 6 10 8 50% (2)
NFM 4 0 0 0

Owner—Dominck Di Miscio
Kennel—Tim-Tom Kennel, Inc.
Trainer—Todd Hopwood

11- 6²	5-16	F	31.36	72	6	3	3⁴	2³⁴	31.58	35.20	D	Stretch gain	TimePtch,RaiderBruisr,LibrtyMs
10-31¹x	5-16	F	31.47	72½	5	6	8	2⁶	31.83	8.20	D	Offstr 1st tn	RiverDark,TipperTary,DutchDisco
10-27²x	5-16	F	31.43	72	4	7	12	11	5³	31.67	10.40	D	Tired stretch	GHsLynd,TriMeBruce,JBsSnowman⁷
10-21⁴	5-16	F	31.50	72½	6	3	4	4¹²	32.32	8.40	D	Slight fade	DKsFormul,JBsSnowman,LittleMaud
10-16³	5-16	F	31.58	71½	7		7¹¹	32.29	2.50	D	Offstr 1st tn	RunningRoom,CVilleLisa,EddiesBug
10- 9²	5-16	F	31.74	72		4	3⁵	31.52	2.40	D	Led to stretch	MDsAppleAnnie,SillySue,EddiesBu⁴

6 YELLOW — **BANJO BOOGIE** (64)
Red Brindle D., March 27, 1980. Pecos Pepper—Lean On Me

PLN 47 3 9 7 5 25% (4)
LV 4 0 2 1

Owner—Albert B. Raver
Kennel—Raver
Trainer—Henry Guzman

11- 6²	5-16	F	31.36	64½	2	8	7	7⁸	31.82	8.40	D	Shutoff break	TimePatch,JetPower,RaiderBruiser
10-28³	5-16	F	31.29	64½	3	5	3	8⁷	31.87	5.20	D	Hard try wd	BYFBiz,NowFreddie,YouNiteBabe
10-24⁵x	5-16	F	31.74	65	4	11	2	2½	32.02	4.50	D	Main threat	DiamondDog,NowFreddie,StickAndy
10-19²x	5-16	F	31.39	65	6	7	6¹⁴	32.19	4.50	D	Some gain	BobbyJ,DutchMarilynE,StickAndy
10-11³x	5-16	F	31.39	64½	3		8¹	32.29	5.40	D	Slow break	WahooSTip,StickAndy,CutyyWagsy
10- 6⁸⁵	5-16	F	31.89	64	2	4	3⁵	32.25			Late gain	IANewsboy,StrikingBlue,Puddietum⁵

7 GREEN & WHITE — **FREEDOM WAY** (71)
Red Fawn D., January 10, 1981. Oshkosh Larry—Center Of Action

PLN 10 0 0 0 0%
PLN 13 1 0 3

Owner—John W. Thomas
Kennel—Ko Kennel, Inc.
Trainer—Tina Mayo

11- 6⁵	5-16	F	31.33	70	3	1	4	7¹⁴	32.58			Bumped 1st trn	GingersGone,BMNeighbor,KsPare
10-30⁵	5-16	F	31.09	70	5	4	5²⁶	32.88			Early speed	RebelsRebl,PecosHead,GiantHrnuse
10-27⁵	5-16	F	30.92	70	4	2	4⁵	32.18			Crowded	JackieSmarty,WishyJack,KsPare
10-23⁸⁵	5-16	F	32.39	70½	2	4¹⁵	32.43			Early leader	JoMarKan,KsPare,PalominoHope⁷

(BELOW AT WHEELING DOWNS, 1982)

9-13³	D11-01	73	7	4	3⁵	31.30	D	Stretch fade	Witchlike,ItsMyTime,VividColrr

8 BLACK & YELLOW — **SOUL ANGEL** (56)
White Brindle B., August 13, 1980. SL's Dumb—Ectoplasm

PLN 8 0 0 0 0%
SGP 9 0 1 2

Owner—S.C. or S.L. Williams
Kennel—Track Road
Trainer—Herman Creagar

11- 3⁵	5-16	F	31.41	57	7	5	3	4⁴	32.02			Outfinished	JSRcyLcy,Gin,JxGn,TatteredMiny
10-30¹¹	5-16	F	31.00	56	2	1	4³⁸	32.92			Shutoff 1st trn	HandPainter,TimPatch,DutchSlike⁷

(BELOW AT SEMINOLE PARK, 1982)

8-31³	318	F	39.92	56½	2	2	11	2	4²½	40.12	5.00	D	Tired str., ins.	ChbasBody,FnsFaithl,ShasyUin
8-26²	318	F	39.97	56	4	3½	31	3½	39.95	17.90	D	Caught str ins.	CHsTim,Flirt,BlueGil
8-23¹³x	318	F	40.79	56	4	2	7	6⁴	41.08	*2.40	D	Early speed	SuddnStru.Br'sExprrs,GrwnDoor

PROGRAM: 3—5—2

costing you money. If you can't see any good data to make decisions with, that doesn't mean you can consider a dog not to be a contender, and hence ignore him. In fact, this entire concept is exactly why *you cannot figure a maiden race,* and shouldn't try, and shouldn't bet!

Speaking of dog #7 and dog #8, the fact that they have arrived at this track (Plainfield, Conn.) from other (or "foreign") tracks, makes them difficult to figure, even without the layoffs and the schooling races. In a case like this, your best move is to pass on the race. Nothing says that you must bet on a certain number of races every night, and in some cases the answer is not to bet. If you feel that you must figure the foreign-track dogs, you can get a notion of how fast they have been running at their home track by consulting the reference table in the back of this book. This table gives you the average running time for each course at most tracks in the country (per the author's computation). About all that you can tell from this, however, is whether the dog has been running slower or faster than the average time back at his home track, compared to how the other entries have been doing at the track that you're at. The catch is, dogs often seem to like one track better than another, and often do far better, or worse, at their favorite track. This can certainly fog up your handicapping, and while it may provide good races for those folks who like to bet on lucky numbers, you'll be moving on to the next race.

Notice that on dog #4, *Little Maude,* we did a little interpretation of her recent times. In the past performance lines, two of her last six races were schooling races. These we ignore. (Almost.) Two of her four non-schooling races were troubled, with a "forced wide" and a "shutoff break." This leaves us with only two times to look at. One is 31.61, and the other is 32.08. Usually, we would average these out to about 31.84, but we note on her troubled races that she got 31.73 and 31.63. This has got to mean that her average is going to be better than 31.84. Let's consider that the race in which she was given 32.08 was a troubled race which the chartwriter failed to note. Or that the track condition, though marked "F" (fast), may have been off to some degree that afternoon. ("X" signifies a matinee race, at most tracks.) So, if one is determined to handicap this race, we are left with assigning her only an arbitrary average time, based on our notion of how fast she really is. In this case, I estimated that she was about a 31.60 speed.

Note that my numerical system gave two dogs the same number of points in this example. That happens occasionally, but not often. It won't make a great deal of difference if we are betting trifectas, boxed perfectas, or quinielas. If, however, we had reason to want to know whether #5 or #3 was the better dog, we would have to devise a tie-breaker. Frankly, I cannot recommend one. Everything that you have researched and applied is telling you here that you have two dogs with equal chances of winning. Accept that, and bet—or don't bet—accordingly. If something in their history gave one dog an edge over the other one, then you should have applied that factor or weighting in the initial scoring! If, for instance, you feel that the dog which seems to be slightly faster (#3) has a little real edge, then you had better give *speed* a little more weight in your system. Probably the best thing you can do, in this case, is to hope that #3 or #5 *scratches,* to resolve your tie!

Would you like to know how that race came out, and how *Little Maude* did? Figure 23 shows the chart for that race.

Little Maude didn't do so good. According to the chartwriter, she got "Bumped in the first turn." (Three other dogs had trouble in this race too, and that is quite normal at the dog races.)

The author's *first, fourth,* and *fifth* selections finished in the money/ trifecta. Had we boxed our five top choices, which would have cost $60, we would have won $146.80. Had we boxed our first *four* choices in a quiniela (costing $12), we would have won $37.60. Had we bet our top two tied dogs each to win, we would have cashed one ticket but lost 25% of our money. The crowd made #2 their favorite, so we were at least more right than they were—and that's what this system is all about!

Figure 23

—	11- 7·x	Royal Patch⁰	52	1	2	3	4	5²³	32.80	10.20	M	Bumped 1st tn
.....	11- 7²x	Dutch Krisp³	58	5	4	8	8	6²⁴	32.90	14.40	M	Offstr 1st tn
.....	11- 7x	KB's Kicker¹⁰	68	8	6	7	7	7²⁴	32.91	13.20	M	Forced wd 1st
.....	11- 6⁸s	Much Danger³	54	7	7	6	6	8²⁷	33.08	22.40	M	Blkd 1st tn

R.J. Barber's Brindle B., March 21, 1981. Eastern Leader—Dusky

ADE D	BEST BLEND	9.80	5.00	6.40	Quiniela 3-6—73.20
.....	SHEER ELEGANCE		11.60	6.40	Trifecta Box—335.40
.....	FANCY MAY			7.60	Trifecta 6-3-4—1006.20

11—11—2   5-16 MILE COURSE—GRADE D   TIME—31.54—FAST

.....	11- 6³	Lord Fantastic¹⁰	68	3	1	1³	1⁴	1⁹	31.54	3.00	D	Never headed
.....	11- 6²	Sallisaw Joe¹⁷	67½	1	3	3	3	2⁹	32.14	6.20	D	Stretch gain
ADE C	11- 6²	Liberty Ms.¹²	56	2	2	2	2	3⁹½	32.18	*2.40	D	Forced erly pace
...·	11- 6²	Banjo Boogie¹	65	6	6	6	6	4¹¹	32.26	13.20	D	Wide closing
.....	11- 3⁵s	Soul Angel¹¹	56½	8	7	4	4	5¹¹	32.28	5.40	D	Slight fade
·..··	11- 6²	Little Maude⁹	56	4	5	8	8	6¹²	32.34	5.20	D	Bumped 1st tn
·.··	11- 6	Jet Power¹³	72	5	8	5	5	7¹³	32.40	7.40	D	Crowded early
ADE C	11- 6⁷s	Freedom Way¹⁵	71	7	4	7	7	8¹⁸	32.78	25.20	D	Blocked 1st tn

Whirlwind's White and Blue Brindle D., July 31, 1979. Big Boy Billy—Nipa Fan*

·.··	LORD FANTASTIC	8.00	3.80	3.00	Quiniela 1-3—37.60
·.··	SALLISAW JOE		4.80	4.00	Trifecta Box—146.80
·.·	LIBERTY MS.			4.80	Trifecta 3-1-2—440.40

Daily Double 6-3—45.80

11—11—3   5-16 MILE COURSE—GRADE D   TIME—31.73—FAST

ADE A	11- 6⁴	Rock Rainey⁴	69	3	2	2	2	1¹½	31.73	5.30	D	Closing outside
.....	11- 6³	Regal Line¹²	53	6	6	4	3	2¹½	31.81	5.40	D	Steady effort
.....	11- 6²x	Tipperary¹⁸	66	5	1	1²	1¹	3¹½	31.82	*1.20	D	Early speed
.....	11- 6²x	Paso Peyton¹	70	2	4	6	5	4²	31.86	7.20	D	Offstr 1st tn
.....	11- 6⁶s	Jimmy's Kojack¹⁴	69	7	8	7	7	5⁶	32.13	8.40	D	Crowded early
DE B	11- 6³	C How UR⁵	62½	8	7	3	4	6⁷	32.21	13.20	D	Early factor
....	11- 6x	No Flirt¹⁷	58	4	5	8	8	7¹⁰	32.37	9.40	D	Wide 1st tn
..·.	11- 6⁷	Prime Contender¹⁰	78	1	3	5	6	8¹⁰	32.40	12.20	D	Shuffled far tn

British Connecticut's Black Brindle D., December 3, 1978. Tell Jimmy—Little My Rose*

..·.	ROCK RAINEY	12.60	4.60	2.60	Quiniela 3-6—37.80

Chapter 12

Factors Seldom
Worth Handicapping

Many other race factors will occur to the thinking handicapper, or be brought to his attention by various books or articles. The author of *this* book feels that most of the considerations not already discussed here are too minor to incorporate into your regular system. In fact, I sincerely feel that one can *over*-handicap a race, and find too many conflicting factors. However, if you should find other considerations which seem to have some merit at *your* track, incorporate them in your system after testing them out by the dry run methods described. There is no way a person can test out everything at every track. Discussions of the more or less "secondary" factors follow.

Frequency of Trouble

How often does a dog collide? Bump? Get bumped? Get caught in traffic? Let's say that, for a certain dog, the last six performance lines listed in the program show this kind of trouble in three or four of these races, while another dog in the same race had zero trouble in his last six races. Doesn't this indicate that one dog is a better bet? Shouldn't one downgrade the dog who had so much trouble, or maybe even eliminate him from consideration? If he's had that much trouble, don't the odds indicate that he is more likely to have trouble in this race? No—not necessarily! There are far too many extenuating circumstances to allow this to be a meaningful criterion. In some cases, the "trouble dog" does indeed have a problem with traffic; just not enough smarts to stay out of trouble. In this case, this dog will most likely never work up through the grades, and may not even be around the track much longer. If you see this factor in a dog that won a maiden race, but then never got beyond Grade D, it may be that simple.

On the other hand, the dog that gets into some tangles now and then may do so because he doesn't *fear* the risk of a collision, for the sake of catching that darn rabbit. He will go hell bent for leather, *regardless.*

Sometimes it works, sometimes it doesn't, but he'll *try!* This is the kind of courage that you might want some of your money on. If he wrecks *all* of the time, he won't be around too long. If he tends to be in the money when he *doesn't* wreck, then he most definitely is a contender. Maybe that dog with no trouble in his history stays out of trouble by giving ground, or being too polite. He may get in the money sometimes, but if push comes to shove, he'd as soon not put it all on the line to win.

All in all, it's best to simply cross out the troubled races from a dog's past performance, right along with the schooling races, and *ignore* those races. Run your own samples, but you are quite likely to find that points shouldn't be added or deducted for the number of clean races a dog runs, or doesn't run.

Weight

Will the dog run slower if he is a pound heavier than his normal weight? Will he speed up if he has shed a pound or two? Will a smaller dog tend to get a faster start than a heavier one? Or do better in the turns? How can a 53-pound dog compete with one that weighs 83 pounds? Shouldn't they handicap dogs with added weight, as they do for thoroughbreds? What do weight changes really mean? Why do they show weights in the program, and announce them at the parade call-out? Will it matter if a dog has a bowel movement just before the race?

There are no clear-cut or meaningful answers to any of these questions. You will hear a lot of theories about weight, but I have found none that hold up to analysis at any of the tracks I have tested. I recommend that you simply ignore weight considerations.

Parade Behavior

Can one spot any worthwhile clues by observing the dog's parade? When dogs seem eager or reluctant when being handled by the lead-outs, does it foretell the dog's race performance? What does it mean if the dog's tail is between its legs, or wagging happily? The answer is: *nothing!* About 1200 races ago, the author noticed a dog who seemed to be favoring one foot while standing with the lead-out. The dog was one of my selections otherwise, but I dropped him from my bet on the grounds of that tender foot. He fizzled. I was right. I won. It was a good payoff. I watched for limps for the next 1000 parades, but haven't seen one since. I've stopped watching. I suggest that you not waste your time watching, unless you want to enjoy the comments of some of the folks around you:

"Harry, get me a ticket on the #3 dog! He looks *fast!*" or "Geez, look at the long legs on that #7 dog! I'm going to put *him* in my trifecta box!" or "Look at that #1 dog straining at her leash—let's use her instead of #4— he's holding back!" And so forth. Just smile, and think to yourself that the odds are good you'll end up with some of the money from these "eyeball handicappers."

Age

Are older dogs slower? More experienced? Inconsistent? More likely to fade in the stretch? In general, age is of little concern. The dogs must be retired at a given age, so you have no real old-timers running, as you do at some harness horse racing tracks. Far more important than age alone is how well the dog has been doing *lately,* as per his performance charts in the program. Age is bound to take its toll eventually, though, and with the average aging greyhound, the typical outcome is the onset of an erratic performance record, i.e., perhaps three to five sharp races followed by two to four lousy ones. This, of course, makes it far more difficult to handicap an older dog, since it isn't likely you can accurately predict his cycles of hot and cold. But a decent dog deserves no point deductions for age alone. If his performance is down, it will show up in your other categories. If it is up, then he or she is a contender, regardless of age.

Lineage (Ancestors)

This could be a factor only in a maiden race, where you have absolutely nothing else to go on (and which you therefore shouldn't be wagering on).

Forget who the doggy's mommy and daddy were. Whatever good or bad traits were inherited, the dog is operating on his own by now, and daddy ain't gonna help now if the dog doesn't know how to win! This philosophy will draw some flack, since it seems quite knowledgeable and elitist to be able to track a dog's family back to a great champion. Much is made of this in horse racing, for sure, and the higher priced the seats, the more of this talk there is. But you could leave it off the program, as far as this handicapper is concerned. The dog's record will speak for itself.

Trainer

Sure, it matters how well the dog has been trained, conditioned, nurtured, and entered, but you will pick up all such results in the performance charts. If you try betting on kennels or trainers, you will lose. Top kennels are tops because they handle dogs of better (more expensive) bloodlines, and have more dogs to enter. Even so, many of their puppies and entries don't turn out at all well. Don't add kennel or trainer points to a dog who isn't performing on his own. If the trainer's training "took," you will be looking at a decent past performance record for the dog. If it didn't take, the trainer's name ain't gonna help that dog a bit!

Matinees

If you have a choice of going to either the afternoon or the evening race, do something else in the afternoon. More lower-grade races tend to be run in the afternoon, times tend to be somewhat inaccurate (in my judgment), and several other factors are different, to at least some degree, from the evening programs. For these same reasons, when weighting an evening race, less credibility should be given to those past performance lines that were matinee races.

This is more than just a personal opinion. There are a number of tracks at which the afternoon races and the evening races are so different it is almost like two different tracks! Even the type of fans, and how they bet, is different. If one is determined to attend the matinees, a separate system should probably be developed.

On the other hand, some folks find it convenient and/or enjoyable to attend the afternoon races. Just keep in mind that because things may well not be the same, in several categories, you should act and bet accordingly. (And do your best to ignore the maiden races, which many tracks run in the afternoons.)

Course Change

Is it an advantage or disadvantage for a dog to change from a longer course to a sprint course, or vice versa? In many cases, it isn't that much of a factor, though one has the difficulty of translating the probable time factor.

In some cases, at some tracks, it can be a factor, and it can be different from one grade to another, and from one track to the other. It is worth checking at *your* track, and this is just as easy to research as are grade change values. Simply look through a number of recent programs and, from the past performance lines, note and record those instances in which a dog switched from one course to the other, and of this number of instances and how many ended up in the money—or not. Break this down grade by grade, for you will almost certainly find a difference. If you do discover a recognizable trend, make note of this on the bottom of your scoring system form.

In general, you will see that a course change is most often (but not always) a disadvantage to some degree. Owners and trainers enter a different course with a dog for a number of reasons, but the most common is that the dog wasn't doing as well on the one course as they thought it should, and they felt that it might do better on the other course. Often, you will see that a dog which has been gaining ground in the stretch on a short course, but not quite getting into the money, will be entered on a longer course, in hopes that this "indication of late speed" will be more advantageous on the longer track. (A logical theory, but it often doesn't work out that neat.) A dog which has been running the longer course, and doing well until the stretch, may be switched to a short course for the same kind of reasoning. Sometimes this works, sometimes it doesn't. For some reason, though, the switch from one direction to the other does seem to work better or worse in some grades than others. If, for example, your research reveals that dogs being switched from short to long courses in the D grade have not been in the money one time out of 20, you've got a real advantage going for you when you spot this situation.

In the instances where you determine that this can be a factor, it will very likely hold true only for the *very first* course change that a dog makes, after at least six races on the other course. For those dogs whose past performance indicates a repeated shifting back and forth from course to course, this logic will not apply.

Most often, when you spot an *advantage* in course change, it will show up in a change from long course to short course. (But not always . . .) At many tracks, this has been found to be a consistent and profitable factor. However, some trainers obviously miss noting this advantage, and seem to waste the opportunity by first entering their dog in a schooling race, on the shorter course, to see how he performs. At least partially because of the advantage, the dog walks away with the schooling race. The trainer feels that his judgment is vindicated, and he enters the dog in a sprint race. This time out, the advantage has already been used up, and the dog gets no benefit from it and places out of the money. (Will any trainers read this?)

One last note on this matter. When you are scoring a race in which one or more of the dogs are changing courses, the computing of those dogs' times is complicated. In fact, it is more than complicated—it is nearly impossible to do with any reliability at all. Unless the dog involved is obviously going to be in or out of your selection based on other factors, you would do well to skip the race, rather than let your determination of the dog's "probable" time be your deciding factor. The best handle you can get on this is to have your own figures worked out on how to translate times at your track. Some handicappers use the track *record* on the various courses as their guideline here. If, for example, at a given track the speed record for the sprint course was :30.44, and the record for the 3/8 course was :39.50, one could use the nine-second difference as the "translation factor." Another way to obtain this is from the various tracks' average speed for each course, found on the table in Appendix B of this book. Or you can work it out yourself, for your own track. The catch is that there is no guarantee a dog is going to run equally fast on one course or the other—and you must be aware that you are not measuring fixed factors here. That is why you should not let this factor be your deciding reasoning in a race of this type.

Dogs From Another Track

I hear many "instant handicappers" throw out "any dog from an outside track." Their theory, I guess, is that no "stranger" is likely to do as well as the dogs who are running on their own "home track." One certainly can't afford to do this, because outside, or "foreign," dogs very often do win! However, because it is so difficult to tell if a stranger is likely to do well or not, races with "strangers" in them should usually be passed. Recognizing, however, that this "passing a race" is one of the most difficult things to do, a table of comparative speeds at all U.S. tracks is included in the back of this book. With this, you can at least "translate" a dog's likely time from one track to another. (No, one track's 3/8-mile course is not rated at the same speed as the 3/8-mile course at another track.)

Another consideration when sizing up these strangers is that the Racing Secretary at most tracks requires a dog moving in from another track to start in at a grade one notch higher than that in which the dog had been running at its home track. When that is the case, it would seem to *definitely* create a disadvantage for the dog. There is a catch, however. Though the grading system was developed to regulate greyhound racing and give it a large measure of continuity, the fact remains that different tracks operate it differently—or at least use different terminology. One track, for example, may have grades M, D, C, B, A and AA, with a few special stakes and sweepstakes races thrown in from time to time. Another track, however, may have no maiden races, but instead move a dog up from a schooling race win to an E grade, which then becomes almost exactly like an M race at another track. Furthermore, though AA is the top bracket at some tracks, A is the top grade at others. And on top of this, many tracks have a BB grade in-between the B and the A, and so on.

So, if that stranger you're trying to figure out ran an A race at his last home-track race, but tonight is entered in an AA race at *your* track, has he really been moved up a grade? The chart in the appendix of this book will let you at least see what the top grade at each U.S. track is. However, a further difficulty in sizing up these strangers is the unknown factor of how they will take to this new track. Many times, a dog which has done miserably at one track will catch fire at another, or vice versa. You can get a *little* insight into this if you can see the results of a number of schooling races which the stranger has run at the new track before he is entered in a race. But for the same reasons that schooling races are unreliable in general, this isn't a very firm handle. You can't afford to throw the stranger out, just because he's a stranger. If he looks like a contender otherwise, include him in your bet if you can afford to. If you can't, pass the race.

This, of course, makes it quite difficult to handicap at the start of a meet, when *all* the dogs are strangers (except for those few tracks which run year round, and break their year up into three or four meets, but still use mostly the same dogs). The answer here is obvious: simply stay away from the track for the first few weeks of the season! Let the dogs establish their pattern at *this* track, before you attempt to *guess*(!) their chances. During this period, you'll notice that the average payoffs are higher, exactly because everyone else is having a fit trying to weight these foreign dogs. You will almost certainly have a bigger bankroll at the end of the meet if you will let these first three or four weeks go by. There—I told you so. But if you see me there the first night of the meet, just assume that I'm doing research . . .

Rested Dogs

What should you figure if you notice that it has been an unusually long time since a dog's last race? (The majority of dogs are raced about every four to five days.) The answer is to search for a reason. Trainers do not usually "rest" healthy dogs, as is done for thoroughbred horses. More often than not, a dog is rested only for a negative reason, such as illness, injury, or a slump attributed to "old age." Sometimes, after a rest, a dog is placed in one or more schooling races before getting back into real races. The question then becomes, for both you the bettor, and the dog's owner and trainer, "Is the dog now healthy/ready or not?"

In reality, this same question could be asked about any other dog in the race, even if they haven't had a lay-off. So, you are left with considering that this dog quite likely *is* as ready as any other dog in the race, and trying to glean whatever useful information you can from his history shown in the past performance lines available to you. In other words, you cannot automatically throw him out of your bet just because he's had a lay-off for a while, unless you can read something more meaningful into his particular set of circumstances.

Track Condition

Rain, mud, sleet, snow or fog... None of this makes much difference in the outcome of a race, at least in my experience. Your tailor-made system should work as well wet or dry, and there is no need to stay away from the track on rainy days. You will at least be far better off at the dog track than the horse track on such days!

Strangely enough, on many tracks the dogs' speed seems to not be affected much by the condition of the track. (There are some exceptions to this, due to the actual composition of certain tracks, so be sure to know the circumstances for *your* track.) In fact, at many tracks, even faster times are often recorded on wet tracks. Likewise, one would think that more collisions, falls, skids, etc., would occur on the "slow," "sloppy" or "muddy" tracks, but this is seldom the case.

An "Inside Dog" Starting
From an Outside Box, and so on...

You find that a dog starting from the #1 or #2 box has a record which indicates a habit of running wide or midtrack. Or, you find an "inside running" dog starting from the #7 or #8 box. Or, you find a dog starting from the #4 box, and his record indicates that the last two times he started from the #4 box he did terribly. Have you got some valuable information there? Should points be subtracted, or added?

Probably not, in this author's opinion; or at least not automatically, without some further considerations. There often are dogs, though, that do historically perform poorly from outside or middle boxes, and when they are forced by the luck of the draw to start from their "bad boxes," they should be down-rated, to a degree. The catch is that the six races of past performance listed in most programs is simply not enough information to positively identify this factor in a dog. The only way to reliably check out this factor in a suspect dog is to look at more performance lines in other recent race programs, or to buy a *past performance chart* at your track. These charts list many more races for each dog, and can be somewhat valuable for your purposes, if the information isn't too stale. (Don't bother buying them when they are so old that they are marked down.) A subscription to the *Greyhound Racing Record* can provide you with this type of information, too, on a very current basis, as will all of the programs which you have saved for your records. (You *will* save them, right?)

At every track that I'm familiar with, the dog's starting box position is drawn by chance. The trainer has no opportunity to select the starting box which he feels his dog will do the best from. If his dog comes out backward from the #8 box every time he is started there, and the draw gives his dog the #8 box, the trainer either scratches the dog (not likely) or hopes that for once he will come out right end first. If your research uncovered this nifty little fact about this dog, you can arrange your bet based on *your* notion of which end of the dog will come out first this time!

In any case, do not drop a dog from contention simply on the basis of seeing one or two instances in his past performance in which he performed good or bad from a certain box. Likewise, a few words from the chartwriter are not descriptive enough for you to form much judgment. A dog whose past performance lines include several remarks indicating a midtrack race by that dog does not necessarily mean he'll break for the outside right away and therefore suffer a disadvantage from an inside box. He may well not seek his "midtrack" route until coming out of the first turn (or whatever).

On the other hand, a dog which regularly is reported to seek an early rail may well suffer from an outside box start, unless he happens to be the fastest-breaking dog in *that* particular race, in which case in *this* race he can write his own ticket. Much has been written on handicapping methods which are designed to predict whether a certain dog in a certain race has more or less chance of getting crowded, bumped, or involved in some other kind of trouble. If, for example, the three dogs inside of the #4 dog, in a certain race, are inside or rail runners, and the two dogs immediately to the #4 dog's right are outside runners, the #4 dog is likely to have a clear, unhampered start down the middle of the track, right? Not if he's so slow getting out of the box that the other seven dogs are jammed into the first curve before he even catches up with them, in which case he'll probably trip over some dogs' tails, or get 'em in his eyes!

The starting and running characteristics of a dog can absolutely be a factor in a race. Under a certain set of circumstances, his odds of either a wreck or a good race can well be a factor of his good or bad starting boxes. There are two major catches in using this factor as a foundation in a handicapping system, however. First is the difficulty in getting an accurate description of exactly how a given dog's style or personality suits each box. You would have to watch hundreds of slow-motion race replays, and make thousands of notes, to get anything at all meaningful or consistent on every dog. You can, especially by researching 20 to 30 races on each dog from programs or past performance books, spot some of the contenders who have glaring likes or dislikes for certain boxes; the chartwriter's remarks are simply not adequate enough to give you a real feel for how every dog will behave.

Secondly, even if you have a pretty good feel for how a dog will perform from an inside, middle, or outside box, that type of performance may serve him well with a certain group of other dogs, and may be a disadvantage when he is racing another group of dogs, each with its own pattern. And, of course, on top of this determination, which is extremely difficult to make, you still have to determine the weight of all the other factors we have already discussed.

This handicapper feels that in order to build a system around this "trouble prediction" method, one would have to do an exhaustive study on each and every dog's racing patterns, and then devise a method of fitting each pattern in with the patterns of the other seven dogs in each race. Since one cannot do this or identify this with any style of numerical designation, it would require an enormous amount of concentration and memory, and therefore leave too much room for error.

Watch for and identify any glaring examples of box preference, and modify your numerical system when it is thereby indicated. Otherwise, an attempt to identify the probability of a dog getting into trouble—or staying out of trouble—is probably a matter of over-handicapping. After all, at the average track, on the average program, some 25% to 38% of the dogs which come out of the box are going to get into some kind of trouble. (Imagine how a percentage like that would blow the mind of a horse handicapper!) Some of these dogs are going to *cause* trouble, others are going to be the *victims* of it. I firmly believe that it can be predicted, to a degree. I also firmly believe that if you were following the career of one certain dog, you could eventually be able to achieve a degree of accuracy in determining his chances of getting into or staying out of trouble under a specific set of circumstances. However, I also firmly believe that the concept is of little use to the handicapper unless he knows *every* dog that well, and few people have the time or inclination to master that.

Maiden Races

By now, you probably anticipate what I am going to say again about maiden races: *forget 'em!* Don't waste your time and/or money in trying to handicap them. No logic applies to the dog maiden race. In a few cases, there will be such a wide difference in the quality and apparent readiness of the contestants that one dog will appear to be a "walk-away." He will likely go off as an odds-on favorite. More often than in most other grades (at most tracks), he will win, but *pay too little to profit from.* Lots of other fans will wheel him in quinielas, perfectas, trifectas, etc., so those payoffs will be tiny, too. When there is *not* a stand-out favorite, then it is purely a roll of the dice. If you buy a ticket, you have bought a lottery ticket. (Which is OK, I guess, if you believe in the lottery—I sure don't!)

A few tracks don't include maiden races in their program; they conduct them at other times. Several other tracks tend to have most maiden races at the matinee performances—another good reason why the author enjoys different afternoon delights!

Tip Sheets

Tip sheets are mostly for lazy fans who think there is an easy way to win at the races. They figure, "Why spend two to three hours working a program when you can get the inside scoop for a buck?" They're wrong. Most tip-sheet writers spend about as little time figuring the program as do the track handicappers—those fellows who work out the so-called morning odds. Try betting with either of them, and it's likely you will lose your bankroll.

Your own system, done at all accurately, will score far better than most tip sheets. (If the tip sheet was a science, then how can two or three different tip sheets disagree so widely?) Not only that, but the tip sheets influence so many fans that when they do hit, the payoff is usually quite small. (At least you don't have 1200 people looking over your shoulder at *your* sheet, do you?) When your system comes up with different selections than the tip sheets, and you are right and they are wrong, you will enjoy some really nice winnings. On the other hand, there will be times when you agree with the tip sheets, and your selections go off at very short odds. Sometimes, in this case, it's best to pass the race. Cashing tickets is definitely fun, but it is profitable only if you cash them for more than you laid out.

Other Factors

Look around, listen in, read enough, and you will come across even more handicapping factors than already discussed here. Evaluate any that sound worthy, of course, but try hard to keep your system as simple as you can, and still have it be a winning system. There is a definite hazard in over-handicapping, and it is not at all impossible to reach a point of weakening your system by adding too much to it.

Chapter 13

Betting Your System, and Money Management

Now...you're ready to go to the races. If you have some betting capital, you're ready to put your system to work. (You've already put it to the test by making many, many dry runs.) You'll be entering the track *not* with a fool-proof system, *not* with a can't-lose method, and *not* with a bet-the-farm sure thing; but you *will* be walking through the gates with a far better chance of success than almost anyone else there! Smirk, if you like, but just don't get greedy. There will be some nights when nothing works, and some times when you wish you could stick this book in my ear. But if you've done it at all right, and stick to intelligent betting, you will come out not only ahead of the track's take (you're about 20% smarter than the rest of the crowd if you just break even!), but you'll find that your bankroll is bigger at the end of the month than it was at the start.

Before you put your money on the line, there are some things you must understand. The most important of all is that no matter how sharp your system, no matter what percentage of winners you pick, it is entirely possible, even easy, for the best handicapper at the track to still *lose* money.

Doing your homework, building your system, scoring your programs, and making sharp selections takes a certain measure of time and effort. When you have done this, *you are only about halfway to a profit.* The other half is intelligent betting and money management. While *there is no way to make money by smart betting without a good system,* a good system *alone* is absolutely *no* guarantee of a profit.

In other words, you can't do all of your selecting at home, go to the track with your program scored, go to the bar, get smashed, bet your system willy-nilly, and count on going home with a profit. It is possible and highly desirable to have your betting moves worked out in advance, as you score the program, but you will still have a number of last-minute decisions to make on certain races. More on that later. For now, repeat to yourself five times, "Betting correctly is just as important as handicapping correctly."

The most intelligent question one could ask at this point is, "How much money do I need to bet with?" That's hard to answer, but we'll try. First, you must decide what *your* level of betting should be. It isn't as simple as deciding how much income you'd like to have from the races, and it isn't as simple as deciding how much you can afford (to lose?). More than anything, at least at the start, you've got to determine what betting level you are comfortable with. Some of us are simply born as $2 bettors, and feel stressful whenever we exceed that level. (By "$2 bettor," I mean buying tickets on that level, be they $2 win or place tickets, $2 quiniela tickets, six $2 trifecta tickets, or whatever.) For many folks, it just feels more natural to buy five $2 tickets on a bet than it does to instead go to the $10 window. Know what I mean?

On the other hand, if you have refined your system into a reliable profit-producing method, and keep it fresh, you can increase your winnings, *up to a point,* by increasing your wagers. You cannot, however, get out from under a losing method by increasing your wagers, as some "progressive wagering" proponents would have you believe.

It is often said that one should not risk more than one is "prepared" to lose. That's easier said than figured out. I, for one, am not "prepared" to lose even $5! It doesn't give me pleasure to lose. A fan once turned to me just before the last race and said, "Boy, it sure is *tiring* to lose!" That's the truth! Nobody likes it. It makes the drive home at least twice as long. But on the other hand, a $5 loss won't push me into bankruptcy, or make the grandchildren's Christmas presents much smaller next year. In fact, I could "stand" losing $500 this week, if I am already further ahead than that—or know that I'm going to be—by the end of the week or month.

The thing is, nobody can tell you how much is too much but yourself. There are few rich enough to pursue a losing system or a losing betting practice. Even with moderate betting, say an average of $10 per race, you are wagering about $120 per night. If you lose half of that, and keep doing so three times a week for six months, that would be a total loss of $4680! I don't know about you, but that would hurt me badly! On the other hand, if you have a system that is producing profit, say an average of $100 per night, that same three times per week for six months would have you $7800 ahead, and how much of an investment would that be worth? If you had to push $300 per night through the mutuel windows to generate that kind of profit, no one could say that betting $300 in one night was "too much."

Your starting point should be based on the following:

You are entering a part-time business. Instead of a business of selling products or services, and being smarter than those you buy from and sell to, your business is going to involve being smarter than the average dog race fan at selecting winning combinations. Instead of selling at a price greater than you buy for, you are going to work hard at cashing in tickets for more than it has cost you to wager. You won't have much overhead, but you'll have to burn some midnight oil to develop your methods. You won't need to advertise, for your "customers" will be readily available. You'll have to get yourself to your "place of business" regularly, but you won't need to punch a time clock. You'll have to keep your mind on what you're doing at all times, but it sure won't be dull. You will need some capital to start the business; you either have it, or you don't—you can either save enough up, or you can't. Since there is an element of risk involved, you don't want to borrow it. (Don't fool yourself. If you've never started a "real" business, you may not know that it is nearly impossible to borrow money to start a business with. The reasons are valid. If your business idea doesn't work, where will the repayment dollars come from?) The question then becomes, what can you afford to lose if your methods or willpower become faulty—if your "business" doesn't succeed? That's your loss limit. It may be higher than the actual start-up amount, but you had better determine in advance exactly where the line is, so you will know when you get there, and *stop*. Or, better yet, recognize when you are *headed* there, and re-trench before you blow away the working capital!

So, you have to draw that line. By all means, don't be a sucker and go past it! Your relatives and neighbors may sympathize with you if you opened a little store and it folded, but if you fail at the pari-mutuel windows, it will seem like a black mark on your character, for whatever reasons—that's human nature. Keep your "maximum investment" well within the bounds of affordability for this reason, as well as for common sense.

You are left, then, with determining how much "start-up" capital you will need. (It is possible that this amount will also equal your "maximum investment"; in this case, you'll have just one chance.) First, you'll need to determine which types of bets you will build your system around. Though we will be discussing several alternative game plans, the heart of the system we are exploiting here is the *trifecta* bet. Furthermore, the author's experience indicates that for reliable profits, a method of boxing four or more selections is required. To go with this plan, and presuming that we might find eight races worth betting in a typical evening, we could be betting $192 or more. We might hit the first bet, and never have to take another dollar out of our pocket again. Or, we might lose the first bet, and the second, and the whole night—in which case we are not only out that $192, but we need some more to bet with the next night. (Some nights like that will happen, and you must be "prepared" to accept them. How *many* to accept is a topic discussed a little later.) We might be well into that second night before we get a winner. That winner could be $594—or it might be $36. In any case, I recommend that you have start-up capital, for this system, of something around $500. If you have too little, you'll tend to lay off some bets, and those might well be the ones your system would have caught. (Boy, does *that* make you mad!)

That $500 ain't peanuts, and it may well be more than you are willing to risk. In this case, you can find some betting methods in the discussions to follow that, played conservatively, intelligently, and cautiously but consistently, will build up a bankroll *for* you. A little slowly, maybe, but if you don't blow it all on pretzels, beer, and dumb races, you can build up enough to cross the threshold into betting for a larger return.

In the pages to come, you will repeatedly see this admonition: *Don't bet when you can't bet smart.* That's simple and easy to say, and nobody will argue the logic of it, but wow—is it hard to do! Steel yourself! Patience! Pass on the races that you should pass on! Hypnotize yourself! Go out the front gate and take a walk! Get into a line that you know will shut you out!

No matter how much time you spend on handicapping, and no matter how good you get at it, *nobody* can ever devise a smart bet on each and every race. There are always a few races on every program for which it is impossible to handicap yourself an advantage. An all-day meeting of the ten best minds in greyhound handicapping could not come up with the probable outcome of these kinds of races. Either there is not enough information to base an intelligent decision on (as is likely to be the case in a maiden race, or any race in which sufficient data is not available on one or more of the dogs), or it is a race in which you can learn all you need to know about every dog, but all the information indicates that it will simply be too close of a race among too many of the entries.

The ability to recognize these types of races is one of the prime advantages of a numerical scoring method. Your bottom line will indicate whether you have an extremely close race or an outstanding selection. More on that later.

The point here is that you will quite often, if you are doing things right, recognize that you are looking at your handicapping results on a given race, and seeing, in your imagination, NO BET written across the page. If you never see that happen, you are not doing things right. The thing to do is to actually write NO BET clear across the page. Now, this is far easier said than done. Your mind will say to you, "Hey! We spent 30 minutes figuring this race out! Are we just going to waste that time, and not even make a bet?" You must develop the ability to answer back, "That's right! That 30 minutes we spent is going to *save* us $24 this time!" In other words, you spent the time to find out if you had a good bet on the race, and your system answered: No! So, you should say "Thanks, system!" and count it as time well spent. The catch is, though, that that is far easier said than done, for you will often find yourself staring at the page concentrating on an effort to see if there isn't some way to salvage all that time spent and make *some* type of bet on the race. Well, it is true that one needs to develop the ability to change one's game plan to fit the circumstances. If you have been mainly betting boxed trifectas, and a particular race doesn't look like a good trifecta bet for you, it is possible that you could spot, for instance, a quiniela play. We'll discuss this in more detail later.

When a race simply looks bad, develop the ability to pass on it. The lack of this ability can easily wipe out all the profits that a good system can win for you! On average, one should anticipate at least two or more races in a card on which no intelligent bet can—or should—be made. Now and then, one of these races would have won for you, anyhow. That's when it's easy to weaken, and swear that you'll never pass another race. Don't weaken! And don't kick yourself when one of the passes would have won. You know it's bound to happen now and then, but there is *no way* you can profit over the long run from betting poor races.

Once you have determined your *stop loss* maximum, and the *start-up capital* needed, you will need to decide how large to keep your bankroll, how much to take to the track, *where* to keep the capital not taken to the track, and what to do with the "excess," or winnings. For example, let's say your game plan calls for wagering about $190 per night. Though you hope to win the first race, you recognize that you may not win at all until the last race, or maybe not even at all this night. So you do need to take the whole $190 to the track. But your business plan calls for maintaining a $500 bankroll. Where will you keep the other 310? I suggest *not* in your pocket—simply in a safe place. Banks work fine for this, and even pay interest! Don't keep it in an account with your other personal funds, though, for it is often too tempting to borrow from it for the car payment, or other purposes.

When your bankroll grows beyond the intended balance, what do you do with the surplus? If your system is strong and reliable, and your nature is such that you can tolerate larger betting without developing facial twitches, you could possibly increase your earnings by simply increasing your average bet; that is, if you want or need more income from the track. There are those who make a quite decent living from the races. I must say here, though, that most find it is not an easy living, and if you go about it for your bread and butter, it could even become boring.

If, instead, you undertake the whole thing more as a challenge and as a source of some extra funds, rather than as your livelihood, you will need to remove the surplus from your bankroll now and then and do what you will with it. I could not begin to make recommendations in this respect, though I suggest that you share at least some of it with your loved ones, who are probably giving up some of their share of *you*, for the time it takes you to accumulate these funds. In any case, I suggest you keep your bankroll intact, don't use it for any other purposes, and remove the excess regularly.

For some reason, it seems far easier to spend track winnings on pleasures, vacations, "toys," and some of those other things that one "has always wanted," than it does to spend wages—even if the wage money is available to spend. No matter how much work and concentration you put into your system, the winnings still somehow feel like "free money," and it seems like more fun to spend it.

Just how "free" that money is, is up to Uncle Sam, to a certain degree. The money that you come out ahead with is called *profit,* any way you look at it, and Uncle looks on profit just as he does on wages. That is, he wants some of it! Your winnings at the track are taxable, just like any other income. That is, your *profit* is taxable, (your winnings minus your wagers). You may deduct the cost of your bets, but only up to a level that doesn't exceed your winnings. In other words, you cannot declare a *loss.* To the letter of the law, one should actually save all tickets purchased, to prove expenditures. Most people do not, of course, but I cannot recommend not keeping or at least recording them.

Part of the complication at the track, of course, is that no one but you is keeping track of how much you spend and how much you win. You do not buy the tickets in your name, and the winnings are not paid out to you by name (with certain exceptions noted below). Therefore, Uncle is not receiving a W-2 Form from the tracks on your winnings, so it will be between him and you at filing time. Obviously, he doesn't have much of a handle on what you're doing. On the other hand, if a jealous neighbor reports you for "unseemly spending," Uncle might very well want an accounting of how you've "been doing." Just as other businessmen are trusted to report accurately on how many "whatevers" they sold last year, you have to be trusted too.

There is one exception to this lack of records, however. At all U.S. tracks, if you win more than $600 on one $2 ticket, or more than $900 for a $3 bet, you must collect your winnings at a certain designated window. At this time, you must divulge your name, Social Security number, etc., and sign for the winnings. All of this goes on a form, a copy of which the track will then send in to the IRS. At filing time, you must be able to prove how much you *lost* before you cashed that big winning ticket. Further, if your winning payment is $1000 or more, at most tracks, the track will "withhold" 20% of your winnings right then and there, and forward it in to the IRS "for" you! (Under certain circumstances, you can sign another form and get your 20% back, on the spot.)

Now, it seems that the majority of people fortunate enough to face this situation do so with mixed emotions. Obviously, they are pleased to have hit a big winner, but at the same time, they recognize that they may now be called on, by the IRS, to do a lot of paperwork to prove those losses which offset some or all of the reported winnings. Otherwise, they may need to pay full tax on the entire gross winnings. For these kinds of reasons, many people would rather hit a $599 ticket than a $601 ticket. Some people even wager that hitting such whoppers is rather unlikely; boxed trifectas, for example, are less likely to exceed this level than are straight trifectas. In any case, your own method of reporting is between you and your uncle, in the end.

Profiting From Your Research

Now we will get into the matter of developing your own basic betting pattern. You will develop this from two factors: first, your available capital, or bankroll; secondly, you will bet *only* in the way that your system indicates that you *can* bet—*profitably*. This will come into perfect focus on your Results Tabulation Chart. This is the form which we've called RT-1, illustrated in Figure 21. This is produced again in this chapter, for we will be referring to it often in this discussion.

Actually, the Figure 21 example shows a rather poor sequence of results. It is not indicative of particularly good results; the track involved was a little cold during the period that these results were achieved. (It was near the end of a meet, and this sometimes happens.) I hope that your average (and mine) is usually far better than this! But it makes for a good example, because it creates some head-scratching, and it represents the kinds of frustrations one may face now and then.

You will note that in Chart RT-1 we rounded off the payoffs to even dollars and eliminated the cents. These are real figures, from a real track, and are quite typical of the payoff scales for trifectas (boxed), perfectas and quinielas. We have a few dashes entered in the 7 and 8 columns; these indicate that there were scratches in those races.

Next, notice that there is no specific pattern in the relationship of the trifecta payoff to the perfecta, or to the quiniela payoff. In other words, the perfecta is not always one-third of the trifecta, or the quiniela one-half of the perfecta, and so on. This is purely a factor of how the crowd has bet each pool. It is not at all impossible for the quiniela payoff to be larger than the perfecta, or even the trifecta box. In general, though, one can estimate that the quiniela will *average* about half of the perfecta, over a span of time, when the tickets cost the same.

One will often see a pattern develop which indicates that the average payoffs in certain grades will be larger or smaller than in other grades. You can spot this easily from your RT-1 chart. This can be a very useful factor in your betting pattern (but ask 10 other fans at the track about this and few, if any, will have ever even noticed it.) In general, you will see that the higher grades, which tend to be more "form-ful," usually provide lower than average payoffs (except for when the favorite *doesn't* hit the board). There are certain tracks at which the author considers trifecta betting on the top grade to be a poor investment, simply because the average payoff is too small. At most tracks, the longer courses provide bigger average payoffs, mostly because the longer courses tend to be somewhat more difficult to reliably handicap.

Looking at the illustrated chart in Figure 21, scratch out the fluke races with the whopper payoffs; these would be the $1748, the $1110, and the $1974 payoffs. They were almost certain to be races in which big crashes or weird circumstances created a totally unpredictable outcome. These are the races which perhaps only two or three "house-number bettors" collected on.

Other than spotting a difference in the average payoff level between grades, can one anticipate whether the payoff on a forthcoming race is going to be larger or smaller than the average? Yes. You can often get a pretty good notion of this, and it can be a tremendous help in determining your wager. For instance, when there is no *odds-on* favorite (extremely short odds, such as 1–2, or 2–5), the payoff will generally tend to be larger. If such a strong favorite does develop in the betting, and does win, you can see box trifecta payoffs of as little as $25 or so. It is when you see three to five dogs showing win odds of about the same, especially if these odds are 3–1 or better, that you can be fairly well assured of a decent-sized payoff, even if three of the shortest-odds dogs come in. What has happened is that the crowd has no stand-out strong dog for *everyone* to put in their bets, or to wheel, and they are playing several different dogs in their pool bets. More will lose, and the payoff will therefore be larger.

There will be times when your handicapping on a certain race agrees almost 100% with that of the crowd, and you both have arrived at one very strong choice which is showing on the tote board at very short win odds. Here is a situation where, if you are right, the payoff will be quite small. The major handicapping factors which you used were so obvious on this particular dog that nearly everyone else caught them too. Often, the solution is to simply pass up this type of situation; if you don't, you will find yourself reaching out to make some bets on long shots, and rooting for the dogs to *lose* that your own system says are the best dogs.

Developing the ability to judge the probable size of the payoff on a given race will serve you well in a number of instances. One such case would be a situation in which you have selected four dogs to box, but your fifth choice is so close that you feel you should also include *it* in a few combinations. To do so will cause a larger investment. In fact, if you are contemplating boxing all five dogs instead of four, it will cost you $60 instead of $24. In this case, it will be a definite advantage to have an idea of what the payoff will be before you decide whether to go for it. In the end, the largest factor in your estimation of the payoff is whether or not your selections agree with those of the crowd. When you agree, the payoffs will be smaller. When you don't agree, and you turn out to be smarter than the crowd—that is, when your selections are in the money and their's aren't—you will reap some big rewards. (And that is exactly why you're reading this book!)

Keep in mind that there's no place on the tote board where you—or the crowd—can see the actual trifecta odds. You will have to make your own estimation of this from your own experience, and by looking at the win odds. You must remember, though, that the two are *not* tied together, and that the trifecta, quiniela, and perfecta pools are held separate from both each other and from the win, place, and show pools. Recently, some tracks began showing the totals bet on the various dogs in the trifecta. This doesn't translate quickly to odds or specific payoffs, but it does help one to see which dogs the crowd is betting on in the trifecta pool. This will be shown on various TV monitors, not on the tote board. Several tracks do show probable quiniela and/or perfecta payoffs or odds, either on the tote board or on TV monitors or both. Actually, you can get a better idea of how the crowd might be betting a certain dog in the trifecta by noting how they are betting that dog in the quiniela or perfecta pools, rather than in the win pool.

All of this is a little beyond the scope of many of the fans present. It is another little edge that you can gain for yourself by developing and using this knowledge in your betting. At least the tote board and the TV screens make it not too difficult, when you know what to look for. In some other countries, one has neither of these—just the morning odds, and the announcer's occasional verbal announcement of which entry is currently receiving the heaviest betting.

Keep in mind that at many tracks, especially the smaller ones and especially on the nights when attendance is light, the win odds that are showing are being determined from some very light betting. In most cases, far more dollars are being spent on the other bets than on win, place and show. Sometimes, the win pool can be so small, even two or three minutes before post, that a bet of as little as $10 can actually change the odds quite a bit.

This brings up another point: will the payoffs be larger when the crowd is larger, and vice versa? No, not usually. The size of the crowd makes a difference to the track owners, of course, since their profit is based on the totals wagered and a bigger crowd will wager more, but to the bettor it is simply a matter of more or fewer winning tickets splitting a larger or smaller pool. When the crowd is small, fewer winning tickets are being cashed, so the average ticket will pay nearly the same as when the crowd is larger. It can happen that there can be an exception to this, in the case of the trifecta pool. With a very small crowd, it can happen that only *very* few winning tickets might be held on a given race—maybe as few as three or four! In this case, it can make a *big* difference if there should be one or two more or fewer tickets. In fact, it can happen that on some races, *no one* will hold a winning *straight* trifecta ticket, and the entire pool gets divided among those who hold boxed tickets. This can make some semiwhoppers, and is far more likely to happen with a small crowd.

On the other hand, a certain number of decent handicappers will frequent any given track. Most of these relatively knowledgeable people attend more races than the average fan, and on any certain night, a number of them are likely to be there whether the rest of the crowd is large or small. This means that on a night with slim attendance, a larger percentage of those who are present have some handicapping skill. This will tend to dilute the payoffs, to a degree. If this is much of a factor at your track, you might be better off attending when the crowd is larger—especially if the crowd is made up mostly of tourists, dinner parties, and other kinds of "fun players" who don't know or care about how to bet intelligently. You, and the other studious handicappers, will have more of their money to share.

In a rural community, where more of those who are attending are at least familiar with the track, if not expert, the size of the crowd tends to make little difference in the payoffs—Other than the fact that on a low-attendance night the betting lines are shorter, and the noise level is lower. . .

How to Develop Your Betting System

Now, back to that RT-1 form. We are going to look at this history to see how we should bet. All of our handicapping is behind us here. We used our best shot at making our selections, and this is a report card on how we did. Remember when we turned to that casual fan and asked him if he did better betting in certain grades than others, and he didn't even *know?* Well, with your RT-1 form, *you* will know how *your* system does, in each grade. Furthermore, you will see if there are any grades or courses in which you should *not* bet. Even further, you will see *which kind* of betting pattern will produce a profit, in which grades, and on which courses. What a tremendous tool you have here! This is what all of your studying, research and homework have been directed toward. This is your blueprint to profit. With this in your pocket, and your handicapping methods kept fresh, you have a fantastic *edge* on nearly everyone else at the track—even the dog owners, the tellers, the waitress in the clubhouse, or anyone else who hasn't prepared themselves as well.

To get a first look at our use of this chart, suppose that our prime intent is to bet mostly the box trifecta. Look first at the Grade A history. (Note: in this example, we have only seven races to look at. That's really not much history, and it would be well to have at least another six to 12 races to study. For the sake of this example, though, we'll make some judg-

Figure 21

TRACK **Doggy Downs**   COURSE **SPRINT**

GRADE	DATE	1	2	3	4	5	6	7	8	BOX TRI $	PER $	QUIN. $
A	11-23	0	0	2	1	0	3	0	0	413	112	41
	11-23	3	1	0	2	0	0	0	0	156	61	19
	11-29	0	2	1	0	3	0	0	0	210	54	16
	11-29	1	0	0	2	0	0	3	0	91	36	11
	12-7	0	3	2	0	1	0	0	0	418	170	62
	12-7	2	0	3	1	0	0	0	0	219	104	49
	12-9	2	1	0	3	0	0	0	-	86	34	9
B	11-23	0	1	2	0	0	0	0	3	194	41	18
	11-23	1	0	3	0	0	2	0	0	240	110	49
	11-27	2	3	0	0	1	0	0	0	509	210	90
	11-27	0	2	1	3	0	0	0	0	218	78	29
	12-6	0	0	0	1	0	0	3	2	1748	340	129
	12-6	1	3	0	2	0	0	0	-	107	69	21
	12-7	3	0	0	1	2	0	0	0	540	126	74
	12-14	0	2	0	1	0	3	0	-	604	181	44
	12-14	3	0	2	1	0	0	0	0	257	141	39
	12-17	0	0	1	2	3	0	0	0	490	102	57
C	11-23	0	1	0	0	3	2	0	-	394	210	64
	11-27	1	3	0	2	0	0	0	0	292	80	36
	12-6	1	3	0	0	0	0	2	0	63	42	10
	12-6	2	0	3	1	0	0	0	0	370	143	67
	12-7	3	1	2	0	0	0	-	-	69	28	16
	12-14	0	0	1	0	2	3	0	0	1110	224	100
	12-14	0	1	3	2	0	0	0	0	189	89	34
	12-17	2	0	3	0	1	0	0	0	372	194	86
D	11-23	0	0	1	0	0	3	0	2	1974	408	161
	11-25	0	2	0	1	0	3	0	0	209	104	30
	11-30	3	0	2	1	0	0	-	-	46	40	31
	12-6	0	1	0	3	0	0	2	0	319	106	109
	12-14	0	3	2	0	1	0	0	0	166	84	33

CHART RT-1: *Results tabulation, by overall ranking sequence.*

ments based on just these seven races.)

Let's look first to see how we would have done if we had simply boxed our top four selections for all seven races. This would have cost $24 per race, so we'd have had to lay out a total of $168 to make these bets. That's quite a bit of money. But we would have won the second, sixth, and seventh races shown, for a total income of $461, and made a profit of $293! Wow! Yes, I'd usually tend to agree, that's a fine return. But, in this example, let's go one more step and examine what would have happened if our method had instead been to box five dogs instead of four. We'd have had to invest a total of $420 in these seven races to do so, *but*—we'd have won *two more* of the seven races, and these were good-sized ones. We'd have cashed tickets for $1089, for a total profit of $669. Wow! If we could only get a system holding like that for ourselves consistently, we might just want to go to this track and bet only Grade A races. Well, I'm here to tell you that it is indeed possible to have these kinds of results. (Not easy, but possible.)

If boxing five dogs in these races made us more money than boxing four, would we make even more by boxing six? Let's look. We'd lay out $840 for the seven races. We'd win even one more of the races (in fact, we'd have won six out of the seven). We'd make a profit of $661. That's a darn good profit, but it isn't any more than we would have made boxing the five dogs. It is true that we would have won the very first race, and therefore would not have had to get back into our bankroll again. But even so, this six-dog box method, though it produced a profit of over 90% (which isn't a bad return in anyone's book), didn't produce nearly as good a *percentage* of profit on *risk* as did the five-dog box method, which gave us about 150%, which is super!

Besides, it takes a good deal of nerve to lay out even $60 on a bet, let alone $120. We're all put together differently, but I, for one, just don't feel comfortable betting this much. If the system proved that this would produce these kinds of profits reliably, it wouldn't be a matter of risking so much—in fact, it might well be the most intelligent thing to do, in this case. It's just that it goes a little beyond the character of most folks. One couldn't afford to let his system go stale for very long, playing at that level.

At the other extreme, let's look at how we would have done boxing only three dogs on that fine system that produced such great results with the four-, five-, and six-dog boxes. We'd have cashed *zero* tickets, a net *loss* of $42! If it is not *impossible* to profit from betting only a single three-dog box, even for an ace handicapper, I'm here to tell you that it is pretty darn close to impossible. Just pick any three dogs in any race—good, bad, or indifferent—and at least one of them is almost certain to get bumped, or into some kind of trouble. Betting a single three-dog box costs only $6, but a really good handicapper will hit only about one out of 50, and that is a long time between wins. (And, the one win would have to be for $300 to break even.) In the examples in our illustration, we would have won only one $69 payoff in the 30 races shown, for a net loss of $111. And, the one race we would have won happened to have two dogs scratched, which made it a bit of an exception.

Let's stop right here and go back to our Grade A illustration to make one more very important point. Suppose that instead of boxing four, five, or six dogs, we instead study some different patterns. Can we find a way to increase our profit even further? Yes! If we were to box our first four dogs, 1, 2, 3, 4, and also box our first, second, and fifth choices, and our first, third, and fifth, and our second, third, and fifth, we'd cover the most logical combinations out of a five-dog box, but have only $42 invested per race instead of $60. We'd catch the same winners that we would have caught with the five-dog boxes, but have much less invested, and increase our profit to $795—a super super return! This is a perfect example of increasing our profit by eliminating poor return betting. If "A penny saved is a penny earned," then the $126 we saved in this example goes right on top of our profits. Very, very rarely will your third, fourth, and fifth dog come in the money together, or even your second, fourth, and fifth. (Your first, fourth, and fifth *might* come in often enough to be worth including, though. Check it out.) The pattern which I just described would be known to me as a trifecta pattern 1-2-3-4, 1-2-5, 1-3-5, 2-3-5. *Be sure to explore each grade for this type of opportunity.* Avoiding wasted bets can, alone, be the key to a winning system.

Now, isn't it neater to look at a page like this to develop your profitable betting patterns, instead of having to push your money across the window to find out? All of this information—your entire RT-1 form—can be developed from dry-run testing of your plan. You don't have to make real bets to get real information. (On the other hand, it will happen now and then, as it did in this particular Grade A example, that you actually lose money by not betting your theory. Chalk that up to research.)

Your Game Plan

As you develop your system, you will find there can be certain grades, certain courses, and even certain tracks where your best methods produce no reliable winning pattern. So be it. If you can't improve your handicapping enough to produce a profit opportunity in a certain grade, etc., then your study has served you well. The next best thing to making money is not losing it.

What needs to be done, once you have enough history on the RT-1 form, is to develop your *normal betting pattern* for each grade. You then usually stick with that pattern as long as it produces a profit, though you will also develop an alternate plan or two for the occasional set of unusual circumstances.

Your main pattern for a given grade might be a simple four-dog trifecta box bet. Your first alternative, for when the opportunity arises, might be to buy a $2 box, instead of the normal $1 box ($48 instead of $24, but twice the payoff). Or, on another grade, your best primary pattern might be a $4 quiniela *wheel,* with the alternative of a $2 four-dog quiniela *box.* Or perhaps in another grade it may be a $1 trifecta *partial wheel,* with an alternate three-dog $2 *perfecta box.* And so forth.

In other words, you've got a pretty good handle going into the program of the types of bets you intend to make on each grade. You also have some back-up ammunition to use when circumstances indicate. Don't, however, fall into the trap of thrashing around between different betting patterns in *desperation* because your intended system didn't seem to work well for a few races in a row. If your basic pattern is sound, and proven out on your history, stick with it! Jumping around in semi-panic will usually cost you money. Likewise, if you're trying to stick with a proven pattern but are short on capital for some reason, you will experience a lot of discomfort—and probably a loss.

Alternatives

Suppose your "favorite" betting pattern is a four-dog trifecta box, but your research indicates a certain grade or course in which that plan will not generate a profit. For an example, look at Grade D in Figure 21. A four-dog pattern on these five races would have cost $120 and brought in only $46, for a net loss of $74. A five-dog box pattern would have caught one more winner, but still would have produced a net loss of $88. Obviously, we need to either pass on this grade until and unless we can improve our handicapping on it, or search for another betting pattern that might produce a profit. Stop right here and look at Figure 21 to see if you can spot a good pattern by yourself. (Again, these five races do not really provide enough history to build a good system around, but we will proceed for the sake of making the point.)

Suppose that we boxed four dogs in a quiniela. This costs a minimum of $12 per race, for a total outlay of $60. We would have cashed two tickets, for a total of $61—not too good. (Better than losing, for sure, but hardly worth the risk.) What if we boxed four dogs in a perfecta, instead of a quiniela? This would have cost $24 at this track, or $120 for the five races. (Note: certain tracks have a minimum $3 perfecta bet, so that a four-dog box would cost $36.) In this example, we would again cash two tickets, for a total of $144; a little more profit than on the quiniela bet, but still not enough return on our risk. If we tried boxing five dogs instead of four, we'd do decently on the quiniela but lose on the perfecta.

While it is true that the first of these five races certainly must have been a fluke race, our example seems to be telling us that we have a very questionable opportunity here. You can easily see that we also have no chance for a profitable win, place, or show bet either. And, if one of the Daily Double races happens to be a race of this grade, we'd better pass that as well. The answer seems to be to go back to the drawing board on our handicapping of this grade, or hope that a little more history will bring a better situation to light.

Look at the other grades in our example. Can you spot some betting pattern opportunities? Work some out, to get the feel of it. You'll see that both Grades B and C would pay a profit on a four-dog trifecta box. How much? The C-grade races would produce even better than the B races. By how much? How much would the "short five-box," which was described earlier, produce? (Pretty darn good, in either grade.) Would a three-dog quiniela box pattern produce? (No, in either grade.) How much profit, if any, would a four-dog quiniela pattern produce?

Though we don't show any win, place, or show payoffs on our chart, assume that the average win pays $8, place pays $6, and show pays $3.50. Are there any win, place, or show opportunities in the B or C grades? You'd get a lot of *action* (cash a lot of tickets) if you bet, for example, your first two selections to *place* in every B and C race, but would you make any money?

You should also be able to spot, in these two grades, some nice opportunities for some profitable *short box* quiniela bets. For instance, check the results of boxing the first, second and third choices, and adding 1-4, 1-5, 2-4, and 2-5. This system would cost $12 per race. It would produce a 58% profit in the B grade, and a 300% profit in the C grade. In a situation like this, it may well pay to up your basic bet to $4, $5, or even more. If you bet too much, of course, you'll start diluting the size of your own winning tickets.

IMPORTANT: Do not set up your own betting plan based on the examples we are making here. This is simply one person's results, from one course, at one track. The betting patterns that prove out from this example will almost certainly not work under all conditions.

Selecting the Losers

From all that has been discussed, you can see that you are trying nearly as hard to *eliminate* entries with your handicapping, as you are to select winners. Your object is to keep as many zeros in the sixth, seventh and eighth columns as possible. *In fact, at most tracks, if you can score well enough to keep your sixth, seventh and eighth selections from being in the money at least 80% of the time, you can devise a winning betting pattern!* Look hard at any of your weighting factors which could indicate when a dog is *out* of contention. Deciphering this is a valuable skill.

You Can't Win 'em All

No one can come out ahead on each and every race. The world's best handicapper is *never* so sure about a selection that he would put his entire stake on it.

If you should be sitting next to me at the next race you go to, and looking over at my program, you might see some pretty "impressive" markings. But, you might see me go three or more races in a row without cashing a ticket. By then, I may not be humming anymore, but you can be sure I'll buy a ticket on the next race that my system shows as a good bet. I might even lose that one, too, but I will still probably go home that night ahead of the game. If not, I will almost certainly be ahead for the two nights by the end of the following night. If I have determined that I cannot do this, at this track, *you won't see me there anymore* until I can get the track figured. In fact, at any given time, there will be certain tracks at which my system or pattern just doesn't work. I'll continue to work on them, and when I can modify or improve my system so that it works there, I'll go back. But at least my system and my records are able to prove to me when this situation occurs, so that I don't continue sending good dollars after bad chances.

You may very well get better at this game than I am, but you will still *never* get so good that you can figure out a way to make money on every race. In fact, if you are cashing a ticket on every *third* race, and making a profit, you are doing *super!* In other words, don't look upon a race that you just lost as a failure; look at it as a segment of a three- or four-race "package" you are betting. In other words, get your head prepared to accept the fact that you are shooting for a longer-range profit, and it is *not* necessary to win at each and every race to achieve that goal.

In short, don't feel that you must hit every race to be "good," or to make money. A losing ticket in your hand is not a sign of failure or embarrassment. In fact, if you have 10 losing tickets in your hand, but one winning ticket that will cash for more money than the 11 tickets cost you, you can consider those 10 losers just an important part of your plan.

Summary

(1) Start with good handicapping practices. Concentrate on the *useful* factors, disregard the meaningless. Update regularly.

(2) *Test* your handicap weighting on paper, with sufficient numbers of examples to provide good input.

(3) *Record* the results your handicapping system provides. Use a format that will allow you to easily evaluate the data.

(4) Establish a wagering pattern that will provide a profit based on your handicapping skills.

(5) Be faithful to your handicapping and wagering methods. Don't back down because of a short-term loss if your system has been strong. Don't pile money on a weak system, on losing grades, or at losing tracks.

(6) By whatever powers you can bring to bear, invoke all the *good luck* you can gather. One can *never* engineer lady luck completely out of the picture. After all, you certainly don't want to get run down by a car on your way into the track on the night you would have hit the $1000 trifecta!

In Cuba, the English pronunciation of "dog" sounds almost exactly like "duck."

May all of *your* ducks fly straight and fast! Good Luck!

Chapter 14

Kennels, Champions, and the Hall of Fame

Who raises, owns, and trains the greyhounds? If a track has 12 races in a program, eight dogs in each race, and eight programs a week, that indicates a grand total of 768 different greyhounds! However, most of the dogs run about twice per week, meaning that about 400 dogs are active during a meet, with many more being trained and raised.

Obviously, few of these dogs are being brought to the track one at a time by individual one-dog owners. Though absolutely *anyone* can own a single dog (or two, or 10), the training, handling, conditioning, and the entering into the races is almost always done by a *kennel*. The kennel takes a cut of the animal's winnings, and shares it with the actual owner (deducting the expenses first, of course). As with horses, any one dog may have more than one owner. Many kennels also directly own some of the dogs they race, and some kennels race only their own dogs.

A typical greyhound track has about 30 to 35 registered kennels contracted to enter dogs in races. Each kennel usually has between 20 to 50 dogs in various stages of training, racing or breeding. Many kennels are local, and usually only race dogs at their local track or tracks, occasionally traveling with a top-class dog to compete at a distant track in a championship race. Other kennels may have "branches" at many tracks around the country. Still others pick up and move their whole stable of dogs to various tracks as the seasons change.

In any case, many of the higher-class greyhounds end up doing a lot of traveling, sometimes in their owner's or kennel's dog campers, vans, trailers or pick-ups, and sometimes by commercial airlines and trains. Most tracks provide several buildings on their grounds for the housing and training of dogs—mainly for those which are in from other areas.

Is there any money in owning a racing greyhound? Yes, if he wins often enough!—Lots, if he wins a lot!—None, if he doesn't win enough! As with horses, it's that simple. And, just like horses, the cost of a champion is high; some have changed hands for as much as $150,000. Untried pups

137

from promising bloodlines may, however, sell for as little as $500 or even less. Unlike horse racing, there are no claimer races in which a price tag must be put on the entrant to enter him in a given race. Several of the industry publications listed in this chapter carry useful information on obtaining and owning greyhounds.

If you own a kennel and I own a kennel, the most logical way for us to decide which one is the best is by the number of dollars that our dogs win. This, of course, is what the racing-dog kennel business is all about. Like any other business, to *stay* in business a kennel has to take in more than it has to pay out. The kennel's only income is track winnings. (No, the owners and trainers do not clean up at the pari-mutuel windows. Historically, they are rotten handicappers, being too partial to their own dogs to

Lantana Glamour, *in the process of winning the 1982 World Greyhound Racing Classic on March 12, 1982, at the Hollywood Greyhound Track. The $175,000 purse was the richest in greyhound racing history. Photo by Jack Desch, courtesy of Hollywood Greyhound Track.*

make any profitable betting.) Most tracks print a "kennel standings" report from time to time in their program, showing the total winnings of each of the kennels racing there.

The records on racing dogs do not go back as far as those on horses, and for years the purses were so small it was impossible for an outstanding *champion* to emerge. Furthermore, it has only been in recent years that records of winnings have been kept and that championship-level races have been staged.

Many of the "champions" from the past were given the title more by legend than by documented records. *Mission Boy* was the first dog to be given legend status (circa 1920) though no history of his record is in existence. *Traffic Officer* and *Perfect Day,* from the 1928 season, were also remembered long after they were gone, though no one can presently quote their percentages.

The development of different types of lures, the varying course lengths, and the absence of a commonly-used grading system prevented the emergence of any really giant names in the first 30 to 40 years of the sport. This period also saw many tracks come and go, many of which did not keep adequate records. Much of the history of the sport and a number of interesting displays are available to the public at the Greyhound Hall of Fame, 405 South Buckeye St., Abilene, Kansas 67410. Phone (913) 263-6000.

As the tracks gradually prospered and persevered, some top dogs began to stand out, and derby races, invitationals and championship races eventually began to develop. Some of the big-money winners of the late 60s and early 70s established their bloodlines into many of today's great racers, and the greyhound as a breed continues to be tuned even finer by selective breeding.

Any "dog man," and many fans, too, will recognize names like *Rooster Cogburn, Rural Rube, Handy Nemo, Lucky Pilot, Rocket Jet, Pecos Cannon, Newdown Heather, Miss Whirl, Blue Diamond, Dawn Tullera, Miss Gorgeous, Venerated, Great Flyer, Butterflies, Kithed, Downing,* and *Hobby Hour.*

In 1982, championship and elimination races from throughout the country culminated in what was billed as the World Series and Super Bowl of greyhound racing. Representatives from nearly 30 tracks were selected by elimination races at their home track, then taken to Hollywood, Florida for the preliminary rounds, and then eventually to the biggest greyhound race of all time, the Purina Grand Prix. A $150,000 purse was divided among the finalists, and *DD's Jackie,* the winner, was acknowledged as the top dog of 1982. Other finalists were *Kingsford, Reunited, Certainly Will, Forward Press, Leo Not Lion, Marine Trader,* and *Gator Joe.*

In 1983, the Grand Prix (this time sponsored by Autotote, Ltd., manufacturer of the computer systems used at many race tracks for parimutuels) was held at the Palm Beach Kennel Club in West Palm Beach, Florida. The finals featured the largest first-place purse of the season: $75,000. Twenty-three tracks, from 12 different states, sent a total of 48 of the best dogs in the country. *Comin' Attraction,* a 17 to 1 long shot from Colorado, beat the field, which included *Army Brat,* owned by Joan Steinbrenner, wife of New York Yankee owner George. *My Problem* was another favorite, as was *Saucy Tabasco.* Other finalists were *Gentleman Jim, Land, Hail The Chief,* and *High Glass.*

Several associations and publications offer printed material, industry news, and other information on greyhound racing. . .

The American Greyhound Track Operators Association (AGTOA) is the home base for the industry. Formed in 1946, it is a non-profit corporation composed of greyhound track owners and operators throughout the United States. A full-time staff is headed by Executive Director George D. Johnson, Jr., with offices at 1065 N.E. 125th St., Suite 219, North Miami, FL 33161. The AGTOA is a founding member of the World Greyhound Racing Federation, which is involved in promoting international greyhound racing throughout the world.

The AGTOA is also the majority stockholder in Greyhound Publications, Inc., which publishes the *Greyhound Racing Record,* a very popular and useful weekly newspaper which covers all aspects of the sport and includes a results chart from almost all of the tracks running. Several other publications and books are also available from their book service. Steve Gulko is the editor, Mildred Hopkins the business manager. Offices: 1065 N.E. 125th St., Suite 211, North Miami, FL 33161. Mailing address: P.O. Box 611919, North Miami, FL 33161. (305) 893-2101.

The National Greyhound Association publishes a monthly, the *Greyhound Review.* Director Gary Guccione has written a number of books on greyhound breeding. Address: P.O. Box 543, Abilene, KS 67410. (913) 263-4660.

Another monthly, *Turnout,* is relatively new and primarily directed to the industry, but also has features for the fans. It is published by the New England Greyhound Association, 209 Squire Road, Suite 26, Revere, MA 02151. Editor, Greg Farley.

Publications from other countries include:

Irish Sporting Press, Irish Coursing Club, Davis Road, Clonmel Cty., Tipperary, Ireland.

The Greyhound Magazine, Ltd., 1 Green Road, Benfleet, Essex SS75JT, England.

Greyhound Recorder, 72 Carlton Crescent, Summer Hill, Box 84, Summer Hill, N.S.W., 2130, Australia.

Queensland Greyhound Magazine, 881 Stanley St., East Brisbane, Queensland 4169, Australia.

National Greyhound News, P.O. Box 628E, Melbourne 3001, N.S.W., Australia.

Award presentation of the 1982 Purina Grand Prix prize money to winner DD's Jackie. *Photo by Jack Desch, courtesy of Hollywood Greyhound Track.*

1982 Major Stakes Champions

Date	Purse	Stakes	Feet	Time	Track	Winner	Kennel
3/12/82	$175,000	8th World Greyhound Racing Classic	1650	31.39	Hollywood	Lantana Glamour	Nova
1/30/82	$150,000	Purina Greyhound Grand Prix	1650	31.81	Hollywood	DD's Jackie	Ralph Long
8/28/82	$150,000	48th Annual Wonderland Derby	2045	39.27	Wonderland	Ijusplanowinner	D.Q. Williams
5/22/82	$135,000	30th Annual Huestis Marathon Championship	2310	44.55	Wonderland	Two On Dolly	Kansas
2/ 5/82	$130,000	The Floridian	2310	44.79	Hollywood	Pecos Wheeling	Kansas
4/26/82	$125,000	11th Hollywoodian	1980	37.72	Hollywood	Unruly	F.B. Stutz
6/ 4/82	$125,000	26th International Classic	1940	37.84	Flagler	Hail the Chef	Big Red
8/ 6/82	$125,000	13th Annual Irish-American Classic	1815	33.51	Biscayne	Carouse	Klein
2/20/82	$100,000	23rd Derby Lane Distance Classic	1980	37.82	St. Petersburg	Cayenne	Carroll Blair
5/15/82	$100,000	Hecht Marathon Championship	2310	44.53	Flagler	Marathon Hound	Dick Andrews
6/30/82	$100,000	Tom Benner Super Marathon Championship	2970	58.90	Flagler	Sizzling Lite	Kerry Patch
9/ 4/82	$100,000	5th Great Greyhound Race	1650	31.43	Seabrook	O K Troy	W.H. O'Donnell
10/ 1/82	$100,000	West Virginia Classic	2033	37.98	Wheeling	Mr. Wizard	John Seastrom
10/ 8/82	$100,000	Hecht Marathon Championship	2310	45.03	Flagler	Wired to Win	D.Q. Williams

Date	Purse	Stakes	Feet	Time	Track	Winner	Kennel
10/30/82	$100,000	Tom Benner Super Marathon Championship	2970	59.33	Flagler	Marathon Hound	Dick Andrews
11/ 6/82	$100,000	5th Annual Grady Sprint Championship	1650	31.31	Wonderland	Stride Along	Wayne Strong
11/26/82	$100,000	Biscayne Derby	1815	33.40	Biscayne	Gold Coast Mel	Dick Jordan
12/17/82	$100,000	U.S. Marathon Championship	2585	52.50	Biscayne	OV's Love Always	Silvero
3/20/82	$ 85,000	7th Derby Lane Sprint Classic	1650	30.64	St. Petersburg	Gene's Spur	Mulberry
9/ 3/82	$ 75,000	Marathon Invitational Championship	2585	48.85	Biscayne	Cajun Angel	Fritz
7/30/82	$ 55,000	City of Wheeling Stakes	1643	30.47	Wheeling	Lil Miss Marker	Kansas
5/14/82	$ 50,000	4th Annual Cloverleaf Classic	1650	31.37	Cloverleaf	JW Rocket One	Wilbert Hart
6/ 6/82	$ 50,000	6th Annual Connecticut Derby	2040	39.20	Plainfield	Win I Do	Teddy Meadows
7/31/82	$ 50,000	Rhode Island Derby	2010	38.46	Lincoln	Stormy Encounter	Classic
7/ 3/82	$ 35,000	Battle of the Ages—Juniors vs. Seniors	1650	30.83	Wonderland	Hondo Monopoly	Kansas
10/23/82	$ 35,000	33rd American Greyhound Derby	1980	38.39	Taunton @ Raynham	Mr. Wizard	John Seastrom
12/ 4/82	$ 35,000	29th Annual Juvenile Championship	1650	31.21	Wonderland	Vision Man	Teddy Meadows
8/ 7/82	$ 29,000	50th Annual Multnomah Kennel Club Derby	2070	39.23	Multnomah	Foxy Red	Roy Grober
4/ 3/82	$ 25,000	Orange Park State	1650	30.75	Orange Park	Snap's EZ Terms	Fred A. Clark
8/ 7/82	$ 25,000	32nd Annual Timberline Stakes	2045	38.81	Mile High	Pat C Misfire	C. Blair
8/20/82	$ 25,000	5/16th Open Sprint	1650	30.20	Biscayne	Lantana Glamour	Nova
9/18/82	$ 25,000	Sprint Championship	1650	31.59	Flagler	Joey Jones	Kogen's
10/30/82	$ 25,000	Jacksonville Stake	1650	30.96	Jacksonville	Logan's Champ	W.F. Muth
7/ 4/82	$ 22,500	Connecticut Oaks	1650	30.85	Plainfield	Erma Lee	H. Caswell
10/30/82	$ 21,000	Westote Classic	1650	30.81	Tucson	RT's Penrose	Joyce Spear
3/ 5/82	$ 20,000	Naples-Ft. Myers Derby	1980	38.13	Naples-Ft. Myers	Kansas Stripper	Dick Andrews

Courtesy: American Greyhound Track Operator's Association.

143

Chapter 15

Greyhound Track Locations

Greyhound racing is presently conducted in 14 states at 44 tracks, and in Ireland, England, Australia, Spain, Mexico and Guam. Several other states presently have dog racing under consideration, as the popularity of the sport continues to grow.

LOCATION OF U.S. GREYHOUND TRACKS

Courtesy: AGTOA.

Each track in the United States is represented by an abbreviation which identifies that track.

When dogs are transferred from one track to another, the past performance charts follow, and will be printed in the program and identified by these abbreviations. At the end of this chapter is a speed chart to assist the fan in relating the speed of a dog on one track to that of another track. In Appendix B is a similar chart showing *average* winning times on each course, instead of record times. Some handicappers will find this more useful.

ABBREVIATIONS OF OTHER GREYHOUND TRACKS
Used in Past Performance and Starts Records

AM—Amado Greyhound Park, Amado, Ariz	**MH**—Mile High Kennel Club, Commerce City, Colo.
AP—Apache Greyhound Park, Apache Junction, Ariz.	**MOB**—Mobile Greyhound Park, Theodore, Ala.
BAY—Bayard Raceway, Jacksonville, Fla.	**MUL**—Multnomah Kennel Club, Fairview, Ore.
BIS—Biscayne Kennel Club, Miami, Fla.	**NFM**—Naples-Fort Myers Kennel Club, Bonita Springs, Fla.
BC—Black Canyon Greyhound Park, Black Canyon City,Ariz.	**OP**—Orange Park Kennel Club, Jacksonville, Fla.
BH—Black Hills Dog Track, Rapid City, So. Dakota	**PB**—Palm Beach Kennel Club, West Palm Beach, Fla.
CAL—Caliente Greyhound Club, Mexico	**PEN**—Pensacola Greyhound Park, Pensacola, Fla.
CL—Cloverleaf Kennel Club, Loveland, Colo.	**PH**—Phoenix Greyhound Park, Phoenix, Ariz.
CS—Rocky Mountain Greyhound Park, Colo. Springs, Colo.	**PLN**—Plainfield Greyhound Park, Plainfield, Conn.
DB—Daytona Beach Kennel Club, Daytona Beach, Fla.	**PUE**—Pueblo Greyhound Park, Pueblo, Colo.
EB—Ebro Dog Track, Ebro, Fla.	**RAY**—Raynham Park, Raynham, Mass.
FLA—Flagler Kennel Club, Miami, Fla.	**SP**—St. Petersburg Kennel Club, St. Petersburg, Fla.
GM—Green Mountain Race Track, Pownal, Vt.	**SO**—Sanford-Orlando Kennel Club, Longwood, Fla.
GT—Greene County Greyhound Park, Tuscaloosa, Fla.	**SAR**—Sarasota Kennel Club, Sarasota, Fla.
HIN—Hinsdale Dog Track, Hinsdale, N. H.	**SEA**—Seabrook Greyhound Park, Seabrook, N. H.
HOL—Hollywood Greyhound Track, Hollywood, Fla.	**SGP**—Seminole Greyhound Park, Casselberry, Fla.
INT—Interstate Kennel Club, Byers, Colo.	**SOD**—Sodrac Park, North Sioux City, S. D.
JAX—Jacksonville Kennel Club, Jacksonville, Fla.	**TAM**—Tampa Greyhound Track, Tampa, Fla.
JC—Jefferson County Kennel Club, Monticello, Fla.	**TAU**—Taunton Dog Track, Taunton, Mass.
JUA—Juarez Race Track, Mexico	**TUC**—Tucson Greyhound Park, Tucson, Ariz.
KW—Key West Kennel Club, Key West, Fla.	**WD**—Wheeling Downs, Wheeling, W. Va.
LR—Lakes Region Greyhound Club, Belmont, N. H.	**WM**—Southland Greyhound Park, West Memphis, Ark.
LGP—Lincoln Greyhound Park, Lincoln, R.I.	**WON**—Wonderland Park, Revere, Mass.
LV—Las Vegas Downs, Henderson, Nevada	**YU**—Yuma Greyhound Park, Yuma, Ariz.

Courtesy: Hollywood Greyhound Track

The following names and addresses for greyhound tracks were furnished by the American Greyhound Track Owner's Association:

Amado Greyhound Park
(Gillett Greyhound Racing, Inc.)

Location: Town of Amado, AZ 85614
Mailing Address: 2601 S. Third Avenue,
  Tucson, AZ 85713
Telephone: (602) 884-7576

Apache Greyhound Park, Inc.
(American Greyhound Racing, Inc.)

Location: 2551 West Apache Trail,
  Apache Junction, AZ 85220
Mailing Address: 3801 East Washington Street,
  Phoenix, AZ 85034
Telephones: (602) 273-7181 (Track);
  (602) 955-0900 (Executive Offices)

Bayard Greyhound Track
(Bayard Raceways, Inc.)

Location: U.S. 1 & Racetrack Road, 17 miles
  south of Jacksonville, FL 32224
Mailing Address: P.O. Box 41309,
  Jacksonville, FL 32203
Telephones: (904) 268-5555, 388-2623

Berenson's Belmont Greyhound Track
Location: Route 106, Belmont, NH 03220
Mailing Address: P.O. Box 287,
  Belmont, NH 03220
Telephone: (603) 267-6561

Biscayne Dog Track
(Biscayne Kennel Club, Inc.)

Location: 320 N.W. 115th Street,
  Miami Shores, FL 33168
Mailing Address: Above or 848 Brickell Avenue,
  Suite 1100, Miami, FL 33131
Telephones: Track (305) 754-3484; Broward
  County (305) 524-0747; Downtown Office (305)
  374-6028; Publicity (305) 754-6330 off-season;
  Florida WATS line to track 1-800-432-0230

Black Hills Track
(Black Hills Greyhound Racing Association, Inc.)

Location: Business Loop I-90 & State 79,
 Rapid City, SD 57701
Mailing Address: P.O. Box 9045,
 Rapid City, SD 57709
Telephones: (605) 787-4642;
 (605) 348-0579 (off-season)

Black Canyon Greyhound Park
(American Greyhound Racing, Inc.)

Location: Black Canyon City, AZ 85324
Mailing Address: 3801 East Washington Street,
 Phoenix, AZ 85034
Telephones: (602) 273-7181 (Track);
 (602) 955-0900 (Executive Offices)

Cloverleaf Kennel Club, Inc.

Location: I-25 & Highway 34,
 Loveland, CO 80537
Mailing Address: P.O. Box 88,
 Loveland, CO 80539
Telephone: (303) 667-6211

Daytona Beach Kennel Club

Location: West on Volusia Avenue (Rt. 92)
 Daytona Beach, FL 32014
Mailing Address: P.O. Box 2360,
 Daytona Beach, FL 32015
Telephone: (904) 252-6484

Flagler Kennel Club
(West Flagler Associates, Inc.)

Location: 401 N.W. 38th Court,
    Miami, FL 33135
Mailing Address: P.O. Box 35-460.
    Miami, FL 33135
Telephone: (305) 649-3000

Greenetrack
(Greene County Greyhound Park, Inc.)
Location: Exit 45 off Interstate 59, near
    Eutaw, AL 35462
Mailing Address: P.O. Box 471,
    Eutaw, AL 35462
Telephone: (205) 372-9318

Green Mountain Race Track
Location: Pownal, VT 05261
Mailing Address: U.S. Route 7,
    Pownal, VT 05261
Telephone: (802) 823-7311

Hinsdale Dog Track
(Hinsdale Greyhound Racing Association, Inc.)

Location: Route 119, Hinsdale, NH 03451
Mailing Address: P.O. Box 27,
    Hinsdale, NH 03451
Telephone: (603) 336-5382

A full house at the Hollywood Greyhound Track. Courtesy: Hollywood Greyhound Track..

Hollywood Greyhound Track
(Investment Corporation of South Florida)

Location: U.S. Route 1 at Pembroke Road,
    Hallandale, FL 33009
Mailing Address: P.O. Box 2007,
    Hollywood, FL 33022
Telephones: (305) 944-3205 from Miami;
    (305) 454-9400 from Broward County

Interstate Kennel Club
(Interstate Racing Association, Inc.)

Location: 40 miles east of Denver at Mile
  322 Exit of I-70 near Byers, CO 80103
Mailing Address: Star Route Box 57A,
  Byers, CO 80103; 6200 Dahlia Street,
  Commerce City, CO 80022 (out of season)
Telephones: (303) 825-6864;
  (303) 288-1591 (out of season)

Jacksonville Kennel Club, Inc.

Location: 1440 North McDuff Avenue,
  Jacksonville, FL 32205
Mailing Address: P.O. Box 41309,
  Jacksonville, FL 32203
Telephone: (904) 388-2623

Key West Kennel Club
(Keys Racing Association, Ltd.)

Location: 5th Avenue & Shrimp Road,
  Stock Island, Key West, FL 33040
Mailing Address: P.O. Box 2451,
  Key West, FL 33040
Telephone: (305) 294-9517

Las Vegas Downs

Location: 711 Racetrack Road,
  Henderson, NV 89015
Mailing Address: P.O. Box 501,
  Henderson, NV 89015
Telephone: (702) 564-6666
Closed until further notice.

Lincoln Greyhound Park

Location: Louisquisset Pike,
   Lincoln, RI 02865
Mailing Address: Louisquisset Pike,
   Lincoln, RI 02865
Telephone: (401) 723-3200

Mile High Kennel Club, Inc.
Location: 6200 Dahlia Street,
   Commerce City, CO 80022
Mailing Address: 6200 Dahlia Street,
   Commerce City, CO 80022
Telephone: (303) 288-1591

Mobile Greyhound Park

Location: I-10 West at Theodore-Dawes Exit,
   Theodore, AL 36582
Mailing Address: P.O. Box 43,
   Theodore, AL 36590
Telephone: (205) 653-5000

Multnomah Kennel Club, Inc.

Location: N.E. 223rd Avenue, between Halsey &
   Glisan Streets, Fairview, OR 97024
Mailing Address: P.O. Box 9,
   Fairview, OR 97024
Telephone: (503) 667-7700

Two views inside the brand new clubhouse area at the Lincoln Greyhound Park, Lincoln, RI. This is one of the most luxurious racetrack dining areas in the U.S. Courtesy: Greyhound Racing Record.

Naples-Fort Myers Kennel Club
(Bonita-Fort Myers Corporation)

Location: Old U.S. 41,
   Bonita Springs, FL 33923
   Halfway between Naples & Fort Myers
Mailing Address: P.O. Drawer M,
   Bonita Springs, FL 33923
Telephones: (813) Bonita Springs, 992-2411;
   Naples, 597-7181; Fort Myers, 334-6555

Orange Park Kennel Club, Inc.

Location: U.S. 17 South & Wells Avenue,
   Orange Park, FL 32073
Mailing Address: P.O. Box 41309,
   Jacksonville, FL 32203
Telephones: (904) 264-9575, (904) 388-2623

Palm Beach Kennel Club
(Investment Corporation of Palm Beach)

Location: Belvedere Road & Congress Avenue,
   West Palm Beach, FL 33409
Mailing Address: Belvedere Road & Congress
   Avenue, West Palm Beach, FL 33409
Telephone: (305) 683-2222

Pensacola Greyhound Park, Inc.

Location: Dog Track Road, just off U.S. 98,
   Millview, FL 32506
Mailing Address: P.O. Box 803,
   Pensacola, FL 32594-0803
Telephone: (904) 455-8595

Phoenix Greyhound Park
(American Greyhound Racing, Inc.)

Location: 3801 East Washington Street,
  Phoenix, AZ 85034
Mailing Address: 3801 East Washington Street,
  Phoenix, AZ 85034
Telephones: (602) 273-7181 (Track);
  (602) 955-0900 (Executive Offices)

Plainfield Greyhound Park

Location: Lathrop Road,
  Plainfield, CT 06374
Mailing Address: P.O. Box 205
  Plainfield, CT 06374
Telephones: (203) 564-3391, Kennel Club;
  Reservations: CT (800) 932-1159; others
  (800) 243-0114

Pueblo Greyhound Park
(Pueblo Kennel Association, Inc.)

Location: 3215 Lake Avenue,
  Pueblo, CO 81005
Mailing Address: P.O. Box 2220,
  Pueblo, CO 81005
Telephones: (303) 566-0370,
  (303) 288-1591 (Off-season, Mile High)

Raynham Park
(Massasoit Greyhound Association)

Location: 1958 Broadway,
  Raynham, MA 02767
Mailing Address: same
Telephone: (617) 824-4071

Rocky Mountain Greyhound Park, Inc.

Location: 3701 North Nevada Avenue,
  Colorado Springs, CO 80907
Mailing Address: 640 Winters Drive,
  Colorado Springs, CO 80907
Telephone: (303) 632-1391

St. Petersburg Kennel Club, Inc.
(Derby Lane)

Location: 10490 Gandy Boulevard,
  St. Petersburg, FL 33702
Mailing Address: same
Telephone: (813) 576-1361

Sanford-Orlando Kennel Club, Inc.

Location: 301 Dog Track Road,
  Longwood, FL 32750
Mailing Address: Box K, Longwood, FL 32750
Telephone: (305) 831-1600

Sarasota Kennel Club, Inc.

Location: 5400 Bradenton Road,
  Sarasota, FL 33580
Mailing Address: same
Telephone: (813) 355-7744

Seabrook Greyhound Park
(Yankee Greyhound Racing, Inc.)

Location: Route 107, New Zealand Road,
   Seabrook, NH 03874
Mailing Address: P.O. Box 218
   Seabrook, NH 03874
Telephones: (603) 474-3065, 474-3031

Sodrac Park
(Southern Dakota Racing Club)

Location: North Sioux City, SD 57049
Mailing Address: P.O. Box 38 or
   1400 River Drive, North Sioux City, SD 57049
Telephone: (605) 232-4321

Southland Greyhound Park
(Southland Racing Corporation)

Location: 1550 Ingram Blvd. at I-40 & I-55,
   West Memphis, AR 72301
Mailing Address: 1550 Ingram Blvd.,
   West Memphis, AR 72301
Telephone: (501) 735-3670

Tampa Greyhound Track
(Associated Outdoor Clubs, Inc.)

Location: 8300 Nebraska Avenue, (U.S. 41)
   I-75, North at Bird Street Exit,
   Tampa, FL 33604
Mailing Address: P.O. Box 8096,
   Tampa, FL 33674
Telephones: (813) 932-4313, 932-4314

Taunton Dog Track
(Taunton Greyhound Association)
Conducted at Raynham Park

Location: 1958 Broadway, Raynham, MA 02767
Mailing Address: P.O. Box 214,
    Taunton, MA 02780; Executive Office,
    1330 Beacon Street, Brookline, MA 02146
Telephones: Track, (617) 824-4071, Raynham;
    Executive Offices, (617) 738-8880, Brookline;
    Off-season, (617) 824-6947, Taunton

Tucson Greyhound Park
(Gillett Greyhound Racing, Inc.)

Location: 2601 South 3rd Avenue,
    Tucson, AZ 85713
Mailing Address: same
    Telephone: (602) 884-7576

Western Racing, Inc.
(American Greyhound Racing, Inc.)

Location: 3801 East Washington Street,
    Phoenix, AZ 85034
Mailing Address: same
Telephones: (602) 273-7181, Track;
    (602) 955-0900, Executive Offices

Wheeling Downs

Location: Wheeling, WV 26003
    Wheeling Island, just off I-70
Mailing Address: South Penn & Stone Street,
    Wheeling, WV 26003
Telephone: (304) 232-5050

Wonderland
(Revere Racing Association, Inc.)

Location: 190 VFW Parkway,
    Revere, MA 02151
Mailing Address: same
Telephone: (617) 284-1300

Yuma Greyhound Park, Inc.
(American Greyhound Racing, Inc.)

Location: 4000 Fourth Avenue,
    Yuma AZ 85364
Mailing Address: 3801 East Washington Street,
    Phoenix, AZ 85034
Telephones: (602) 726-4655, Track;
    (602) 273-7181, Phoenix Track;
    (602) 955-0900, Executive Offices

Greyhound Governmental Supervisory Agencies:

National Association of State Racing Commissioners
    P.O. Box 4216
    Lexington, KY 40504

Arizona Racing Commission
    1645 West Jefferson, Room 437
    Phoenix, AZ 85007

Arkansas State Racing Commission
    P.O. Box 3076
    Little Rock, AR 72203

Colorado Racing Commission
110 State Services Building
1525 Sherman Street
Denver, CO 80203

Connecticut Commission of Special Revenue
P.O. Box 11424
Newington, CT 06111

Florida Division of Pari-Mutuel Wagering
1350 N.W. 12th Avenue, Room 332
Miami, FL 33136

Greene County Racing Commission
P.O. Box 542
Eutaw, AL 35462

Massachusetts State Racing Commission
1 Ashburton Place, Room 1313
Boston, MA 02108

Mobile County Racing Commission
P.O. Box 1886
Mobile, AL 36601

National Racing Commission of Mexico
P.O. Box 34-050, C.P. 11619
Mexico, D.F.

Nevada State Racing Commission
3850 Lakeside Drive
Reno, NV 89509

New Hampshire Pari-Mutuel Commission
105 Loudon Road
Concord, NH 03301

Oregon Racing Commission
113 State Office Building
1400 S.W. Fifth
Portland, OR 97201

Rhode Island Racing & Athletics Commission
Roger Williams Building
Hayes Street
Providence, RI 02908

South Dakota Racing Commission
State Capitol
Pierre, SD 57501

Vermont Racing Commission
P.O. Box 310
Waterbury, VT 05676

West Virginia Racing Commission
511 Boulevard Tower
1018 Kanawha Boulevard, East
Charleston, WV 25301

TRACK COURSES AND RECORDS

*All time in hundredths of a second except when otherwise noted.

Description name. Distance in feet   *Time

AMADO
SR Santa Rita Course (1104)................18.42
SC Sonora Course (1320)...................25.80
5-16 (1650)................................30.34
AC Amado Course (2055)....................38.43
SCC Santa Cruz Course (2310)..............45.75
NC Nogales Course (2640)..................52.92

APACHE
JC Junction Course (942)..................17.09
TC Trail Course (1320)....................25.92
5-16 (1650)...............................30.04
DC Desert Course (1674)...................31.13
AC Apache Course (2049)...................38.00
PC Pinal Course (2163)....................40.35
SC Superstition Course (2262).............42.55
GC Gold Course (2640).....................54.26

BAYARD
CC St. John's County Course (1490)........28.31
5-16 (1650)...............................30.50
MC Marathon Course (2010).................38.12

BISCAYNE
MSC Miami Shores Course (990).............19.79
5-16 (1650)...............................30.15
BC Biscayne Course (1815).................32.91
MC Marathon Course (2585).................47.91

BLACK CANYON
CC Canyon Course (1650)...................30.26
SC Sunset Course (2049)...................38.71
YC Yavapi Course (2133)...................40.65
BC Bradshaw Course (2310).................43.60

BLACK HILLS
DC Dakota Course (990)....................18.00
FC Futurity Course (1320).................25.85
RC Rushmore Course (1667).................30.83
BH Black Hills (2000).....................38.75
BC Badlands Course (2310).................44.52
RG Reptile Gardens Course (2640)..........52.87
WR West River Course (2970)...............59.82

CALIENTE
RC Rosarita Course (990)..............17.58/60
CC Caliente Course (1566).............30.07/60
TC Tijuana Course (1638)..................30.27
BC Baja Course (2070).....................39.33
SD San Diego Course (2250)................42.52
7-16 (2310)...........................44.02/60

CLOVERLEAF
CC Cloverleaf Course (1650)...............30.41
LC Loveland Course (2035).................38.16
BT Big Thompson Course (2310).............44.25

COLORADO SPRINGS
PC Peak Course (1710).....................31.48
SC Springs Course (2080)..................39.50
PP Pikes Peak Course (2412)...............48.34

DAYTONA BEACH
3-16 (1050)...............................18.32
5-16 (1650)...............................30.44
3-8 (1980)................................37.58
BC Beach Course (2050)....................39.17
7-16 (2310)...............................44.25

FLAGLER
3-16 (1004)...............................18.64
5-16 (1650)...............................30.80
FC Flagler Course (1940)..................36.56
MC Marathon Course (2310).................44.20
SMC Super Marathon Course (2910)..........57.92
FF Five Furlongs..........................65.03

GREENETRACK
5-16 (1650)...............................30.51
3-8 (2070)................................38.99

GREEN MOUNTAIN
5-16 (1650)...............................30.45
3-8 (1980)................................37.81

HINSDALE
5-16 (1650)...............................30.56
3-8 (1980)................................37.74

HOLLYWOOD
SC Sprint Course (938)....................17.58
5-16 (1650)...............................30.26
3-8 (1980)................................36.94
7-16 (2310)...............................43.73

INTERSTATE
5-16 (1650)...............................30.30
3-8 (2020)................................37.88
MC Marathon Course (2301).................44.37

JACKSONVILLE
DC (Duval Course) (1490)..................27.98
JC Jacksonville Course (1650).............30.51
MC Marathon Course (2010).................38.15

JEFFERSON COUNTY
LC Leon Course (705)......................13.30
5-16 (1650)...............................30.30
JC Jefferson Course (2025)................38.25
MC Monticello Course (2970)...............59.19

JUAREZ
3-16 (990)................................18.16
FC Futurity Course (1485).................28.02
5-16 (1650)...............................30.67
5-16 Hurdle (1650)........................31.14
JC Juarez Course (2040)...................39.00
EP El Paso Course (2310)..................44.72

KEY WEST
CC Conch Course (941).....................17.18
KW Key West Course (1628).................30.20
BC Boca Chica Course (1853)...............34.48
MC Monroe Course (1980)...................38.66
Mar Marathon Course (2271)................43.47

LAKES REGION
BC Belmont Course (1650)..................30.57
LR Lakes Region (1980)....................38.48

LAS VEGAS
5-16 (1650)...............................31.07
Henderson Course (2025)...................38.97
Lake Mead Course (2310)...................44.50
Las Vegas Course (2970)...................59.84

LINCOLN
5-16 (1650)...............................30.42
OC Ocean Course (2010)....................37.81
LC Lincoln Course (2330)..................44.35

162

Description name. Distance in feet   *Time

MIAMI BEACH
AC Atlantic Course (1179)................22.75
BC Beach Course (1740)................33.65
Surf Surf Course (2166)................42.60
Mar Marathon Course (2256)................44.45
MILE HIGH
SC Sprint Course (980)................18.21
AC Adams Course (1692)................31.02
CC Commerce Course (2045)................38.42
MC Marathon Course (2404)................46.19
MOBILE
5-16 (1650)................30.62
3-8 (1980)................37.61
MULTNOMAH
5-16 (1650)................30.26
GC Gresham Course (1980)................37.23
MC Multnomah Course (2070)................38.49
FC Fairview Course (2100)................39.68
CC Columbia Course (2310)................43.44
NAPLES-FT. MYERS
SC Sprint Course (868)................17.09
5-16 (1650)................30.02
3-8 (1980)................38.02
MC Marathon Course (2227)................42.84
SMC Super Marathon Course (2970)................57.30
5-8 (3295)................66.71
ORANGE PARK
CC Clay County Course (1490)................27.79
OP Orange Park Course (1650)................30.22
MC Marathon Course (2010)................37.56
PALM BEACH
SC Sprint Course (904)................16.77
RP Royal Palm Course (1635)................29.50
3-8 (1980)................38.01
DC Dixie Course (2213)................41.89
PENSACOLA
EC Escambia Course (990)................17.00
GC Gulf Course (1320)................25.29
NC Navy Course (1605)................29.88
PC Pensacola Course (1980)................38.60
MC Marathon Course (2310)................43.36
BC Beach Course (2640)................52.65
FC Fiesta Course (2970)................59.54
PHOENIX
WC Western Course (1029)................17.24
1-4 (1320)................24.85
5-16 (1650)................30.00
RC Roadrunner Course (1980)................36.48
PC Park Course (2106)................39.08
CC Collier Course (2250)................40.94
PC Phoenix Course (2310)................42.69
TC Thunderbird Course (2679)................50.83
9-16 (2970)................59.44
PLAINFIELD
5-16 (1650)................30.14
YC Yankee Course (2040)................38.36
CC Constitution Course (2310)................43.92
PC Plainfield Course (2970)................58.27
PUEBLO
5-16 (1650)................30.43
PC Pueblo Course (1677)................30.78
WC Wright Course (2079)................38.75
CC Connell Course (2349)................44.62

RAYNHAM
3-16 (990)................18.00
FC Futurity Course (1452)................28.71
5-16 (1650)................30.2/5
3-8 (1980)................37.54
7-16 (2310)................43.81
1-2 (2640)................53.3/5
9-16 (2970)................58.40
SANFORD-ORLANDO
3-16 (1050)................16.98
5-16 (1650)................30.45
SC Seminole Course (1980)................37.80
SLC Sanlando Course (2260)................43.04
SARASOTA
3-16 (990)................17.92
5-16 (1650)................30.17
3-8 (1980)................37.39
SC (Sarabay Course) (2310)................44.19
SEABROOK
3-16 (990)................18.37
5-16 (1650)................30.35
YC Yankee Course (2040)................38.25
SC Seabrook Course (2310)................43.54
9-16 (2970)................57.16
SEMINOLE
5-16 (1650)................30.57
3-8 (2046)................38.58
7-16 (2300)................43.82
SODRAC
3-16 (990)................17.51
5-16 (1650)................30.37
3-8 (1990)................38.30
LC Lewis and Clark Course (2230)................43.85
SOUTHLAND
WM West Memphis Course (950)................17.17
CC Crittenden Course (1003)................17.86
5-16 (1650)................31.15
AC Arkansas Course (1748)................31.85
SC Southland Course (2197)................41.24
MC Memphis Course (2439)................47.62
DC Delta Course (2488)................48.07
ST. PETERSBURG
3-16 (990)................18.21
5-16 (1650)................30.35
3-8 (1980)................37.11
7-16 (2310)................44.72
TAMPA
SC Sprint Course (888)................16.25
CC Columbus Course (1492)................27.95
5-16 (1650)................30.48
3-8 (1980)................37.12
HC Hillsborough Course (2150)................40.69
FC Florida Course (2325)................44.73
TAUNTON
5-16 (1650)................30.30
3-8 (1980)................36.84
TC Taunton Course................40.80
EC Endurance Course (2301)................43.60
TOPSFIELD FAIR
5-16 (1650)................30.44
TC Topsfield Course (2025)................38.21
9-16 (2970)................59.38

Description name. Distance in feet   *Time

TUCSON

MC Mission Course (1004)	17.00
RC Rincon Course (1320)	24.29
5-16 (1650)	30.07
TC Tucson Course (2055)	38.51
NP New Pima Course (2145)	40.53
CC Catalina Course (2310)	42.83
PC Pueblo Course (2460)	51.38
ML Mt. Lemmon Course (2970)	58.58

WASHINGTON COUNTY

BC Beach Course (940)	17.27
CC Chipley Course (1630)	29.63
EC Ebro Course (1881)	35.86
PC Panama Course (2001)	39.10
MC Marathon Course (2280)	43.63
SM Super Marathon (2990)	58.00
9-16 (3183)	60.00

WHEELING DOWNS

PC Panhandle Course (1643)	30.24
KC Keystone Course (2033)	38.19
BC Buckeye Course (2284)	43.39
9-16 (2963)	58.69

WONDERLAND

3-16 (990)	18.1/10
1-4 (1349)	25.38
FC Futurity Course (1485)	27.8/10
5-16 (1650)	30.44
RC Revere Course (2045)	38.53
WC Wonderland Course (2310)	43.95
HC Huestis Course (2669)	51.40
9-16 (2970)	58.1/10
10-16 (3365)	67.3/10

YUMA

3-16 (1004)	18.49
1-4 (1320)	25.33
5-16 (1650)	30.40
YC Yuma Course (2040)	39.17
DC Derby Course (2310)	44.40
1-2 (2640)	53.04

Appendix A:
Glossary of Terms

Appendix B:
Track Abbreviations and Average Speeds

Appendix C:
Book Review

Appendix D:
Sample Forms

Appendix A
Glossary of Terms

ADVANCE WAGERING—Available only at certain tracks. Bets are accepted on any race of the day at any time. One can, for example, wager on the tenth race before the first race is over. In some cases, bets on any race of the day are accepted even hours before the first race starts.

AKC—American Kennel Club. The national organization at which most pure-bred dogs are registered.

BERTILLION CARD—The identification card which lists the 56 specific points by which each dog may be positively identified.

BIG Q—A type of wager in which one selects the *win* and *place* positions (a quiniela) in *two* sequential races. A ticket is purchased on the first race involved. If the ticket wins, it is "traded in," at no additional cost, for another ticket on the following race. In effect, it is a parlayed quiniela wager. Not available at all tracks.

BITCH—A female dog of any age.

BOX—The post position of the dog, or the starting box itself; to *box* a wager is to bet one's selections in different orders of finish.

BLANKET—The "saddle cloth" worn by each dog during the race. The dog's number and colors are designated by the blanket.

BRINDLE—The most prevalent coloration for the greyhound breed. A mottled, streaky combination of colors, including a predominance of brown or tan.

BUMP—A somewhat minor contact with another dog during a race. The dog involved usually loses stride, and seldom finishes in the money. The dog in question may be either the bump*er* or the bump*ee*.

CALL POST—The point on the course where each dog's position is noted and recorded in the race chart (i.e., 1/8 call, stretch call, etc.).

CHART—The printed results of a completed race.

CHARTWRITER—The track employee who compiles the charts and writes the comments on each dog's performance during a race.

CLASS—The *grade* of a race, or of a dog; also a term used to describe the recent performance of a given dog.

COLLIDED—A rather major contact between two or more dogs during a race. This usually will cause a dog to finish out of the money. According to the style of the chartwriter, the dog so noted may be either the collid*er,* or the collid*ee.*

COURSE—The length of the race. Most tracks run races of two or three different distances, varying the starting point to create each course. The majority of races are run at the shorter, or usually 5/16-mile, course. Other common course distances are 3/8-mile and 7/16-mile.

DAILY DOUBLE—A bet in which the winners of two consecutive races are selected. Usually the first two races of the program.

DAM—The mother of a dog.

DEAD HEAT—An exact tie. When two dogs finish in a dead heat for any money position, a payoff is made for that position for each dog.

DOG—A male dog, when used to signify gender.

DRAW—The random process by which each dog's starting position is selected prior to the race. Usually determined by numbered cubes cast from a leather container.

EARLY SPEED—The performance of a dog during the early portion of the race.

ENTRY—A contestant in a race. (There are eight *entries* in most dog races.) Not the same meaning as for horse racing, where an entry signifies two horses being entered under the same number by the same owner.

ESCAPE BOX—The box or trap into which the rabbit lure disappears when the race is finished.

ESCAPE TURN—The track turn or curve in which the escape box is located. Usually the turn to the crowd's right, as they face the track. Usually known in horse racing as the *clubhouse turn.*

EXACTA—A bet in which the first two positions are selected in order of finish. Also known as a *perfecta.*

FARM—This usually refers to the location where dogs are bred. In many cases, pups are whelped at the puppy farm, and then passed to the kennel for training. In some cases, the farm *is* the kennel, or vice versa.

FAST TRACK—A track in fine condition, on which the dogs can achieve their best speed.

FIGHTER—A dog which shows a tendency to nip at other dogs during a race, or actually show aggression. This fault is extremely difficult to train out of a young dog, and usually results in the cancellation of a racing career.

FORCED OUT—A chartwriter's term describing the instance of a dog being crowded to the outside by one or more other dogs.

FORM—A dog's recent performance is referred to as *form.* It is in *good form* if it's been doing well.

GATE—The number of fans attending a race program; the amount of money collected from the admissions to a race program.

GRADE—The grade of a race, or of a dog (A, B, C, etc.). Generally, as a dog wins in one grade, its next race will be in the next higher grade (except in the top grade, of course). Likewise, if a dog does not finish in the money for three races, its next race will be in a lower grade.

HANDLE—The total amount of money wagered during a program.

IMP.—An abbreviation (in the printed program) sometimes used after the name of a dog to indicate that the dog had been impeded in its last several races.

INFIELD—The area surrounded by the oval track.

INSIDE LURE—A mechanical rabbit motorized lure which runs on rails located on the inside track fence.

JUDGE—An official employed by the track to make decisions as to photo finish results, race eligibility, etc.

KENNEL—This refers to the company or the individual owning the facility at which the dogs are housed and trained. Each kennel must be approved and registered with the track in order to enter dogs in the races.

LATE SPEED—The performance of a dog during the late stages of a race, as in the stretch.

LEAD-OUT—The person assigned to escort the dog out to the track for the post parade, place the dog in the starting box, and collect the dog when the race is over.

LENGTH—The length of one dog. Used to denote how far ahead or behind each dog is at the finish. In speed, each length is computed to represent about 7/100 of a second.

LOCK-UP—The place or the procedure for locking the dogs up in isolation prior to the race.

LURE—The motorized rabbit. Operated by an electric motor of variable speed.

LURE OPERATOR—The track employee responsible for controlling the speed of the lure during each race.

MAIDEN—A dog which has never won a pari-mutuel race. Designated as (M).

MATINEE—A race program held in the afternoon.

MEET—The duration of days for which the state has granted license to the track to conduct races. Many tracks have more than one meet per year. In fact, some year-round tracks have four three-month meets per year (Winter Meet, Spring Meet, etc.). Any dog *graded out* (not finishing in the money for four consecutive starts in the lowest grade) may not start again in that meet at that track.

MORNING LINE—Or *morning odds.* The order printed in the program in which the track oddsmaker guesses what the betting crowd will wager on the entries.

MUG—Slang for a race fan. Those fans who use no knowledgeable method of selection; often used in a derogatory manner by handicappers.

MUZZLE—The plastic face-cover worn over the dog's nose during the race. It is used both to create a sharper image for the photo finish camera, and to prevent any nipping. If a muzzle comes loose during a race, the dog is not disqualified, but is sometimes bothered enough by the nuisance that he loses time.

NOSE—The approximate length of a dog's nose, as used to indicate that a dog won or lost "by a nose."

OOP—A chartwriter's term for *Out of the Picture;* too far back to show in the photo finish camera and/or so far back as to make the computation of lengths impractical.

OUTSIDE LURE—A lure which has its motorized carriage tracks on the *outside* fence of the track.

OVAL—The racetrack itself.

OWNER—The person (or persons) who actually owns the dog. This may or may not be the kennel that entered the dog in the race.

PACE—The *speed* of a race or of a dog. The higher the grade of a race, the faster its pace (usually) is.

PACER—A dog which often chooses to run beside or slightly behind the lead dogs; often in the money, but seldom wins.

PADDOCK—The staging area in which the dogs are weighed, numbered, identified and readied for each race. This area is open to public view at many tracks.

PARI-MUTUEL—The style of betting legalized in the states which allow dog racing. In this form of wagering, the fans are actually betting among themselves, with the track collecting and holding the bets and removing a share of the bets for state fees, purses, expenses and profit.

PARLAY—The act of wagering all the winnings made on one race on a following race.

PAST PERFORMANCE—The printed record of a dog's prior performance in previous races.

PERFECTA—A type of bet in which the first- and second-place dogs are selected *in order* of finish. Also known as an *exacta.*

PHOTO FINISH—A finish too close to judge with the naked eye. An automatic camera takes a still photograph of each race's finish, and the judges may choose to look at a print produced by this camera before declaring the official results.

PICK SIX—A wager in which the *winner* is selected in each of *six* consecutive races. The pool for this wager is carried over if there is no winner, though part of it is usually awarded as consolation prizes to the fan(s) who comes the closest. Also known as Select Six, Big 6, and by similar names. Not available at all tracks. Usually a very large payoff.

PINCHED BACK—A chartwriter's comment regarding a dog that got squeezed out of position by one or more other dogs cutting it off.

PLACE—The position of coming in in second place.

PLAY—The act of betting or wagering, as in "I'll *play* the 8 to win."

PLAYER—A person who is betting.

PROGRAM—The afternoon or evening's races are called that day's *program;* also, the printed program, listing entries, past performances, and other such information.

PROGRESSIVE BETTING—A system of increasing the amounts of one's wagers following a loss, with the intent of increasing the amount collected when a win is made.

PUPPY— A young male or female dog of about 15 months or less.

RACING SECRETARY—The track official who determines how many races of which *grades* shall be run on each *course,* for each *program,* during the *meet.* The Racing Secretary also lines up the entries for each race (usually several days in advance) and oversees the make-up of stakes races.

ROUTE—A race held on one of the longer courses at the track. Shorter races are usually called *sprint* races.

SCHOOLING RACE—A training or qualifying race. No betting is allowed. Usually conducted at times other than during regular programs. Signified by an "s" on past performance lines.

SCRATCH—When a dog which had been entered in a race is withdrawn, either by the owner's or the judge's decision.

SHOW—The position of finishing in *third* position.

SHUT OFF—A chartwriter's term for denoting a case of one or more dogs cutting in front of a dog, but without actual contact.

SHUT OUT—The happenstance of being in line at the ticket window when the race starts, and not being able to place your bet in time. (No further bets are taken once the starting box doors open.)

SPOT PLAY—A description of any system which is based on automatically placing a bet whenever a certain set of factors occur concerning a particular race.

SPRINT RACE—A race held on one of the shorter courses at the track. The longer courses are often referred to as *route* races.

STAKES RACE—A race which has been set up by the Racing Secretary for some of the top contenders at a track. Designated by "S" in the program.

STARTING BOX—The box, or row of boxes, in which the dogs are placed just before the race. The entire front of the row of boxes flips up to ensure an even start.

STUD—A male dog used for breeding purposes. (To date, no method of artificial insemination of dogs is being used.)

SUPERFECTA—A bet in which *four* dogs are selected to finish first, second, third and fourth. Like the trifecta, perfecta or quiniela, this bet can be *boxed*.

TAKE—The percentage which is removed by the track from the money that is wagered. The *take* is divided between the track and the state.

TATTOO—Indelible permanent marks on the dog's ears, lip, and other areas to enable positive identification at all times.

TELLER—The clerk at the betting window who handles betting transactions and issues printed tickets to the bettors.

TICKET—The printed paper slip which is given to the bettor as a receipt of his wager. This is what will be cashed in if it wins. (What one does with the tickets that don't win is up to the individual.)

TIP SHEET—Papers sold at the track by vendors. These are published by commercial handicappers, and list their order of selection. Some tip sheets are far more accurate than others. Few are profitable for anyone other than the seller.

TOTE BOARD—The display board in the infield, or behind the backstretch, which records the betting, the odds, the time till the next race, and other information.

"T" RACE—An invitational race made up by the Racing Secretary. May be of any grade, or mixture of grades.

TRAINER—The kennel employee in charge of training young dogs to race and older dogs to race better; often also in charge of conditioning, diet, medical care, etc. The trainer for each dog is listed in the printed program.

TRIFECTA—A bet in which the first three dogs are selected, in order. (Or, this bet can be boxed.)

TURNS—The curves of the track.

QUINIELA—A bet in which the first two finishers are selected, in either order.

WEIGH IN—The pre-race process of checking each dog's weight. If the dog doesn't meet certain weight loss/gain limitations, it will be scratched from the race.

WHELPED—The act of birth.

WIN—The position of finishing *first*.

WINDOW—The place where the betting transaction is made.

WL—Weight loser. A dog which has a recognized history of losing slightly more than the normally allowed amount of weight prior to a race, and is therefore excused from the normal limitations. This is designated on the program. It is rather rare.

WOE—What a loser experiences.

WOW!—What a winner says.

Track Abbreviations and Average Winning Times

The following chart shows track abbreviations and average winning times on each course, in the top grade at each track. (Note: Times shown are *average* winning times, not course records.)

Average Winning Times

Abbrev.	Track	Short	Medium	Long
AM	Amado, AZ	31.13	39.50	
		550	685	
AP	Apache, AZ	30.78	38.84	
		5/16	Apache	
BA	Bayard, FL	31.34	38.77	
		5/16	Marathon	
BC	Black Canyon, AZ	31.32	39.55	
		Canyon	Sunset	
BE	Belmont, NH	31.52	39.30	
		5/16	3/8	
BH	Black Hills, SD	31.78	40.20	45.30
		Rushmore	Black Hills	Badlands
BI	Biscayne, FL	30.60	33.54	48.98
		5/16	Biscayne	Marathon
CA	Caliente, MEX	31.28	39.68	
		Tijuana	Baja	
CL	Cloverleaf, CO	31.39	39.29	
		Cloverleaf	Loveland	
CS	Rocky Mt., CO	32.30	40.54	
		Peak	Springs	
DB	Daytona Bch., FL	31.27	38.35	44.70
		5/16	3/8	7/16
EB	Ebro, FL	30.60	37.04	
		Chipley	Ebro	
FL	Flagler, FL	31.54	37.72	45.43
		5/16	Flagler	Marathon
GM	Greene Mtn., VT	31.57	38.64	
		5/16	3/8	

Abbrev.	Track	Short	Medium	Long
GT	Greenetrack, AL	31.17 5/16	39.74 3/8	
HI	Hinsdale, NH	31.84 5/16	38.53 3/8	46.00 7/16
HO	Hollywood, FL	31.61 5/16	38.95 3/8	45.13 7/16
IS	Interstate, CO	31.11 5/16	38.99 3/8	
JA	Jacksonville, FL	31.09 5/16	39.48 Marathon	
JC	Jefferson Co., FL	31.17 5/16	39.30 3/8	
JU	Juarez, MEX	31.59 5/16	40.19 Juarez	
KW	Key West, FL	31.03 Key West	36.15 Boca Chica	
LI	Lincoln, RI	31.24 5/16	38.57 Ocean	44.71 Lincoln
MH	Mile High, CO	31.85 Adams	39.04 Commerce	
MOB	Mobile, AL	31.22 5/16	38.22 3/8	
MUL	Multnomah, OR	30.98 5/16	39.27 Multnomah	44.29 Columbia
NFM	Naples, FL	30.77 5/16	39.13 3/8	43.99 Marathon
OP	Orange Park, FL	31.07 5/16	38.99 Marathon	44.15 7/16
PB	Palm Beach, FL	30.44 Royal Palm	38.58 3/8	43.09 Dixie
PEN	Pensacola, FL	31.14 Navy	39.85 Pensacola	
PH	Phoenix, AZ	30.81 5/16	37.81 Roadrunner	40.51 Park
PLN	Plainfield, CT	31.28 5/16	39.39 Yankee	45.47 Constitution
PUE	Pueblo, CO	31.96 Pueblo	40.06 Wright	
RAY	Raynham, MA	31.33 5/16	38.75 3/8	44.57 7/16
SAR	Sarasota, FL	31.06 5/16	38.30 3/8	

Abbrev.	Track	Short	Medium	Long
SOD	Sodrac, SD	31.09	39.10	
		5/16	3/8	
SEA	Seabrook, NH	31.01	39.36	43.97
		5/16	Yankee	Seabrook
SGP	Seminole Pk, FL	31.36	39.69	45.19
		5/16	3/8	7/16
SO	Sanford-Orlando, FL	31.22	38.50	43.38
		5/16	3/8	7/16
SP	St. Petersburg, FL	31.22	37.97	
		5/16	3/8	
TAU	Taunton, MA	31.60	38.64	44.58
		5/16	3/8	7/16
TAM	Tampa, FL	31.32	38.08	45.90
		5/16	3/8	Florida
TUC	Tucson, AZ	31.08	39.45	
		550	685	
WD	Wheeling, WV	30.84	39.17	43.43
		Panhandle	Keystone	Buckeye
WM	Southland, AR	32.57	41.84	
		Arkansas	Southland	
WON	Wonderland, MN	31.35	39.54	44.85
		5/16	Revere	Wonderland
YU	Yuma, AZ	31.77	40.20	
		5/16	Yuma	

Appendix C
Book Review: *Capsule Comments on Books Currently Available*

Oliver Graham-Jones, FRCVS, Editor
The Racing Greyhound, Volume 3
World Greyhound Racing Federation, 1981.

This is a report on the veterinary and scientific symposium held in October 1978 in London, England; a collection of the papers presented at that meeting. The book is more for the greyhound owner than for the average race fan. It features good segments on methods of preventing and/or detecting questionable drug use.

Dan Coleman
Greyhound Racing
DGM Publishing (not dated).

Mr. Coleman's book has some good race basics, but they're arranged in a rather random sequence; somewhat broad and brief treatment of several facets of racing and handicapping. Includes some spot-play systems. Ninety pages.

J.J. Sokoloff
Handicapping the Hounds
Joe Sokoloff and Bob Gordon, 1976.

A 73-page book, the first 19 of which consist of a biography of the author and editor. Forty-six of the remaining 54 pages are reproductions of race program pages and charts. The author's major thrust is the identification and playing of *inside dogs* and *outside dogs*. In all, it's a pretty brief treatment.

Gary Guccione
Introduction to Greyhound Breeding
Greyhound Breeding Publications, 1982.

This work consists of 52 pages of meaty basics by one of the foremost authorities in the world. Includes a most concise look at the importance of bloodlines and the development of the breed. The author has written several other more massive works on the topic. This book is mainly for the dog owner or breeder, not the casual race fan.

Bob and Barbara Freeman
Wanta Bet?
Greyhound Publications, Inc.

A study of the pari-mutuel system in the United States; discusses how it works, and the sports on which wagering has been legalized.

Jack Fink
The Science of Greyhound Handicapping
Ten Greyhound Spot-Play Systems Leading to Winners
Jack Fink Publications.

Mr. Fink is an experienced handicapper and author, but most of his works are written in a rambling style that makes it difficult to pick out the useful facts from among the various side-thoughts and reminiscences.

Paul C. Hartwell
The Road From Emeryville
California Research Publishing, 1980.

This is a very thorough and concise history of the sport of greyhound racing—how the sport grew up, and where it is headed. No handicapping or wagering information is presented, but most fans would probably find this book interesting. Mr. Hartwell belongs to one of the first generation of men who have "grown up" with the sport.

Dick Herter
Making a Living at the Dog Track
Managing for Profit
The Chase Manhattan Bank System
The Dutch Shultz System Made Just About Perfect
Dick Herter Publications.

A respected columnist and handicapper, Mr. Herter gets to the point quickly and shows the reader how to understand the angles he has discovered. A little humor helps make for nice reading, too. Any of these books offer good information for the serious handicapping student.

Appendix D

Sample Forms

Factor Weighting

TRACK _____ COURSE _____ DATE _____

	GRADE _____							GRADE _____							GRADE _____						
	PP	EG	AS	MA	SG	PM	GC	PP	EG	AS	MA	SG	PM	GC	PP	EG	AS	MA	SG	PM	GC
1							-							-							-
2							-							-							-
3							-							-							-
4							-							-							-
5							-							-							-
6							-							-							-
7							-							-							-
8							-							-							-
U	-	-	-	-	-	-		-	-	-	-	-	-		-	-	-	-	-	-	
D	-	-	-	-	-	-		-	-	-	-	-	-		-	-	-	-	-	-	

	GRADE _____							GRADE _____							GRADE _____						
	PP	EG	AS	MA	SG	PM	GC	PP	EG	AS	MA	SG	PM	GC	PP	EG	AS	MA	SG	PM	GC
1							-							-							-
2							-							-							-
3							-							-							-
4							-							-							-
5							-							-							-
6							-							-							-
7							-							-							-
8							-							-							-
U	-	-	-	-	-	-		-	-	-	-	-	-		-	-	-	-	-	-	
D	-	-	-	-	-	-		-	-	-	-	-	-		-	-	-	-	-	-	

PP = Post position advantage
EG = Early gain, or jump
AS = Average speed, recent
MA = Maneuvering ability
SG = Stretch gain, late speed
PM = Percentage races in money
GC = Grade change
U = Up in grade
D = Down in grade

Chart RT-1: Results tabulation, by overall ranking sequence.

TRACK _____ COURSE _____ __ __

GRADE	DATE	1	2	3	4	5	6	7	8	TRI $	PER $	QUIN.¢
—												
—												
—												
—												

KEEPING YOUR GAMING KNOWLEDGE CURRENT THROUGH *WIN*

Now that you are well on your way to becoming a proficient Blackjack player, you will want to keep abreast of all the latest rule variations in the game in casinos around the world. *WIN* Magazine (formerly *Gambling Times*) can give you that information.

Since February of 1977, readers of *WIN* Magazine (formerly *Gambling Times*) have profited immensely. They have done so by using the information they have read each month. if that sounds like a simple solution to winning more and losing less, well it is! Readers look to *WIN* for that very specific reason. And it delivers.

WIN is totally dedicated to showing readers how to win more money in every form of legalized gambling. How much you're going to win depends on many factors, but it's going to be considerably more than the cost of a subscription.

WINNING AND MONEY

Winning, that's what *WIN* is all about. And money, that's what *WIN* it all about. Because winning and money go hand in hand.

Here's what the late Vince Lombardi, the famous football coach of the Green Bay Packers, had to say about winning:

"It's not a sometime thing. Winning is a habit. There

is no room for second place. There is only one place in my game and that is first place. I have finished second twice in my time at Green Bay and I don't ever want to finish second again. The objective is to win—fairly, squarely, decently, by the rules—but to win. To beat the other guy. maybe that sounds hard or cruel. I don't think it is. It is and has always been an American Zeal to be first in anything we do, and to win, and to win and to win.''

Mr. Lombardi firmly believed that being a winner is ''man's finest hour.'' *WIN* believes it is too, while being a loser is depressing, ego-deflating, expensive and usually very lonely. ''Everybody loves a winner'' may be a cliche, but it's true. Winners command respect and are greatly admired. Winners are also very popular and have an abundance of friends. You may have seen a winner in a casino, with a bevy of girls surrounding him...or remember one who could get just about any girl he wanted.

Some of the greatest gamblers in the world also have strong views on what winning is all about. Here's what two of them have to say on the subject:

> ''To be a winner, a man has to feel good about himself and know he has some kind of advantage going in. I never made bets on even chances. Smart is better than lucky.''
> —''Titanic'' Thompson

> ''When it comes to winnin', I got me a one-track mind. You gotta want to win more than anything else. And you gotta have confidence. You can't pretend to have it. That's no good. You gotta have it. You gotta know. Guessers are losers. Gamblin's just as simple as that.''
> —Johnny Moss

WIN will bring you the knowledge you need to come home a winner and come home in the money. For it is knowledge, the kind of knowledge you'll get in its pages, that separates winners from losers. It's winning and money that *WIN* offers you. *WIN* will be your working manual to winning wealth.

The current distribution of this magazine is limited to selected newsstands in selected cities. Additionally, at newstands where it is available, it's being snapped up, as soon as it's displayed, by gamblers who know a sure bet when they see one.

So if you're serious about winning, you're best off subscribing to *WIN*. Then you can always count on its being there, conveniently delivered to your mailbox—and what's more, it will be there one to two weeks before it appears on the newsstands. You'll be among the first to receive the current issue as soon as it comes off the presses, and being first is the way to be a winner.

Having every monthly issue of *WIN* will enable you to build an "Encyclopedia of Gambling," since the contents of this magazine are full of sound advice that will be as good in five or ten years as it is now.

As you can see, a subscription to *WIN* is your best bet for a future of knowledgeable gambling. It's your ticket to *WINNING* and *MONEY*.

Take the time to read the following offer. As you can see, *WIN* has gone all out to give you outstanding bonuses. You can join the knowledgeable players who have learned that *WIN* helps them to win more money.

NINE NEW WAYS TO GET 12 WINNING ISSUES OF *WIN* FREE...

Every month over 250,000 readers trust *WIN* to introduce powerful new winning strategies and systems. Using proven scientific methods, the world's leading experts show you how to win big money in the complex field of gambling.

WIN has shown how progressive slot machines can be beaten. Readers have discovered important new edges in blackjack. They've been shown how to know for sure when an opponent is bluffing at poker. *WIN* has also spelled out winning methods for football, baseball and basketball. They've published profound new ways of beating horses. Their team of experts will uncover information in the months ahead that's certain to be worth thousands of dollars to you.

In fact, the features are so revolutionary that they must take special precautions to make sure *WIN* readers learn these secrets long before anyone else. So how much is *WIN* worth to you? Well...

NOW *WIN* CAN BE BETTER THAN FREE! Here's how: This BONUS package comes AUTOMATICALLY TO YOU WHEN YOU SUBSCRIBE...or goes to a friend if you give a gift subscription.

★1.   A CARD that entitles you to a 50% discount at over 2,000 quality hotels in over 400 cities, mainly in North America and the Caribbean. Only the finest hotels are included; chains such as Holiday Inn, Sheraton, Hilton, Best Western, Marriott and Ramada Inns. Discounts are good 365 days per year. Stay as long as you like, subject to availability. Save as much as $100 per night.

★2.   A 50% discount on a one week stay in over 2,000 condominiums, worldwide, including the United States, Canada, Mexico, France, Bahamas, Jamaica, Italy, Spain, Germany, Austria, Aruba and many more! Reservations made by a toll free number.

★3.   Free Kodak film for life when you use our specified National Processing laboratory, which gives a 40% discount off Kodak list prices for developing. Free Kodak Color film, any size, speed or exposure to fit your camera, is provided with each roll of film developed.

★4.   A 5% REBATE on the lowest available scheduled Airline fares in the US and up to a 45% REBATE on international flights when you book through our contract agency, San Diego Travel. Licensed and Bonded since 1963. Reservations can be made by a toll free number.

★5.   A 3 day/2 night FREE vacation for two in your choice of Las Vegas, Reno, Tahoe, Atlantic City or Hawaii, plus Disneyland or DisneyWorld—when you book your air fare and reservations through our travel agency, San Diego Travel.

★6.   A funpack booklet entitling the holder to over $250 in discounts at local businesses in your choice of: Las Vegas, Reno, Tahoe, Atlantic City, Hawaii, Orlando, Carlsbad-Oceanside, Disneyland, Palm Springs or Acapulco, Mexico. Includes cash, meals, chips, Keno, lucky bucks, slot tokens, drinks, entertainment, attractions and much, much more! Outside of Nevada the funpack may not include cash or gambling benefits. Good 7 days a week, including all holidays.

★7. 15% to 50% discounts on over 1,000 cruise trips. Savings can be as much as $1,000 per cruise. Includes a $50 per cabin bar-boutique ship credit. Reservations by toll free number.

★8. A standard discount on car rental from Hertz, Avis, Budget and Alamo car rental agencies. Guaranteed lowest prices, not available to the public. Toll free numbers in US & Canada.

★9. Your choice of a FREE 3-piece, 6-piece or all 9-piece set of English Leather Designer Luggage. Total value of all 9 pieces is $199.90. Gift certificate with each subscription.

To begin your delivery of *WIN* magazine at once, enclose a payment of $36.00 by check or money order (U.S. currency), Mastercard or Visa. Add $5.00 per year for postage outside the United States. Send payment to:

> *WIN* MAGAZINE
> 16760 Stagg St., Suite 213
> Van Nuys, CA 91406-1642

Other Valuable Sources of Knowledge Available Through *Gambling Times Inc.*

Here are some additional sources you can turn to for worthwhile gambling information:

The Experts Blackjack Newsletter.
This bi-monthly newsletter has all the top blackjack Experts working just for you. Features answers, strategies and insights that were never before possible. Yearly subscriptions are $30 for 6 issues.

OTHER BOOKS AVAILABLE

If you can't find the following books at your local bookstore, they may be ordered directly from *Gambling Times*, 16760 Stagg St., Van Nuys, CA 91406. See Page 199 for Details.

Blackjack Books

The Beginner's Guide to Winning Blackjack by Stanley Roberts—The world's leading blackjack writer shows beginners to the game how to obtain an instant advantage through the simplest of techniques. Covering Basic Strategy for all major casino areas from Las Vegas to the Bahamas, Atlantic City and Reno/Tahoe, Roberts provides a simple system to immediately know when the remaining cards favor the player. The entire method can be learned in less than two hours and taken to the casinos to produce sure profits.
Softbound. $10.00. (ISBN: 0-89746-014-6)

The Gambling Times Guide to Blackjack by Stanley Roberts— This book reads like the ''Who's Who'' of the gambling world. The top blackjack authorities in the world today have been brought together for the first time to bring the reader the ins and outs of the game of blackjack; Stanley Roberts, Edward O. Thorp, Ken Uston, Lance Humble, Julian Braun, Jerry Patterson and other experts in this field. This amazing book is clearly the definitive book on blackjack today—not only for the expert and advanced player, but for the casual player as well!
Softbound. $9.95. (ISBN: 0-89746-015-4)

Million Dollar Blackjack by Ken Uston—Every blackjack enthusiast or gaming traveler who fancies himself a "21" player can improve his game with this explosive bestseller. Ken Uston shows you how he and his team won over 4 million dollars at blackjack. Now, for the first time, you can find out how he did it and how his system can help you. Includes playing and betting strategies, winning secrets, protection from cheaters, Uston's Advanced Point Count System, and a glossary of inside terms used by professionals.
Softbound. $14.95. (ISBN: 0-914314-08-4)

Winning Blackjack by Stanley Roberts—It is the simplest, most accurate blackjack system ever devised. The average person takes

about eight hours both to read the system completely and master it. It does not require a photographic memory. All you really have to do is pay attention to the game. Businessmen and housewives alike report consistent winnings of up to $500 a day when using this system. This manual is complete in every way. It not only tells you how to play, it also tells you where to play, how much to bet and some very important tips about the art of casino play. There is a special section for beating multi-deck games and everything you need to know about blackjack in Las Vegas, Reno, Tahoe, Atlantic City and a host of other casino resorts around the world. This book has the power to completely transform your life! *Winning Blackjack* is large, 8½" × 11", and includes pull-apart flash cards printed on card stock.
Softbound. $95.00. (ISBN: 0-914314-00-9)

Poker Books

According to Doyle by Doyle Brunson—Acknowledged by most people as the world's best all-around poker player, twice World Champion Doyle Brunson brings you his homespun wisdom from over 30 years as a professional poker player. This book will not only show you how to win at poker, it will give you valuable insights into how to better handle that poker game called LIFE.
Softbound. $6.95. (ISBN: 0-89746-003-0)

Caro on Gambling by Mike Caro—The world's leading poker writer covers all the aspects of gambling from his regular columns in *Gambling Times* magazine and *Poker Player* newspaper. Discussing odds and probabilities, bluffing and raising, psychology and character, this book will bring to light valuable concepts that can be turned into instant profits in home games as well as in the poker palaces of the West.
Softbound. $6.95. (ISBN: 0-89746-029-4)

Caro's Book of Tells by Mike Caro—The photographic body language of poker. Approximately 180 photographs with text explaining when a player is bluffing, when he's got the winning hand—and WHY. Based on accurate investigation; it is NOT guesswork. Even the greatest of gamblers has some giveaway behavior. For the first time in print, one of the world's top poker players reveals how he virtually can read minds because nearly every player has a "tell." Seal the leaks in your poker game and empty your opponent's chip tray.
Hardbound. $20.00. (ISBN: 0-914314-04-1)

Free Money: How to Win in the Cardrooms of California by Michael Wiesenberg—Computer expert and poker writer par excellence, Michael Wiesenberg delivers critical knowledge to those who play in the poker rooms of the western states. Wiesenberg gives you the precise meaning of the rules as well as the mathematics of poker to aid public and private poker players alike. Wiesenberg, a prolific author, is published by more gaming periodicals than any other writer.
Softbound. $8.95. (ISBN: 0-89746-027-8)

New Poker Games by Mike Caro—In this ground-breaking book, you'll learn Mad Genius Mike Caro's new ways to play an old game. Some of the games are Caro originals, while others are contributed by readers of *WIN* Magazine. Loaded with descriptions and winning strategies for novel forms of poker. Caro is recognized as the leading poker teacher of the Nineties!
Softbound. $5.95. (ISBN: 0-89746-040-5)

Poker for Women by Mike Caro—How women can take advantage of the special male-female ego wars at the poker table and win. This book also has non-poker everyday value for women. Men can be destroyed at the poker table by coy, cunning or aggressive women. That's because, on a subconscious level, men expect women to act traditionally. This book tells women when to flirt, when to be tough and when to whimper. Many of the tactics are tried and proven by Caro's own students. This book does not claim that women are better players, merely that there are strategies available to them that are not available to their male opponents.
Softbound. $6.95. (ISBN: 0-89746-009-X)

The Railbird by Rex Jones—The ultimate kibitzer, the man who watches from the rail in the poker room, has unique insights into the character and performance of all poker players. From this vantage point, Rex Jones, Ph.D., blends his expertise and considerable education in anthropology with his lifetime of poker playing and watching. The result is a delightful book with exceptional values for those who want to avoid the fatal errors of bad players and capitalize upon the qualities that make up the winning strengths of outstanding poker players.
Softbound. $6.95. (ISBN: 0-89746-028-6)

Tales Out of Tulsa by Bobby Baldwin—Oklahoma-born Bobby Baldwin, the youngest player to ever win the World Championship of Poker, is considered to be among the top five poker players in the world. Known affectionately as "The Owl," this brilliant poker genius, wise beyond his years, brings the benefits of his experience to the pages of this book.
Softbound. $6.95 (ISBN: 0-89746-006-5)

Wins, Places, and Pros by Tex Sheahan—With more than 50 years of experience as a professional poker player and cardroom manager/tournament director, Tex lets his readers in on the secrets that separate the men from the boys at the poker table. Descriptions of poker events, playing experiences from all over the world, and those special personalities who are the masters of the game. . .Tex knows them all and lays it out in his marvelous easy-to-read style.
Softbound. $6.95. (ISBN: 0-89746-008-1)

Casino Games

The Gambling Times Guide to Casino Games by Len Miller—The co-founder of *Gambling Times* magazine vividly describes the casino games and explains their rules and betting procedures. This easy-to-follow guide covers blackjack, craps, roulette, keno, video machines, progressive slots and more. After reading this book, you'll play like a pro!
Softbound. $9.95. (ISBN: 0-89746-017-0)

The Gambling Times Guide to Craps by N.B. Winkless, Jr.—The ultimate craps book for beginners and experts alike. It provides you with a program to tackle the house edge that can be used on a home computer. This text shows you which bets to avoid and tells you the difference between craps in Nevada and craps in other gaming resort areas. It includes a glossary of terms and a directory of dealer schools.
Softbound. $9.95. (ISBN: 0-89746-013-8)

How to Win at Casino Gaming Tournaments By Haven E. Haley—Win your share of the millions of dollars and fabulous prizes being awarded to gaming contestants, and have the glory of being

a World Champion. Poker, gin rummy, backgammon, craps, blackjack and baccarat are all popular tournament games. The rules, special tournament regulations, playing procedures, and how to obtain free entry are fully explained in this informative manual. The tournament promoters—who they are, where they hold events—and the cash and prizes awarded are explained in detail. Tournament play usually requires special strategy changes, which are detailed in this book.
Softbound. $8.95. (ISBN: 0-89746-016-2)

General Interest Books

Gambling and the Law by I. Nelson Rose—The definitive work on the subject of law as it relates to the world of gaming. Professor Rose explains all facets of gambling law and how they apply to players, professionals and casino owners and employees. A MUST read for anyone concerned with gambling. Topics addressed include: Taking gambling losses and expenses off your taxes; How to avoid paying gambling debts; What to do if cheated; The legality of home poker; Your rights in the casino; Getting a gaming license and Suing to get your losses back. Destined to be the most influential gambling book of the decade.
Hardbound. $19.95 (ISBN: 0-89746X-066-9)

GT Guide to Bingo by Roger Snowden—Gives bingo history, instructs on how to best play the game, describes over 108 variations and explain how you can increase your chances of winning by selecting the right locations to play. The author is an editor of the *Bingo bugle* newspaper.
Softbound. $6.95. (ISBN: 0-89746-057-X)

GT Guide to European and Asian Games by Syd Helprin—A comprehensive guide to casino gambling in faraway lands. Covers such games as: Australian mini dice, *trente et quarante*, *banca francesa*, *punto banco*, *pai gow*, *kalooke*, *sic bo*, *fan tan* and many others.

Important information for the informed gambler.
Softbound. $7.95 (ISBN: 0-89746-062-6)

The Gambling Times Guide to Systems That Win, Volume I and Volume II—For those who want to broaden their gambling knowledge, this two-volume set offers complete gambling systems used by the experts. Learn their strategies and how to incorporate them into your gambling style. **Volume I** covers 12 systems that win for roulette, craps, backgammon, slot machines, horse racing, baseball, basketball and football.
Softbound. $5.95. (ISBN: 0-89746-034-0)
Volume II features 12 more systems that win, covering horse racing, craps, blackjack, slot machines, jai alai and baseball.
Softbound. $5.95. (ISBN: 0-89746-034-0)

The Gambling Times Guide to Winning Systems, Volume II—For those who take their gambling seriously, *Gambling Times* presents a set of proven winning systems. Learn how the experts beat the house edge and become consistent winners. **Volume II** contains 12 winning systems covering poker bluffing, pitching analysis, greyhound handicapping and roulette.
Softbound. $5.95. (ISBN: 0-89746-033-2)

Gambling Times Presents Winning Systems and Methods, Volume I and Volume II—This two-volume collection of winning strategies by some of the nation's leading experts on gambling will help you in your quest to beat the percentages. **Volume I** includes several chapters on blackjack, as well as methods for beating baseball, basketball, hockey, steeplechase and grass racing.
Softbound. $5.95. (ISBN: 0-89746-036-7)
Volume II contains an analysis of keno and video poker, as well as systems for success in sports betting and horse racing.
Softbound. $5.95. (ISBN: 0-89746-037-5)

The Gambling Times Quiz Book by Mike Caro—Learn while testing your knowledge. Caro's book includes questions and answers on the concepts and information published in previous issues of *Gambling Times*. Caro

tells why an answer is correct and credit is given to the author whose *Gambling Times* article suggested the question. This book covers only established fact, not the personal opinions of authors, and Caro's inimitable style makes this an easy-reading, easy-learning book.
Softbound. $5.95. (ISBN: 0-89746-031-6)

Golf, Gambling and Gamesmanship by Gary Moore—After three decades as a golf course hustler, the author embarked on a six-year search to find winning systems for gambling on golf. The results are presented here. Read this book and dominate your buddies all the way to the 19th hole!
Softbound. $7.95 (ISBN: 0-89746-054-5)

The Mathematics of Gambling by Edward O. Thorp—The "Albert Einstein of gambling" presents his second book on the subject. His first book, *Beat The Dealer,* set the gambling world on its heels and struck fear into the cold-blooded hearts of Las Vegas casino-owners in 1962. Now, more than twenty years later, Dr. Thorp again challenges the odds by bringing out a simple to understand version of more than thirty years of exploration into all aspects of what separates winners from losers. . . knowing the real meaning of the parameters of the games.
Softbound. $7.95. (ISBN: 0-89746-019-7)

P$yching Out Vegas by Marvin Karlins, Ph.D.—The dream merchants who build and operate gaming resorts subtly work on the casino patron to direct his attention, control his actions and turn his pockets inside out. At last, their techniques are revealed to you by a noted psychologist who shows you how you can successfully control your behavior and turn a losing attitude into a lifetime winning streak.
Hardbound. $14.95. (ISBN: 0-914314-03-3)

Winning by Computer by Dr. Donald Sullivan—Now, for the first time, the wonders of computer technology are harnessed for the gambler. Dr. Sullivan explains how to figure the odds and identify key factors in all forms of race and sports handicapping.
Softbound. $5.95. (ISBN: 0-89746-018-9)

Sports Betting Books

The Gambling Times Guide to Basketball Handicapping by Barbara Nathan—This easy-to-read, highly informative book is the definitive guide to basketball betting. Expert sports handicapper Barbara Nathan provides handicapping knowledge, insightful coverage, and step-by-step guidance for money management. The advantages and disadvantages of relying on sports services are also covered.
Softbound. $5.95. (ISBN: 0-89746-023-5)

The Gambling Times Guide to Football Handicapping by Bob McCune—Starting with the novice's approach to handicapping football, and winding up with some of the more sophisticated team selection techniques in the sports handicapping realm, this book will actually tell the reader how to forecast, *in advance,* the final scores of most major national football games. The author's background and expertise on the subject will put money into any sports gambler's pocket.
Softbound. $5.95. (ISBN: 0-89746-022-7)

The Gambling Times Guide to Greyhound Racing by William E. McBride—This complete discussion of greyhound racing is a must for anyone who is just beginning to appreciate this exciting and profitable sport. The book begins with a brief overview detailing the origins of greyhound racing and pari-mutuel betting, and explains the greyhound track environment, betting procedures, and handicapping methods. Includes an appendix of various greyhound organizations, a review of greyhound books, and an interesting section on famous dogs and personalities in the world of greyhound racing.
Softbound. $9.95. (ISBN: 0-89746-007-3)

The Gambling Times Guide to Harness Racing by Igor Kusyshyn, Ph.D., Al Stanley and Sam Dragich—Three of Canada's top harness handicapping authorities present their inside approach to analyzing the harness racing scene and selecting winners. All the important factors from the type of sulky, workouts, drivers' ratings, speed, pace, etc., are skillfully presented in simple terms that can be used by novices and experienced racegoers to find the likely winners.
Softbound. $5.95. (ISBN: 0-89746-002-2)

The Gambling Times Guide to Jai Alai by William R. Keevers—The most comprehensive book on jai alai available. Author Bill Keevers takes the reader on an informative journey from the ancient beginnings of the game to its current popularity. This easy-to-understand guide will show you the fine points of the game, how to improve your betting percentage, and where to find jai alai frontons.
Softbound. $5.95. (ISBN: 0-89746-010-3)

The Gambling Times Guide to Thoroughbred Racing by R.G. Denis— Newcomers to the racetrack and veterans alike will appreciate the informative description of the thoroughbred pari-mutuel activity supplied by this experienced racing authority. Activities at the track and available information are blended skillfully in this guide to selecting winners that pay off in big-ticket returns.
Softbound. $5.95. (ISBN: 0-89746-005-7)

Fast Track to Thoroughbred Profits by Mark Cramer—Here is a unique and effective approach to selecting thoroughbred winners. *WIN* Magazine's horse racing editor and noted handicapping expert Cramer discusses how to distinguish between valuable and commonplace information through a method using handicapping factors in terms of "return on investment." Experienced racing enthusiasts will find many surprises and "edges" in this work, while beginners will appreciate Cramer's clear and lively presentation.
Softbound. $8.95. (ISBN: 0-89746-025-1)

Other Winning Programs From Gambling Times Software

Turn your computer into a home casino!!

COMPLETE CRAPS—Try your dice system without risk at home before you bet your cash in the casino! The experts at Gambling Times Software have devised the most complete craps program available today which includes every conceivable bet and playing system known. Realistic graphics and sound simulate actual casino play. This research and learning tool enables you to select the rules variations of your favorite casino. Select any system you like; a different system for every bet on the table...if you choose! Change your bets with each roll of the dice. Let ''Complete Craps'' play thousands of rolls, then see the results tallied and charted on the screen or printed out. Complete documentation included. (Minimum 256K and a floppy drive required; hard disk recommended. IBM-PC compatible only.) *Add $3 shipping and handling. $5 extra for 3½" version. Only $49.95!

LOTTO CALC—The ultimate lottery players' software! Harness the power of your IBM PC or PC-compatible to capture the data you need to knowledgeably play and BEAT any lotto game in the U.S., Canada or overseas. Three years in the making, this powerful database gives the serious lottery player: hit-and-miss frequencies, complete up-to-date records of every lotto game played in the U.S. from its inception, updating capability, accurate repeat occurrences, file merging plus WHEELING, random number selections and computer system picks. Complete documentation included. (Minimum 256K and a floppy drive required; hard disk recommended. IBM-PC compatible only.) *Add $3 shipping and handling. $5 extra for 3½" version. Only $49.95!

EXPERT BLACKJACK—WARNING: THIS IS NO GAME! "Expert Blackjack" is simply the most powerful analytical and learning tool available. Learn from modern masters of "21." Ken Uston, Julian Braun and Stanley Roberts have contributed their knowledge of blackjack and incorporated it into this learning and playing program designed for experts and beginners alike. Contains exclusive systems, teaches play, advises and charts your results. Don't go into the casino ill equipped to *WIN*. Simulate casino conditions with this program *before* heading for the tables and amaze yourself with the new-found strength of your game. $495

COMPLETE BACCARAT—The ultimate game for high rollers. Learn and practice the game, applying pre-programmed systems or design your own. For all varieties of the game from *punto banco* to *chemin-de-fer*. Single table or *deux tableaux*. Complete statistics charted on screen or printout. Complete documentation included. (Minimum 256K and a floppy drive required; hard disk recommended. IBM-PC compatible only.) *Add $3 shipping and handling. $5 extra for 3 1/2" version. Only $49.95!

COMPLETE ROULETTE—French (0) or American (00) versions complete with the most popular pre-programmed systems, or design and implement your own favorite system. Allows you to run your system prior to laying down cash at a casino. Complete statistics charted on screen or printout. Complete documentation included. (Minimum 256K and a floppy drive required; hard disk recommended. IBM-PC compatible only.) *Add $3 shipping and handling. $5 extra for 3½" version. Only $49.95!

SUPER 7-STUD POKER—This all-new program allows you to program your opponents' playing and betting tendencies. Good for beginners and experts alike. Realistic graphics and sound let you feel like you're sitting in a real game! Results charted on screen or printout. Complete documentation included. (Minimum 256K and a floppy drive required; hard disk recommended. IBM-PC compatible only.) *Add $3 shipping and handling. $5 extra for 3½" version. Only $49.95!

Ordering Information

Send your book or software order along with your check or money order to:

Gambling Times
16760 Stagg St., Suite 213
Van Nuys, CA 91406

Softbound Books: Please add $1.00 per bood if delivered in the United States, $1.50 in Canada or Mexico, and $3.50 for foreign countries.
*Hardbound Books:*Shipping charges for the following books are $2.50 if delivered in the United States, $3.00 in Canada or Mexico, and $5.00 for foreign countries:
Caro's Book of Tells
Million Dollar Blackjack
P$yching Out Vegas
Winning Blackjack (softcover, large format)
Gambling and the Law